THE POLAROID YEARS

Instant Photography and Experimentation

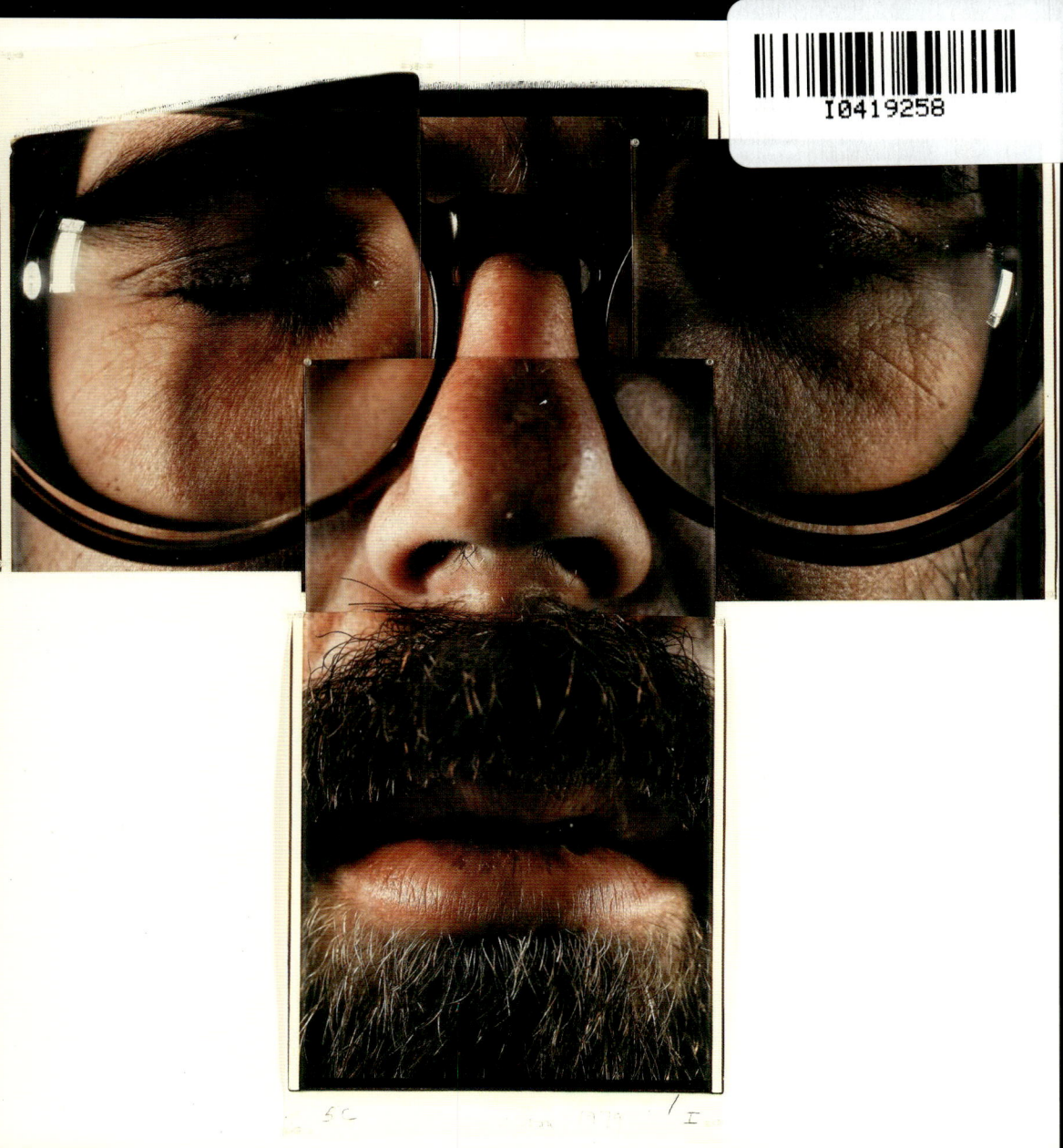

Chuck Close, 5C (*Self-Portrait*), 1979, Five Polaroid Polacolor prints, The Frances Lehman Loeb Art Center, Vassar College, © Chuck Close

Ansel Adams
Jack Butler
Ellen Carey
Carter
Bruce Charlesworth
Chuck Close
Anne Collier
Laura Cooper and
 Nick Taggart
John Coplans
Marie Cosindas
Philip-Lorca diCorcia
Charles and Ray Eames
Walker Evans
Bryan Graf
Richard Hamilton
Robert Heinecken
David Hockney
Barbara Kasten
André Kertész
Les Krims
David Levinthal
Miranda Lichtenstein
John Maggiotto
Andreas Mahl
Robert Mapplethorpe
Joyce Neimanas
Catherine Opie
Lisa Oppenheim
Beatrice Pediconi
Victor Raphael
John Reuter
Lucas Samaras
Dash Snow
Paul Thek
Mungo Thomson
Andy Warhol
William Wegman
James Welling
Grant Worth

Curated by Mary-Kay Lombino

The Frances Lehman Loeb Art Center, Vassar College
April 12 - June 30, 2013

Mary & Leigh Block Museum of Art, Northwestern University
September 20 - December 1, 2013

The Frances Lehman Loeb Art Center | Vassar College | Poughkeepsie | New York | www.fllac.vassar.edu

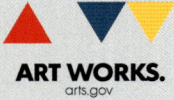
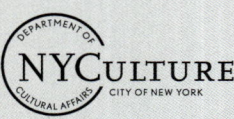
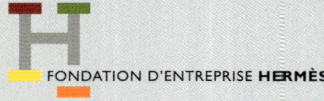
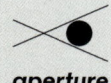

aperture　　Aperture Foundation　547 West 27th Street, 4th Floor, New York, N.Y. 10001　212.505.5555　www.aperture.org

THE PARIS PHOTO-APERTURE FOUNDATION PHOTOBOOK AWARDS

2013 CELEBRATING THE BOOK'S CONTRIBUTION TO THE EVOLVING NARRATIVE OF PHOTOGRAPHY

CALL FOR ENTRIES JUNE 21–SEPTEMBER 13
WINNERS TO BE ANNOUNCED AT
PARIS PHOTO, NOVEMBER 14–17, 2013,
AND IN *THE PHOTOBOOK REVIEW* ISSUE 005
APERTURE.ORG/PHOTOBOOKAWARDS

FIRST
PHOTOBOOK
PRIZE

PHOTOBOOK
OF THE YEAR
PRIZE

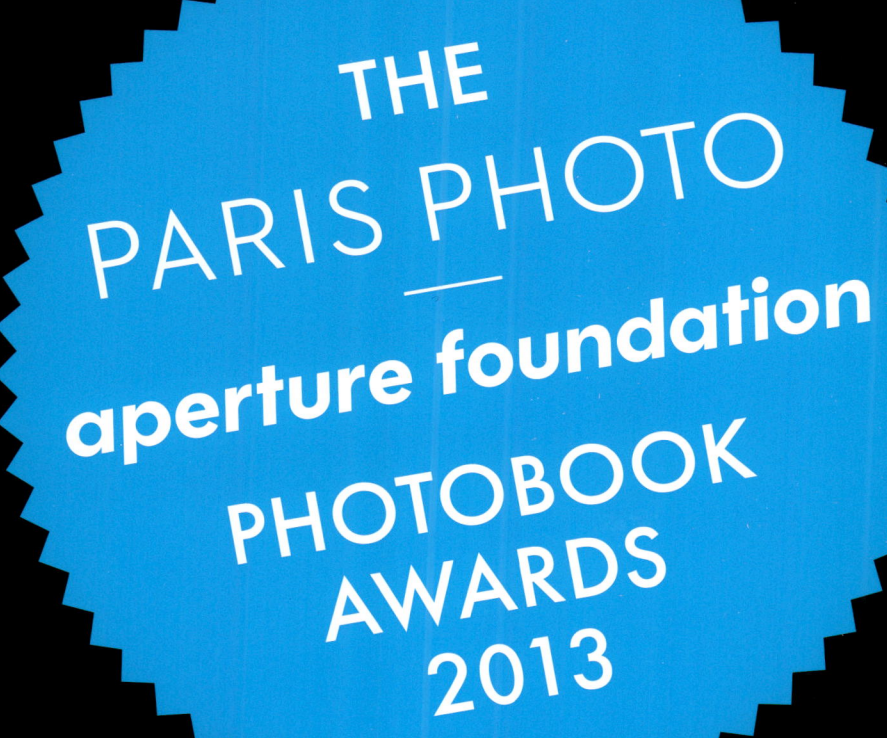

THE
PARIS PHOTO
—
aperture foundation
PHOTOBOOK
AWARDS
2013

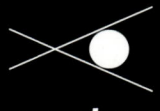

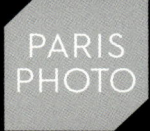
PARIS
PHOTO

aperture

Aperture Foundation   547 West 27th Street, 4th Floor, New York, N.Y. 10001   212.505.5555   www.aperture.org

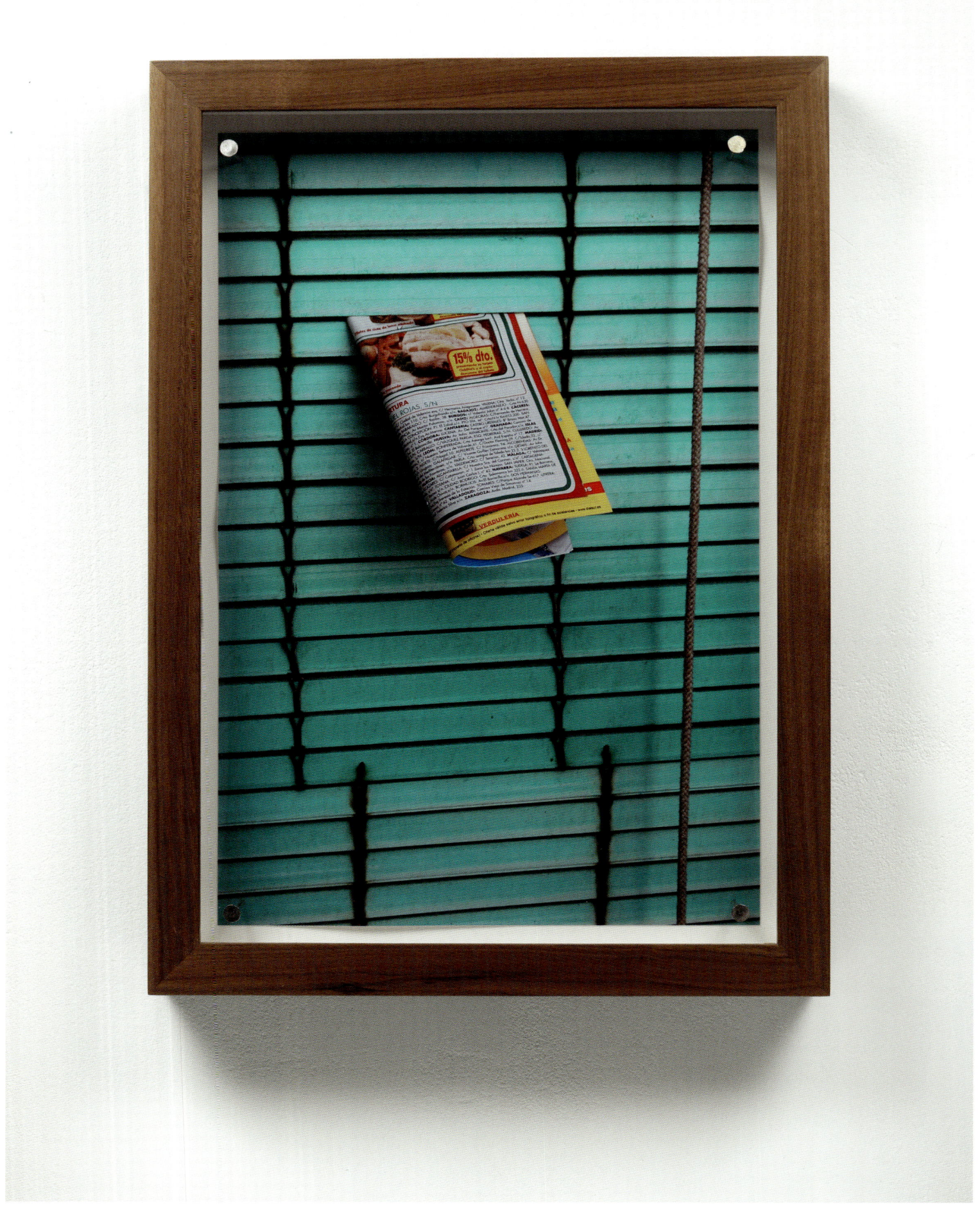

Opposite:
Richard Wentworth,
South East Spain, 2007,
2013 (see Dillon, page 26)
Courtesy the artist and
Lisson Gallery, London

Front cover:
Berenice Abbott, *Static
Electricity,* ca. 1950
© Commerce Graphics,
Courtesy Howard
Greenberg Gallery,
New York and Steidl

Editor
Michael Famighetti

Senior Editor
Diana C. Stoll

Associate Editor
Brian Sholis

Assistant Editor
Paula Kupfer

Production Manager
Matthew Harvey

Work Scholars
Martina Caruso, Luke Chase, Elli Trier

Art Direction, Design & Typefaces
A2/SW/HK, London

Editor-at-Large
Melissa Harris

Publisher
Dana Triwush
magazine@aperture.org

Advertising Representative
Bill Besch
631-665-0467
bbesch1@verizon.net

**Executive Director,
Aperture Foundation**
Chris Boot

Minor White, Editor (1952–1971)

Michael E. Hoffman, Publisher and Executive Director
(1964–2001)

Aperture, a not-for-profit foundation, connects the photo community and its audiences with the most inspiring work, the sharpest ideas, and with each other —in print, in person, and online.

Help maintain Aperture's publishing, education, and community activities by becoming one of our Philanthropists ($5,000), Benefactors ($2,500), Patrons ($1,000), or New Collectors ($500). Donors are acknowledged in *Aperture* magazine and invited to private salon events with artists, receive complimentary publications and special discounts, and enjoy many other benefits. Aperture Foundation welcomes support at all levels of giving, and all gifts are tax-deductible to the fullest extent of the law. For more information about supporting Aperture please visit aperture.org/donate or contact the Development Department at 212-946-7108.

Aperture (ISSN 0003-6420) is published quarterly, in spring, summer, fall, and winter, at 547 West 27th Street, 4th Floor, New York, N.Y. 10001. In the United States, a one-year subscription (four issues) is $75; a two-year subscription (eight issues) is $124. In Canada, a one-year subscription is $95. All other international subscriptions are $105 per year. Visit aperture.org to subscribe. Single copies may be purchased at $24.95 for most issues. Periodicals postage paid at New York and additional offices. Postmaster: Send address changes to *Aperture*, P.O. Box 3000, Denville, N.J. 07834. Address queries regarding subscriptions, renewals, or gifts to: *Aperture* Subscription Service, 866-457-4603 (U.S. and Canada) or email custsvc_aperture@fulcoinc.com.

Newsstand distribution in the U.S. is handled by Curtis Circulation Company, 201-634-7400. For international distribution, contact Central Books, centralbooks.com.

Library of Congress Catalog Card No: 58-30845.

Printed in Germany by optimal media.

aperture.org

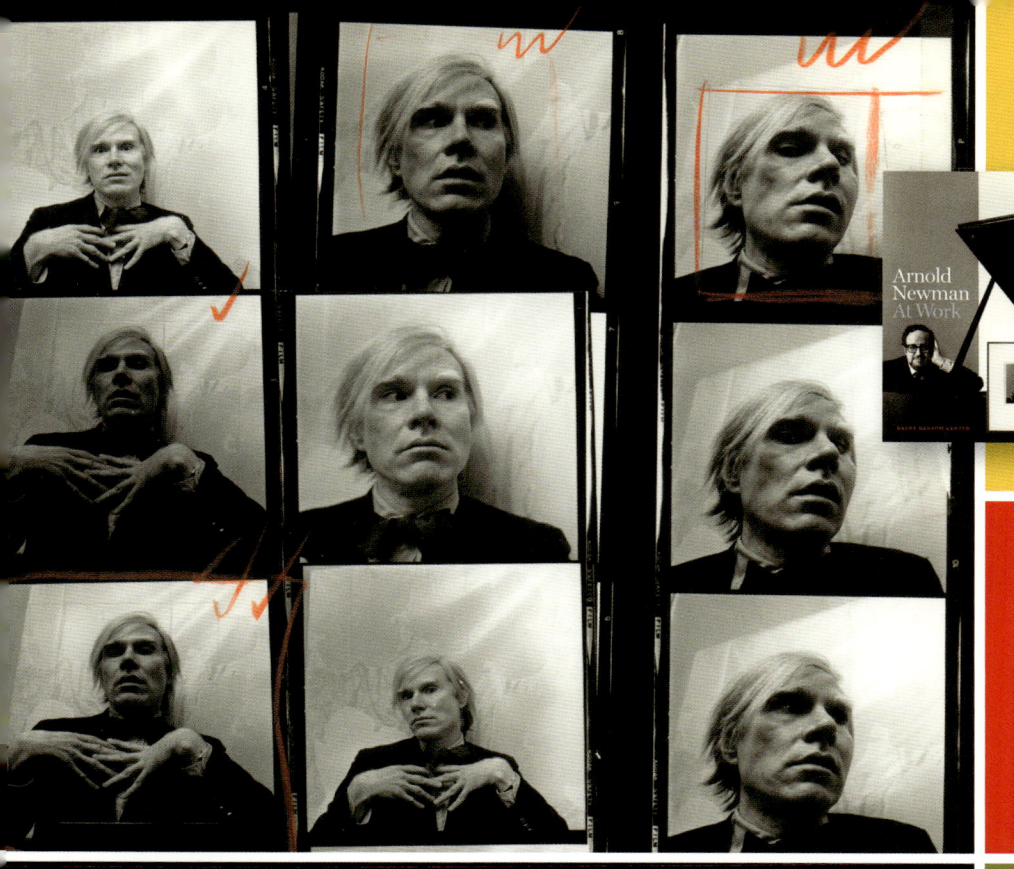

Arnold Newman
At Work

HARRY RANSOM CENTER
BY ROY FLUKINGER
INTRODUCTION BY MARIANNE FULTON

Rich with materials from Arnold Newman's extensive archive in the Harry Ransom Center—contact sheets, Polaroids, work prints, notebooks, calendars, and tearsheets—this volume offers unprecedented, firsthand insights into the creativity of one of the twentieth century's greatest photographers.
HARRY RANSOM CENTER PHOTOGRAPHY SERIES,
Jessica S. McDonald, *Series Editor*
107 color photos and 171 color plates
$60.00 hardcover, $60.00 e-book

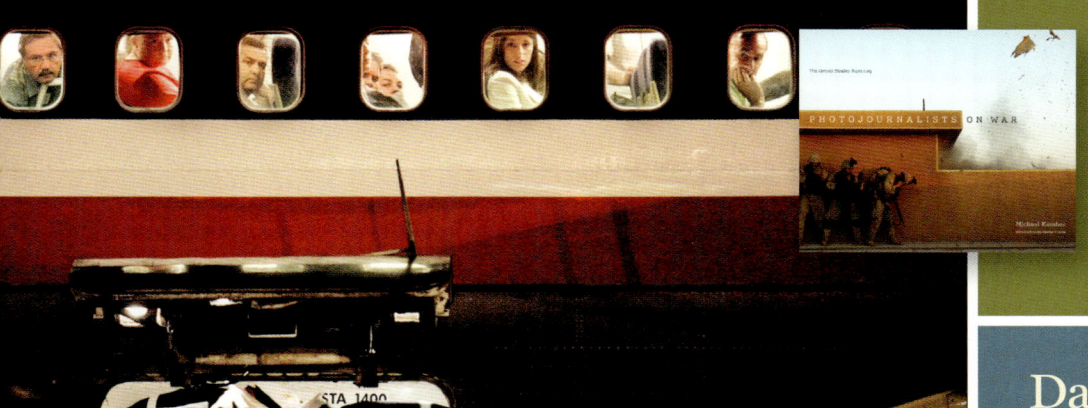

Photojournalists on War
The Untold Stories from Iraq

BY MICHAEL KAMBER
INTRODUCTION BY DEXTER FILKINS

With visceral, previously unpublished photographs and eyewitness accounts from the front lines, three dozen of the world's leading photojournalists reveal the inside and untold stories of the Iraq war in this groundbreaking oral history.
120 color and B&W photos • $65.00 hardcover

Dan Winters's America
Icons and Ingenuity

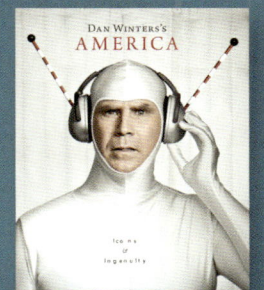

BY DAN WINTERS
ADDITIONAL ESSAYS BY COURTNEY A.
MCNEIL and JOHN GRZYWACZ-GRAY

This lavishly illustrated catalog of the first museum retrospective exhibition of internationally award-winning photographer Dan Winters surveys his entire oeuvre, including iconic celebrity portraits, scientific photography, photojournalism, and lyrical personal expressions.
Distributed for Telfair Books, an imprint of Telfair Museums, Savannah, Georgia
120 color photos • $39.95 hardcover

Unsettled/ Desasosiego
Children in a World of Gangs/ Los niños en un mundo de las pandillas

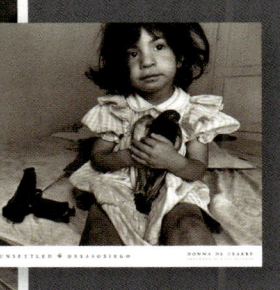

BY DONNA DE CESARE
FOREWORD BY FRED RITCHIN

Culminating thirty years of photographing gang members and their families and collecting images that have been featured in *Aperture*, *Mother Jones*, and other publications, award-winning photojournalist Donna De Cesare uncovers the effects of decades of war and gang violence on the lives of youths in Central America and in refugee communities in the United States in this bilingual book.
105 duotone photos • $65.00 hardcover

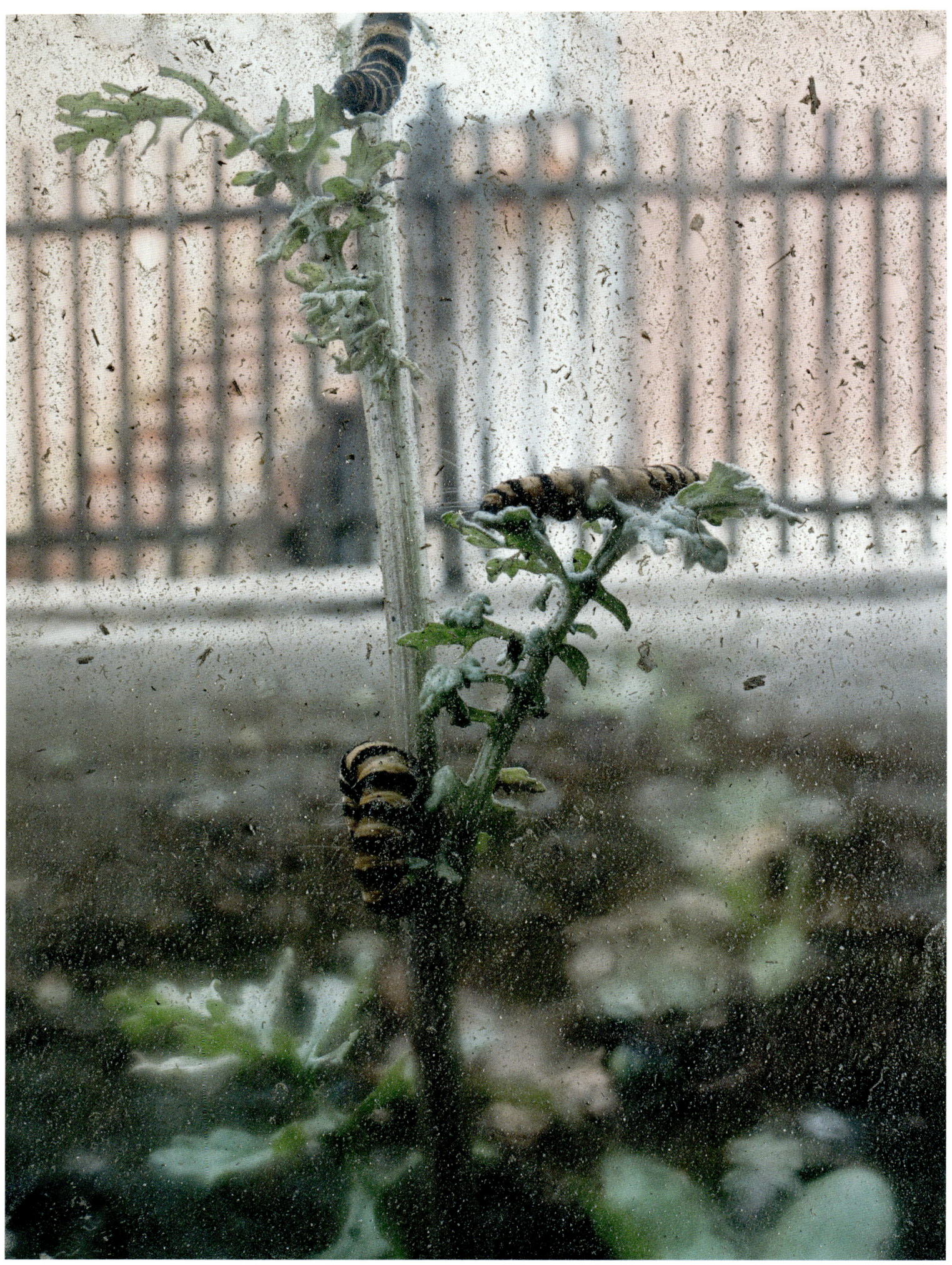

Curiosity

What provokes us to pursue something, to want to find out more? "*Curiosity* is an oddly ambivalent word," notes critic Brian Dillon in this issue. It can lead, he points out, to a range of conditions, from utter distraction to deep concentration, all stemming from the "urge to discover." Photography has long served as a medium of choice not only for the curious practitioner, but also for his or her audience, whose curiosity may be either aroused or appeased by an image. In the following pages, the desire to see and visualize—in the often interconnected fields of science and art—serves as a capacious framework for approaching photography's relationship to curiosity.

As Berenice Abbott once noted, photography is "science's child," a familial relationship well illustrated by revisiting the medium's early decades. Historian Jennifer Tucker looks back into the nineteenth century, when photographic "first glimpses" of microbes, solar eclipses, or the surface of Mars had lives as both news items and entertaining spectacles, and when the young medium of photography was itself still viewed as something of a technical marvel. Tucker points out that in today's atmosphere of image inundation "first glimpses"—if they still exist at all—make a less breathtaking impression. The images recently transmitted from NASA's *Curiosity* Mars Rover, for example, are uncannily similar to familiar photographs of the Earth's deserts. Such comparisons of the terrestrial with the alien are investigated here by David Campany, who discusses photographs by an eclectic group— Man Ray, Frederick Sommer, and Sophie Ristelhueber, among others—that may cause viewers to wonder exactly *what* they are seeing. Curator Joel Smith examines an equally inscrutable group of images, by Katy Grannan, Frank Gohlke, Naoya Hatakeyama, and others, in his guide to making (and making sense of) "photographs of nothing."

While some artists have more or less intentionally confounded viewers, researchers in other realms of image making have used photographs to show us the world as it is, in an attempt to come to a deeper understanding of the phenomena that surround us. Science historian Peter Galison and artist Trevor Paglen discuss the history of objectivity, as well as how images—now digital, searchable, everywhere —may be shifting from being mere depictions to performing specific functions.

Whether obliquely sidling up to our attention or demanding it outright, one thing that photography has always done is *reveal*. Harold E. Edgerton, through his famous flash experiments, slowed time down to unveil what had once been "invisible" actions. Berenice Abbott, too, aimed to bring the strangeness and beauty of scientific subjects to the public— as with her renderings of interference patterns in light, or her illustration of static electricity, featured on this issue's cover. Photography historian Kelley Wilder discusses Abbott's work along with that of Edwin E. Jelley, a little-known research scientist at Kodak who was fascinated by the forms and struc- tures of light. Jelley's work paved the way for the commercially available color processes that would be taken up by artists such as Lázsló Moholy-Nagy, who experimented with color photograms in the 1930s. Moholy-Nagy's images in turn offer a departure point for Thomas Ruff's latest body of work, also featured in this issue: photograms for the digital era, created with 3-D imaging software. German photographer Horst Ademeit was, by contrast, terrified of technology: his enigmatic and obsessive project, introduced here by curator Lynne Cooke, used the instant Polaroid form to document what he named "cold rays," an unseen force he believed emanated from his apartment's electrical sockets. While Ademeit's fraught attentions were absorbed in an intensely insular world, other photographers train their lenses with equal fervor outward, toward the mysteries of the atmosphere and the celestial bodies. Lisa Oppenheim follows this impulse with her recent "lunagrams," heliograms, and more, taking her cue from nineteenth-century astronomical imagery.

Whether investigations originate in the nineteenth, twentieth, or twenty-first century, by using the latest technologies or by reviving older ones, the desire to lay bare the unknown is perpetual. Yet, whether the realm is art or science, photography—like any medium of investigation— may lead not to answers but to further questions: as Joel Smith observes here, photographs can "doubt as well as certify, negate as well as indicate, embody absence as well as substance."

—The Editors

What Matters Now?
Photography, Technology, and the World

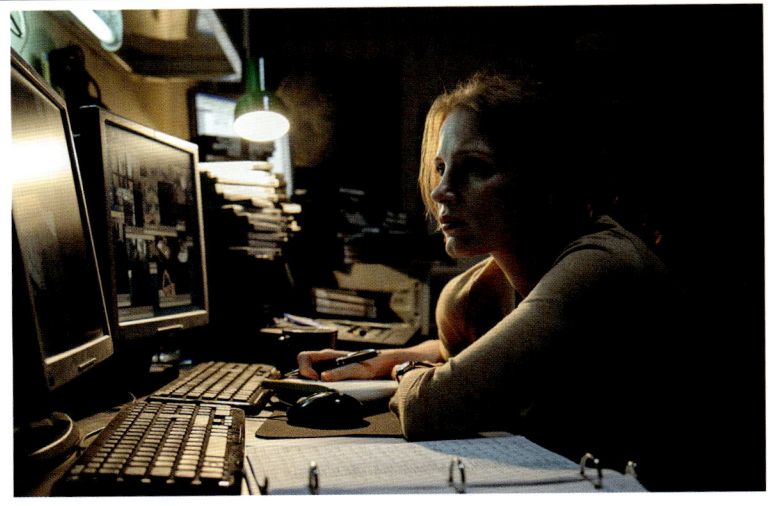

CIA Torture Tapes

For the past several years I have been obsessed with images I've never seen. They were recorded and destroyed. These images document torture. In their absence, fictitious images have emerged.

Jose Rodriguez, the man who in 2005 ordered the destruction of ninety-two videotapes of torture committed by the Central Intelligence Agency, claims: "I was not depriving anyone of information about what was done or what was said. I was just getting rid of some ugly visuals that could put the lives of my people at risk."

Rodriguez, a high-ranking intelligence officer, made the decision to destroy the torture tapes in response to the public reaction to the Abu Ghraib photographs in 2004. It is often forgotten that the abuse at Abu Ghraib was made "public" before those images were released. Four months before the publication of the photographs, the U.S. military issued a press release saying they were investigating claims of prisoner abuse in Iraq. The announcement received little media coverage or interest. Had the photographs not been leaked to the *New Yorker* and *60 Minutes*, Abu Ghraib would likely have disappeared from history.

Without visual evidence of CIA torture, history is being written by Hollywood. In *Zero Dark Thirty*, the CIA torturers are the heroic protagonists. Can we imagine this happening with Lynndie England, the woman holding the end of a dog leash around the neck of a naked prisoner at Abu Ghraib? Or Sabrina Harman, who gives the "thumbs up" sign over the dead body of Manadel al-Jamadi, a man killed during a CIA interrogation?

If the CIA's torture tapes had been made public, how would history be told differently?

—**Laura Poitras, documentary filmmaker and MacArthur Fellow, whose work includes** *The Oath* (2010); *My Country, My Country* (2006); *The Program* (*New York Times* Op-Doc, 2012); and *Death of a Prisoner* (*New York Times* Op-Doc, 2013)

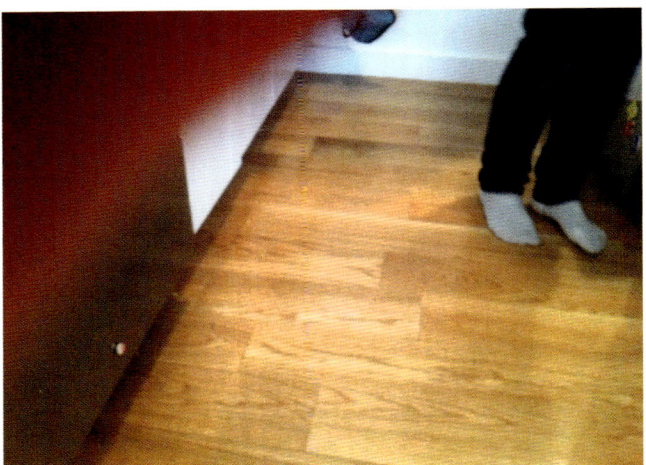

Photographs as Things

Photographs, especially personal ones, have always served as physical manifestations of memory. Held between fingers or hung on a wall, photographic prints had a direct material connection to their subjects, from light to lens to film to paper. Today, of course, our photographs are born digital. Their power as images remains, gloriously so; but their reality as objects is often lost.

In my house, these two ideas collide in the small hands of my three-year-old daughter, compulsively snapping photographs with a phone snatched off the table. She has amassed hundreds of them (mostly of fingers and floors). They are not merely weightless, but evanescent. So in an effort to fix them in the most literal way, we bought a sixty-nine-dollar wireless printer. The effect was strange: a photograph taken with one magic box was magically transferred through the air to another magic box, out of which a photograph (on paper!) slowly emerged. Up it went on the refrigerator door. The images themselves are beside the point. What I am grasping for, perhaps foolishly, is the sense of a photograph as a *thing*, an object of value—something to be cared for in the physical world, as we care for each other.

—**Andrew Blum, journalist and author of** *Tubes: A Journey to the Center of the Internet* (Ecco, 2012)

North Korea's Gulag

After Hurricane Sandy last year, photographer Iwan Baan captured an iconic shot of Manhattan, half in blackout: it is a photograph that will haunt our collective memory for a long time. At the same time, Google Maps recently added North Korean coverage by means of a clever juxtaposition of aerial shots, satellite imagery, and clandestine on-the-ground documentary photos by daring locals and visitors alike, giving us firsthand views of this notoriously media-shy country and its equally notorious death camps. With this ostensibly minor extension of its mapping service, everyone's favorite search engine entered the political arena—and Google deserves great credit for this unexpected advance. In the end, this "citizen documentation" of actual gulags on North Korean ground is more likely to unsettle the restrictive regime than any international sanctions.

Both Baan's image and Google Maps in North Korea have reignited my appreciation for straightforward reportage that channels and politicizes key issues via powerful visual records. When I think about Vietnam, the Cold War, or space-age advances—as well as events that occurred before my lifetime—I consider those times and events through iconic press shots that strike a mental, emotional, and sociopolitical chord. Images help us to contextualize topics, ideas, and historical events. Great press photographs trigger desires, anger, compassion: they get me going. I *expect* photography to play a powerful part in developing my political agenda. I believe that the decline of quality news outlets goes hand in hand with a decline in empathy, political involvement, and democratic engagement. We are ready for a new breed of earnest and enthusiastic photojournalists who can produce those shots that capture our hearts and minds.

—**Robert Klanten, founder and publisher of Gestalten, Berlin**

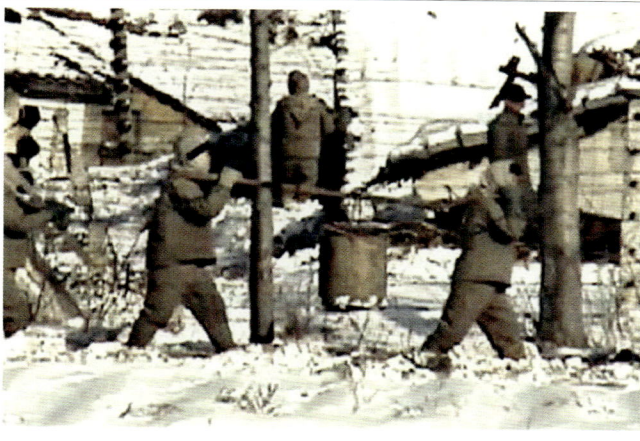

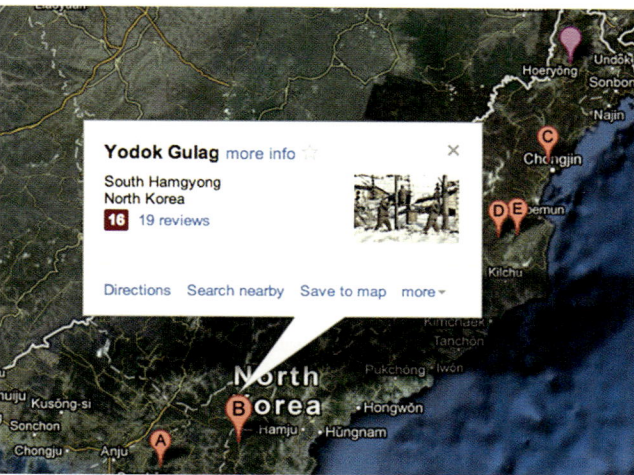

Possibilities of Pleasure

A favorite image from the past few years is by Maha Maamoun. What is depicted is a children's playground in a Cairo park, dominated by an aging tubular metal slide, which is painted in the bright colors of the flag of the Arab Republic of Egypt and bears an inscription in Arabic that translates to: "Baby Land Welcomes You!" Two small girls and a toddler boy are about to climb the stairs to the top of the slide, while a young woman in gray veil is helping another woman, in a black *niqab*, who just slid down, to emerge from the industrial-looking orifice at the bottom of the slide.

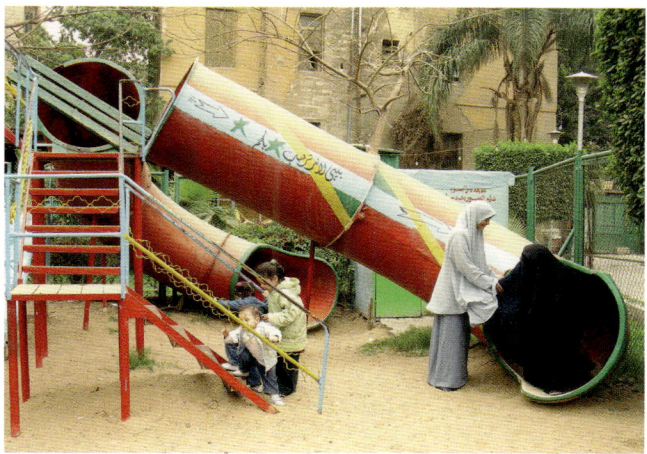

The image, which is humorous, sad, and indicative of a certain psychosis, brings to my mind a 1920 drawing by Max Ernst called *The Hat Makes the Man*, which is full of colorful tubular forms and men's black hats, and bears a cryptic inscription: "seed-covered stacked-up man seedless waterformer [*edelformer*] well fitting nervous system also tightly fitting nerves! (the hat makes the man) (style is the tailor)." Like Ernst's drawing—which suggests a kind of alchemical-industrial transubstantiation of masculinity—Maamoun's photograph delicately charts a cosmology of women's lives and the possibilities of pleasure within a certain conveyor-belt religious order.

—**Anton Vidokle, artist and co-editor of *e-flux journal***

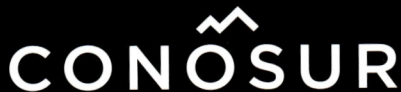

CONÕSUR

PARRILLA & FONDUE

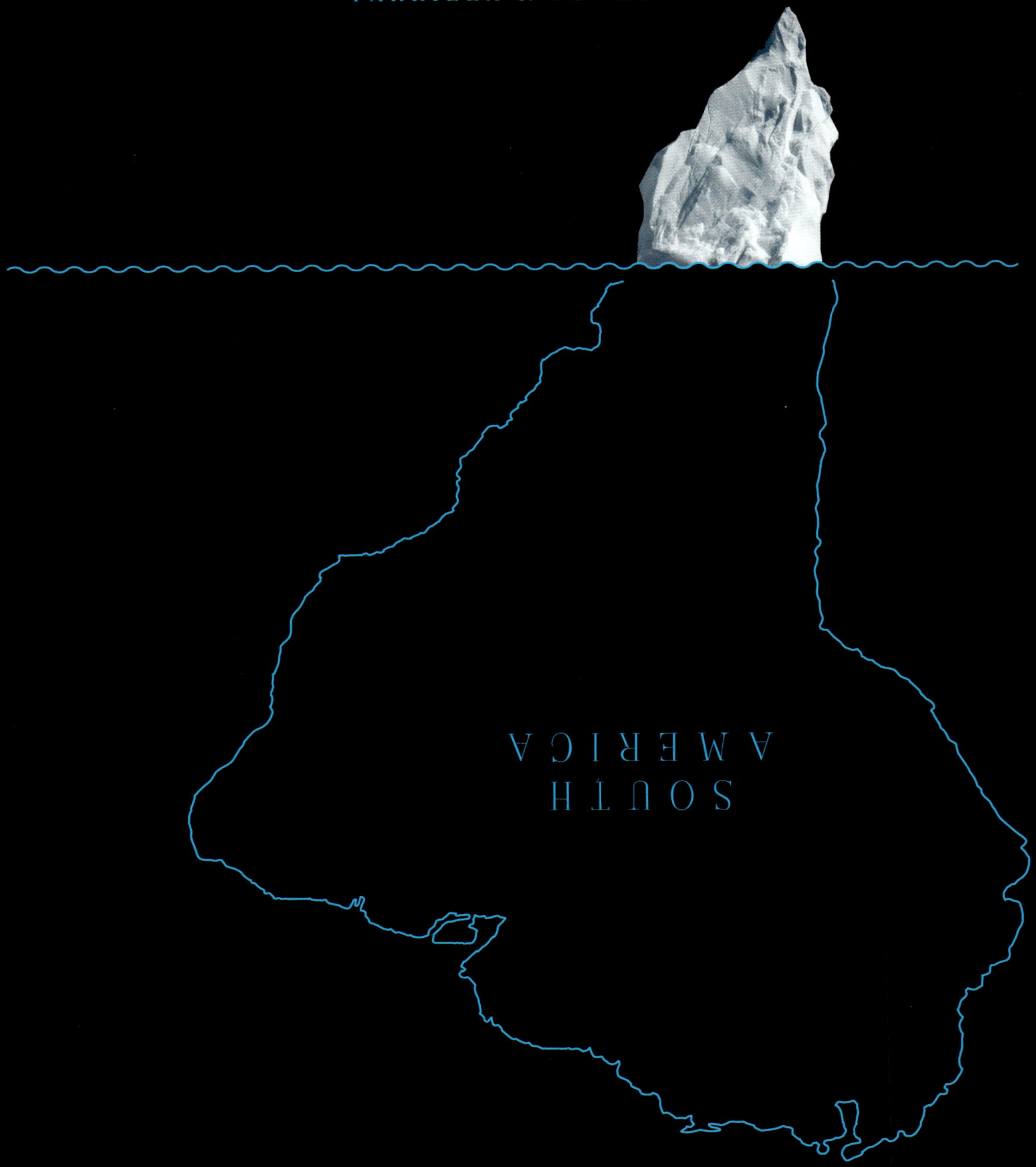

SOUTH AMERICA

HÔTEL
CHELSEA **AMERICANO** NEW YORK

518 West 27ᵗʰ Street, New York NY 10001

www.hotel-americano.com

twitter.com/GRUPOHABITA   **GRUPOHABITA.MX**   facebook.com/GrupoHabitaHotels

Redux
Rediscovered Books and Writings

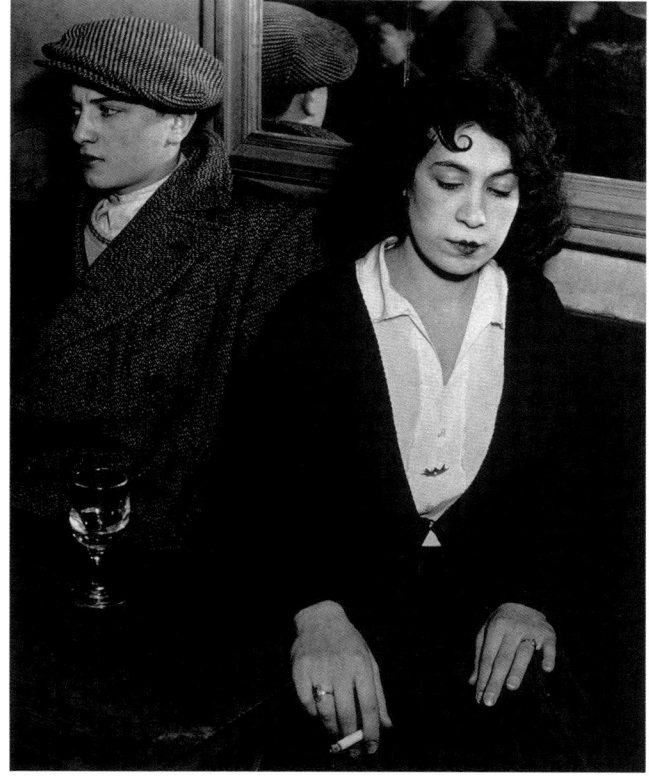

Brassaï's *Proust in the Power of Photography*
Ulrich Baer

Pleasures are like photographs: those taken in the beloved's presence no more than negatives, to be developed later, once you are at home, having regained the use of that interior darkroom, access to which is "condemned" as long as you are seeing other people.
—Marcel Proust, *Within a Budding Grove*, cited in Brassaï, *Proust in the Power of Photography*

Paris in the 1920s teems with foreign strivers, most of them refugees from the far-flung corners of a continent churning with resentments, occupations, and newly minted nations carved like slabs from a bleeding beast. Among those spilling into Paris is a young Hungarian, Gyula Halász, who arrives in 1924 with a dogged determination to become a French artist. Halász has studied in Berlin and comes with that prototypically Hungarian mix of wry sensibility and deep intelligence— shared by the likes of László Moholy-Nagy, André Kertész, and others.

For months young Halász tunnels through the novel that's the talk of the town at the moment: Marcel Proust's seven-volume *In Search of Lost Time*. The Hungarian decodes each unknown word like a spy sneaking through alleys and along boulevards who hopes for hidden meanings in syllables snatched from overheard conversations and random words on street signs. Halász is intoxicated by Proust's finely spun web of social intrigue, glaring passion, and sharp disappointments, and above all by the French novelist's capacity to let each word at once refer to present-time reality and resonate with unspoken and hitherto unremembered truths. *In Search of Lost Time* initially serves as a language primer for the man who rechristens himself Brassaï, after his Transylvanian hometown of Brasso; later, Proust's protracted examination of the dialectics between imagination and reality becomes a guiding principle of the photographer's life. Brassaï reads Proust's novel as a guide to how our present-day existence, with its inevitable contingencies, occasionally opens onto a past that we have yet to understand fully, even if it is ours alone. Proust's insistence that we live as much in time as we do in specific places will inform especially Brassaï's photographs of interior spaces, which in many cases use mirrors and doublings to show one scene from several perspectives at once.

In 1933 Brassaï publishes *Paris by Night* to great acclaim. His photographs present with testimonial intensity, but also compassion, the creatures of Parisian nightlife, with their garishly made-up and sharply lit faces thrust against the unrelenting passage of time, and a few specimens from the French leisure class. But the book's most evocative images are nocturnal scenes patterned by architectural details and lines drawn on glistening pavements by streetlamps. Tucked into those urban spots, patterned like fields meticulously tended by unseen specters, are half-hidden lovers, curvaceous silhouettes of working women, dancing sparks of light beckoning the viewer. With his camera Brassaï succeeded in letting darkness speak on equal terms with light, and allowing the photographically heightened contrast between shade and illumination to imply that the city harbored unknown secrets and seductions. The strength of Brassaï's pictures results from this invitation to the viewer to invest with significance the dark spots in the picture, until then areas that signified an absence of meaning.

With *Paris by Night* Brassaï established himself as a bona-fide French artist. The book resulted in overnight acclaim and provided access that would shape his career—although photography would ultimately be only one of his several media of expression. Brassaï famously portrayed some of France's great artists, befriended among others Pablo Picasso, Jacques Prévert, and Henry Miller, and continued to document the Parisian underworld.

He guarded his pictures against becoming clichés by focusing on form

Previous page:
Brassaï, *Couple fâché
au Bal des Quatre-Saisons,
rue de Lappe* (Quarrel,
Bal des Quatre-Saisons,
rue de Lappe), ca. 1932

This page:
Brassaï, *Allumeur des
réverbères, Place de la
Concorde* (Lamplighter,
Place de la Concorde),
1933
Both photographs
© RMN-Grand Palais/
Art Resource, New York

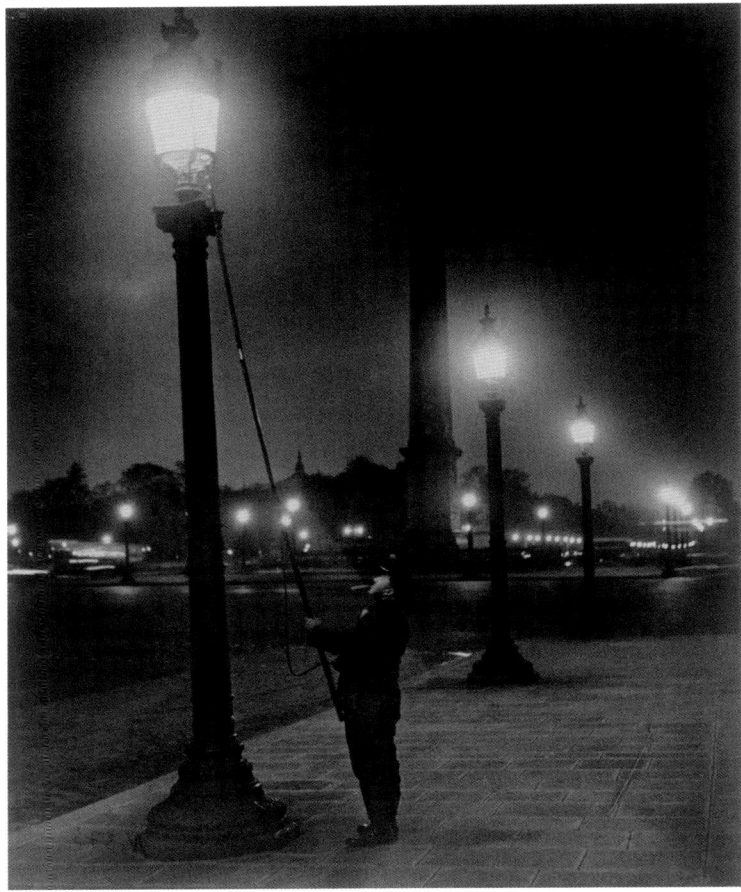

Proust, in Brassaï's inspired reading, constructed his world as one gigantic photograph—that is, the novel that Brassaï first encountered in 1926 is "developed" via the philosophical and narrative digressions for which *In Search of Lost Time* is famous. In Proust, Brassaï discovered a theory of photography's oscillation between the camera's dispassionate gaze and the filter of consciousness by which we see things in light of past experiences and forgotten sights and scenes.

Without saying as much, Brassaï recognized his own technique of shooting like an "impartial witness" while "sensing the magic beneath the surface of reality" in Proust's writing. He backed his reading of Proust with research into the novelist's obsessive collection of visiting cards and photographic portraits, which served the writer especially in later days as triggers for the true vision of people on whom he was modeling his characters.

From Brassaï's book we may see to what extent Proust's project informed Roland Barthes's notion of photography as providing evidence about time itself, rather than simply about the photographed subject. Today we take largely for granted the notion that photography is an investigation into the nature of time and the effects of memory—including forgotten traces of past events— upon our purportedly objective ways of seeing. Brassaï's book illuminates how this assumption became the touchstone for so much contemporary criticism, and to what extent Proust's obsession with photographs and his reliance on photographic phenomena in his groundbreaking novel served as a catalyst in this understanding.

for its own sake, and by capturing a previously unknown vitality and urgency of Parisian nightlife that courses mercurially through even the most languid, lost, and louche courtesan's limbs. (For me he rescues that scene from the aestheticizing, leering, or condescending gaze prevalent among French artists of the time.) Each of Brassaï's pictures was wrested from time, not in a pyrrhic fight against its passage, but by capitalizing upon the meaning in hidden moments. Those are the moments in which we might drown nightly, in either pleasure or pain, were it not for the wheel of time with its mundane ticking of the clock, churning on toward the sober glare of dawn. We want to vanish into the night but also to see the morning sun: that is the tension in us that Brassaï sears into his images.

In 1968 Brassaï reread Proust's novel, this time without the need of dictionaries. By now the photographer's style had become famous, his images iconic. Two lovers tucked into a bistro's mirrored corner; an elderly cocotte resting one splayed hand on a café table while the other clutches her bosom; a cobblestoned gutter snaking along a road like a glistening serpent beckoning us yonder; the Pont Neuf creating four portholes—or camera lenses—by the play of light on the Seine's dark waters.

Brassaï's second reading of Proust resulted in the inspired *Proust in the Power of Photography* (published after his death as *Proust sous l'emprise de la photographie* [Gallimard, 1997; University of Chicago Press, 2001]), in which he showed that *In Search of Lost Time* relies uncannily on photographic phenomena. Proust's novel, Brassaï noted in his second perusal, contains significant moments structured like photographs, where the relation (or gap) between what we know and what we see becomes apparent (for instance when we think a particular photograph captures a person's essence more than others).

Brassaï examined Proust's correspondence, diaries, and various critical studies for this second reading. In doing so, he realized that the novel's key episodes of engagement with time, as both formal and plot devices —undertaken by Proust with the use of involuntary memory, as in the famous scene with the madeleine—resembled the conceit of photography to arrest time's passage, but also to make more apparent how photography shapes our perception of the world. More importantly, Brassaï realized that Proust investigates the distance between appearances and the true nature of things by means of mental processes modeled on the development of a photograph from latency into a full image.

Ulrich Baer is Vice Provost for Arts, Humanities, and Multiculturalism at New York University, and author of *Spectral Evidence: The Photography of Trauma* (MIT Press, 2002). His most recent book is a collection of short stories, *Beggar's Chicken: Stories from Shanghai* (Earnshaw Books, 2013).

The *Paris Review* Print Series

Born, 1964. Revived, 2012.

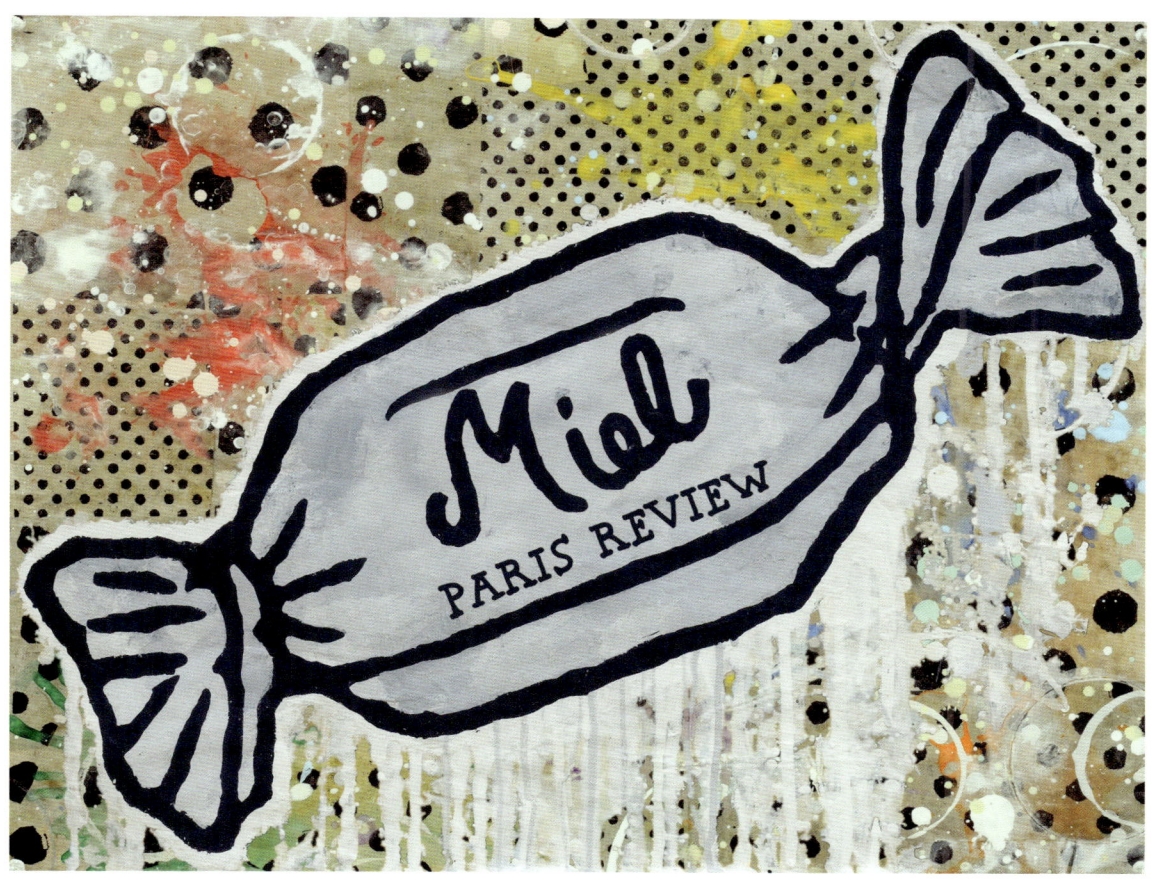

Donald Baechler, 2012, limited edition, $3,500.

In 1964, a gift from Drue Heinz enabled *The Paris Review* to commission a series of prints by major contemporary artists. The purpose was to encourage works in the print medium while publicizing and providing financial support for the magazine. Among the early contributors were Andy Warhol, Robert Rauschenberg, Helen Frankenthaler, and Robert Motherwell. Later contributions were made by Louise Bourgeois, Ed Ruscha, Sol LeWitt, James Rosenquist, and others. Many of the original prints are still available for purchase.

Suspended in 2004, the print series was revived last year with a print by Donald Baechler.

To inquire, visit us online at
www.theparisreview.org/prints *or call* 212.343.1333

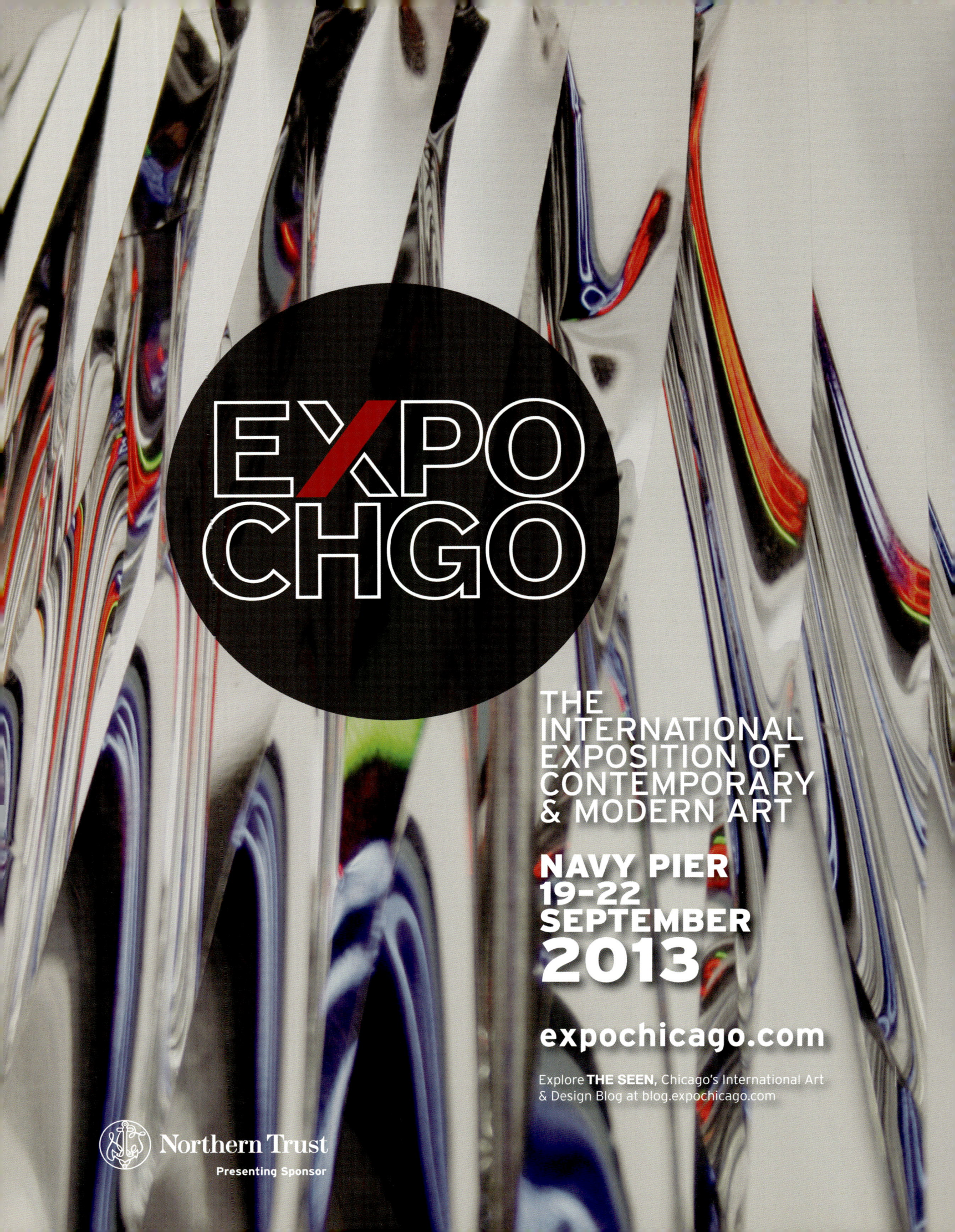

Dispatches
Photography Scenes Worldwide

This festival, created in 1999 by the South African Centre for Photography, routinely elicits sighs, hand-wringing, open letters, public confrontation (notably when photographer Omar Badsha interviewed David Goldblatt at the 2008 edition), and even drunken non sequiturs (from photographer George Hallett at the same event).

Last September, on the same evening that current organizer Jenny Altschuler opened the MoP, Tillim debuted his guitar band Wrong Man at a live venue across town. Like his pal, the journalist Rian Malan (author of the 1990 memoir *My Traitor's Heart*), Tillim has in recent years been making a primitive form of rock 'n' roll. His emergence as a singer-songwriter has been unspectacular—a hundred hits on YouTube. This is a paltry figure compared with the twenty-one million hits racked up by Johannesburg-based Roger Ballen's video for alt-rap band Die Antwoord. That work—"I Fink U Freeky"—was exhibited during MoP as both a video and still portraits at Erdmann Contemporary, one of just a few Cape Town venues to regularly exhibit photography. But Tillim does not make music for public acclaim; rather, like his surfing habit, it is a diversion and a routine.

Music and surfing are useful keys, it would seem, for unlocking the biographies and work of many Cape Town photographers. David Southwood is both a DJ and a surfer—his book *Milnerton Market*, a long-form New Topographics–like photo-essay on a low-rent bric-a-brac market on Cape Town's urban periphery, was published in 2011 by Fourthwall (South Africa's only publisher devoted solely to photobooks). Pieter Hugo was Southwood's assistant for a time. Hugo surfs, too, and he has often spoken to me about how music—in particular the experimental British group Death in June, known for its puzzling symbolism and aesthetics—offers a way into his portraiture, which has polarized local opinion because of its use of pseudo-anthropological and ethnological tropes.

Unlike Southwood and Hugo, photographer Dale Yudelman doesn't surf. He was the winner of last year's Ernest Cole Award, South Africa's newest and best-funded photography prize, named in honor of the country's first black freelance photojournalist, who died in exile in 1990. Yudelman's wry, noir style is, however, elaborated through his love affair with music.

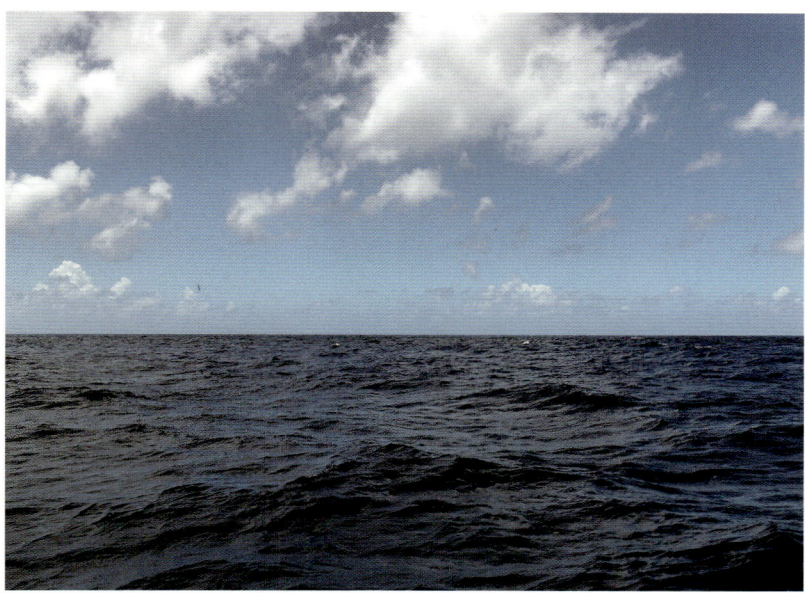

Sean O'Toole on Cape Town

Cape Town, a cosmopolitan port city at the southern meeting point of the Atlantic and Indian oceans, is home to photographers Zwelethu Mthethwa, Guy Tillim, and Pieter Hugo, among others. In the nineteenth century, Cape Town was also the home of German immigrant Carel Sparmann—the city's earliest known photographer—who in 1847 placed an advertisement in a local newspaper: "Daguerreotype Portraits," it read, "taken daily in the Garden."

Last September I found myself in that same garden (actually a tree-lined avenue known as the Company's Garden), running to an interview with Tillim. The tall, graying, soft-spoken photographer had agreed to chat about his impressionistic depictions of conflict, modernist architecture, unfamiliar domesticity, and bureaucracy at a seminar coinciding with the launch of the fifth installment of Cape Town's

This page:
Guy Tillim, *Near Huahine*,
2011
© Guy Tillim, courtesy
Stevenson, Cape Town
and Johannesburg

In the 1980s, exhausted by photographing local conflict for a Johannesburg newspaper, Yudelman moved to Los Angeles with his band. There he met and photographed Frank Zappa ("It was a highlight of living in L.A.," he told me). If Tillim is an amiable, often poetic interview subject, Yudelman—whom I interviewed at the launch of his new book, *Life Under Democracy* (Jacana Media, 2012), a distillation of twenty-eight thousand iPhone photographs of life in contemporary South Africa—is routinely shy and tight-lipped. "Having lived through the dark days of apartheid, I feel grateful that I'm around to witness and enjoy the freedom that many people sacrificed their lives for," I managed to glean from him.

But Yudelman's time in the award spotlight is now up. Ilan Godfrey, a young Johannesburg documentary photographer, has been given the second Ernest Cole Award for his work-in-progress *Legacy of the Mine*, which looks at South Africa's turbulent post-apartheid mining economy. The prize is managed by Paul Weinberg, a humanist documentarian with an amicably grumpy manner and windswept appearance, who last year published a new book himself, titled *Dear Edward* (Jacana Media). An autobiographical portrait of the photographer's family, it begins with the arrival of Edward Weinberg, a Jewish exile from Moscow, in South Africa in the late 1800s, and juxtaposes images from family archives—postcards and old photographs—with recent, color-rich depictions of remote towns where the family traded and settled.

Largely bypassed by the retail galleries, Weinberg is nonetheless an important figure in local photography. In 1982, together with Omar Badsha and others, he founded Afrapix, a self-funded, mixed-race photographic collective. Tillim joined four years later, working the news beat in Cape Town. Despite receiving due acknowledgment last winter, in Okwui Enwezor's exhibition *The Rise and Fall of Apartheid* at New York's International Center for Photography, this now-defunct collective recently passed its thirtieth birthday without a single mention in the local press. "Absolutely nothing," said Weinberg.

In his capacity as senior curator of the visual archives at the University of Cape Town, Weinberg bears some responsibility for repositioning the

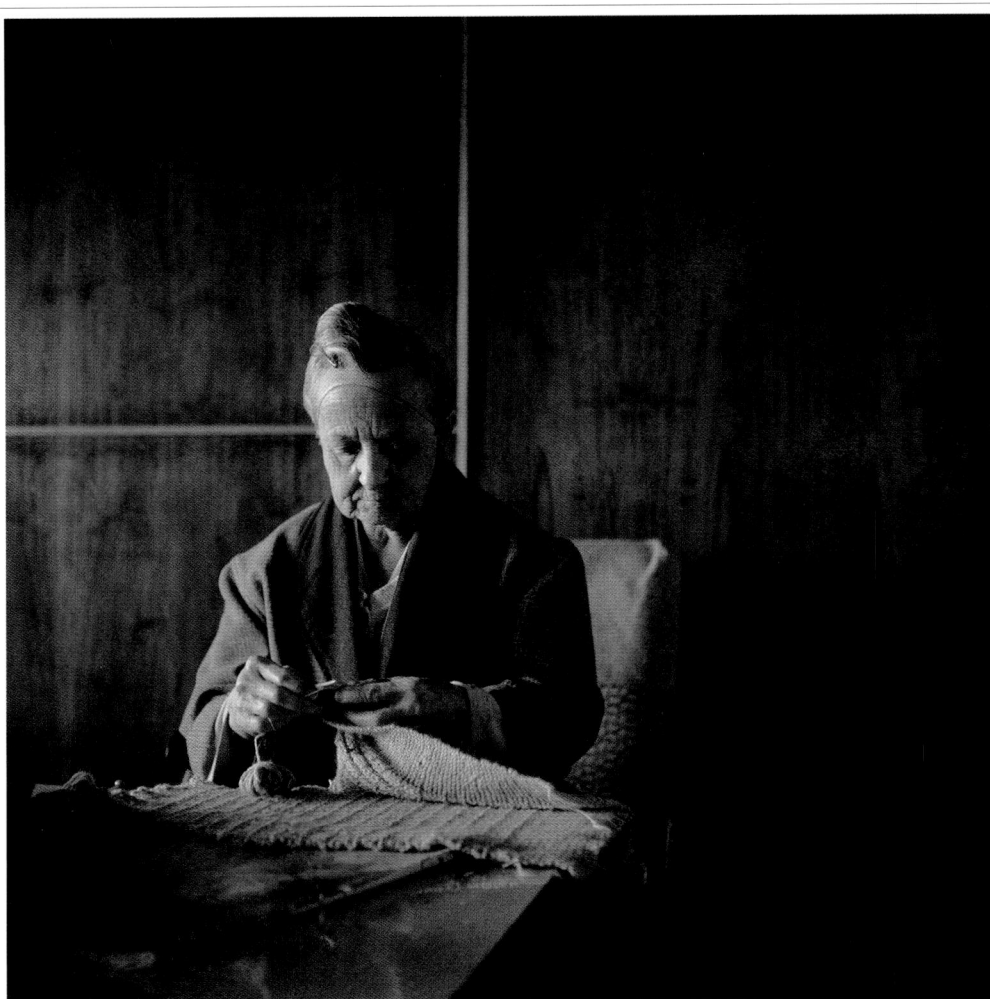

Jansje Wissema,
A resident knits in Cape Town's District Six (before the community's removal), ca. 1970
Courtesy University of Cape Town

Music and surfing are useful keys, it would seem, for unlocking the biographies and work of many Cape Town photographers.

careers of neglected photographers. As part of MoP's dispersed program of events last year, Weinberg organized an exhibition of work by Jansje Wissema (1920–1975), a highly regarded studio photographer with a defined modernist sensibility. The show was held at the District Six Museum, an independent space devoted to memorializing a mixed-race neighborhood razed to the ground after it was declared a whites-only enclave in 1966. Four years later, apartheid bulldozers hard at work, the Cape Provincial Institute of Architects commissioned Wissema to record the neighborhood's disappearing buildings and exiled inhabitants. They were relocated to grim social housing on the Cape Flats, which young photographer Ashley Walters made the subject of his award-winning 2011 undergraduate portfolio at Cape Town's Michaelis School of Fine Arts (the school that trained Mikhael Subotzky, Zwelethu Mthethwa, and the twin brothers Hasan and Husain Essop, who work as a duo). Wissema's portraits of District Six's residents, many of them Muslim, are marked by their decisive stillness and acute observation of the quotidian particulars of a disappeared place. This extends to her depiction of the area's once-animated street life, which was the focus of many workaday essays at the time. A photograph showing three men playing cards—one wears the latest fashions, hat included; the other two are without shoes—recalls a similar photograph made by Jürgen Schadeberg in 1954, an exquisitely lit piece of documentary fiction shot in Sophiatown, a mixed-race neighborhood

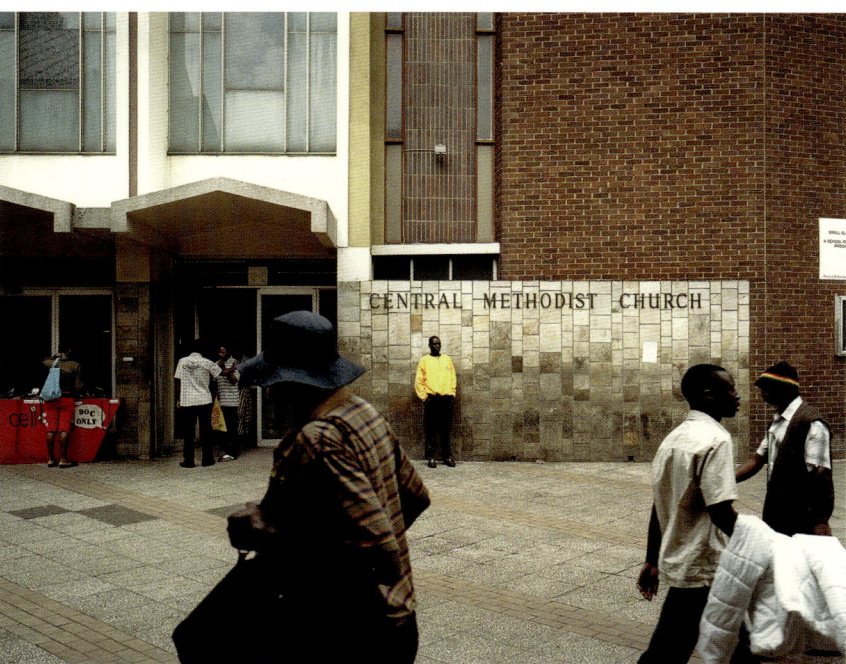

Ilan Godfrey, Entrance to the Central Methodist Church on Pritchard Street, 2008, from the series *Sanctuary of Exile*
© and courtesy Ilan Godfrey

township dwellers in vivid color— "black-and-white photography is attached to a political agenda," he asserted in a 2003 interview. While Mthethwa, who early on adopted a portraiture style reminiscent of the West African studio tradition, focused on subjects staving off poverty with decoration and adornment, Thorne's subjects inhabit a world of formal architecture and curtained windows, of coffee tables and untidy bedrooms. Speaking at his opening, Thorne celebrated the large turnout of black visitors. "Usually I'm one of the only brothers at an opening," he quipped, pointing to the fissures that continue to shape life, after apartheid, under democracy, in Cape Town.

in Johannesburg that suffered a fate similar to that of District Six.

At a walkthrough of Wissema's photographs at MoP, a spirited conversation took place in front of a portrait of a man seated on the ground, his back leaning against a white wall. His eyes were swollen. Was he drunk? The speculation prompted further questions: What are the ethics of portraying the urban poor? When does representation spill over into distortion? How does race inflect such portrayals?

All familiar questions for anyone tuned in to the Cape Town scene— and a useful context for talking about visiting African-American photographer Jared Thorne's exhibition *Black Folk*. That show, a kind of closing bracket to MoP, consisted of portraits—some naturalistic, others stiffly posed and obscure—of a range of middle-class black South Africans. A wall text quoted author bell hooks on the "critical challenge" facing black photographers, particularly in redressing "blatantly stereotypical" representations created by "white people" (photographers included).

It is an urgent idea, one that prompted Mthethwa a decade ago to record the lives of impoverished

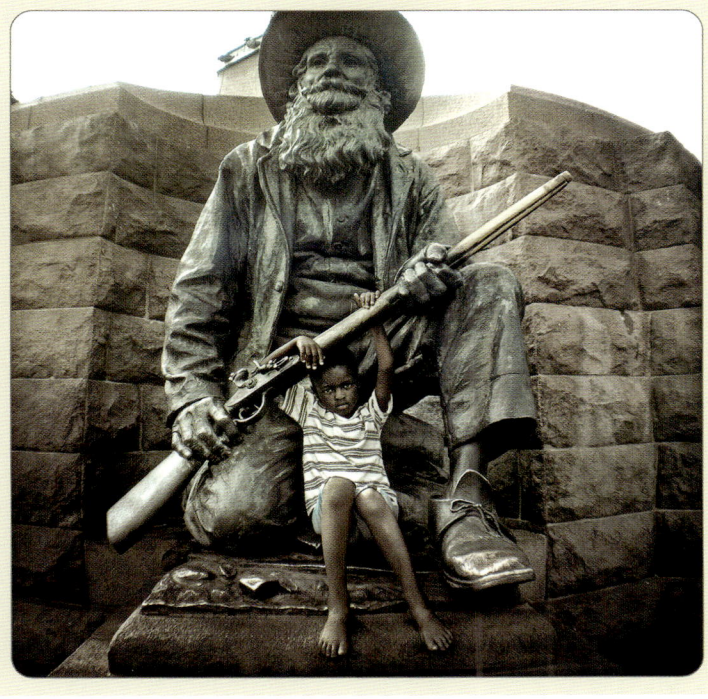

Dale Yudelman, Elia Mashao on statue of Boer soldier, Church Square, Tshwane, 2012, from the series *Life Under Democracy 1*, 2011 and ongoing
© and courtesy Dale Yudelman

Sean O'Toole is a writer of fiction and nonfiction based in Cape Town.

Collectors
The Architects
On Recent Acquisitions

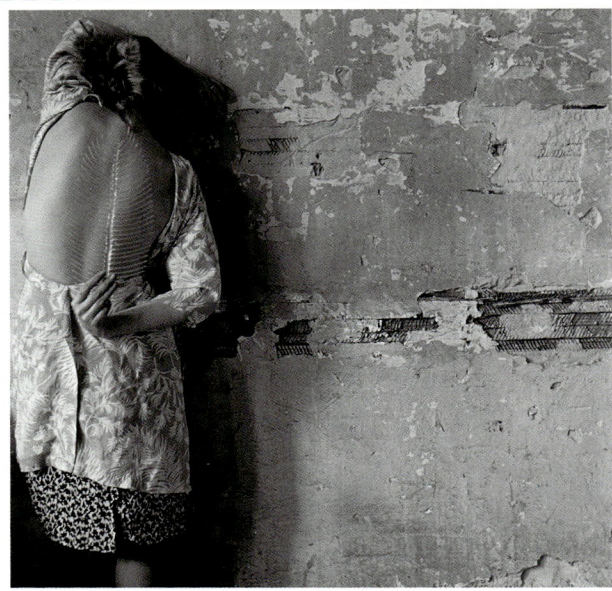

Francesca Woodman, *New York*, 1979–1980. Courtesy George and Betty Woodman

Annabelle Selldorf

I first became aware of Francesca Woodman's work when I stumbled upon a publication from the 1986 exhibition at Wellesley College at Untitled Books in SoHo. I was deeply struck by the images in the catalog; I cannot recall having such a visceral reaction to photographs, or for that matter to *any* art, before that. They were disarmingly disturbing yet completely engaging, with a haunting beauty. One could not help but want to see more—and to know more about the artist. I began the dogged task of acquiring one of her photographs. They were not readily available in the late 1980s, but I persevered. Eventually I was able to acquire two photographs, which I cherish and which have a place in my home; they hang by my desk. They speak to the universal search for identity, and specifically to the search for female identity. And of course in the context of the artist's short life and suicide they are particularly moving.

Annabelle Selldorf is a fellow of the American Institute of Architects and president of the board of directors of the Architectural League of New York. Her firm, Selldorf Architects, has designed many spaces for art, including the recently completed galleries for David Zwirner and Hauser & Wirth in New York and London, as well as the Frieze Masters art fair and the Neue Galerie New York.

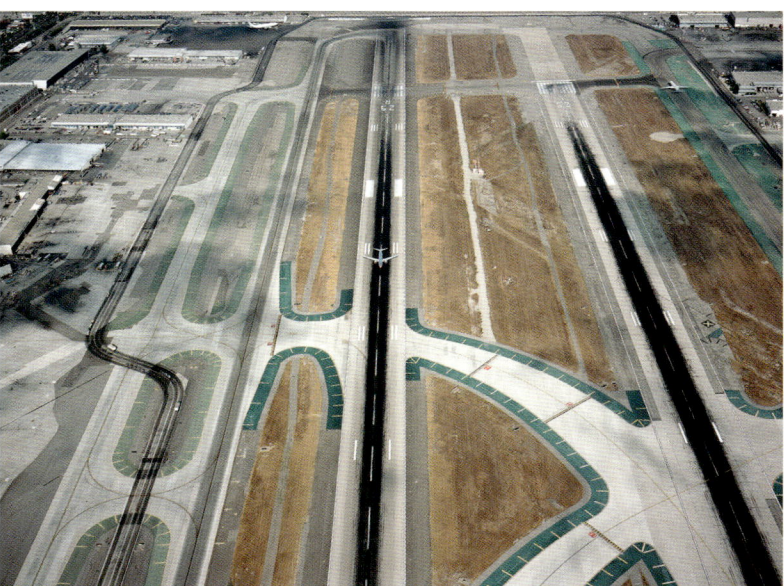

Benny Chan, *LAX Runway*, 2005 © Benny Chan

Neil Denari

I acquired this photograph for its sublime formal qualities and because it captures a moment of transgression in a heavily trafficked airspace. It's a big piece—forty by forty-eight inches—and we keep it over the fireplace in our living room. I have known Benny Chan since 1991. He studied photography in Hawaii, and later, after finishing his studies at the Southern California Institute for Architecture in 1992, he worked in my office for half of 1993. He traveled to Europe to document architecture and began his career as a professional photographer. He has photographed all my domestic projects and models since 1993 and is now exhibiting his fine art work, of which our LAX piece is one. This particular photograph was made on March 17, 2005, 3:36 P.M., over the Los Angeles International Airport North Runway.

Neil Denari was awarded the Los Angeles AIA Gold Medal in 2011. His firm, Neil M. Denari Architects, based in Los Angeles, recently won the international building design competition for the New Keelung Harbor Terminal in Taiwan. It is scheduled to open in 2017.

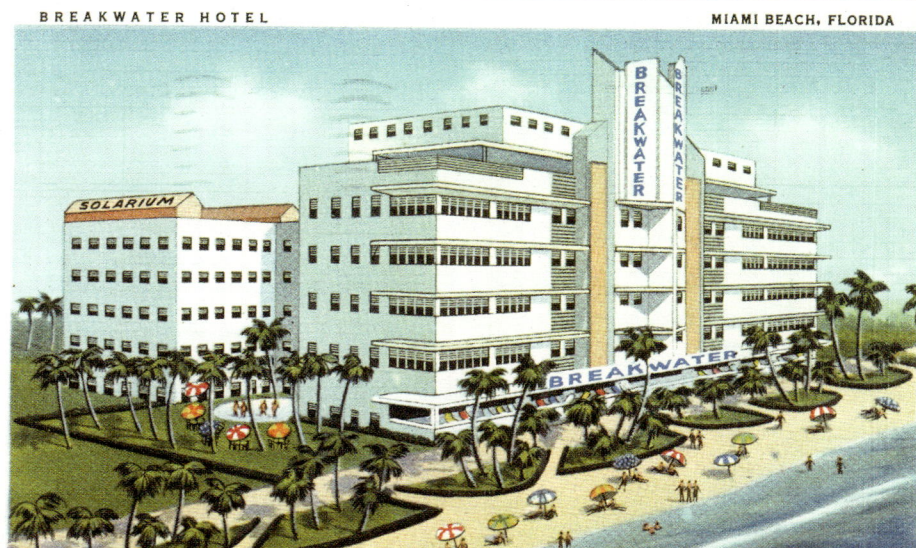

BREAKWATER HOTEL   MIAMI BEACH, FLORIDA

DIRECTLY ON THE OCEAN

Postcard showing Miami Beach's Breakwater Hotel, early 1940s

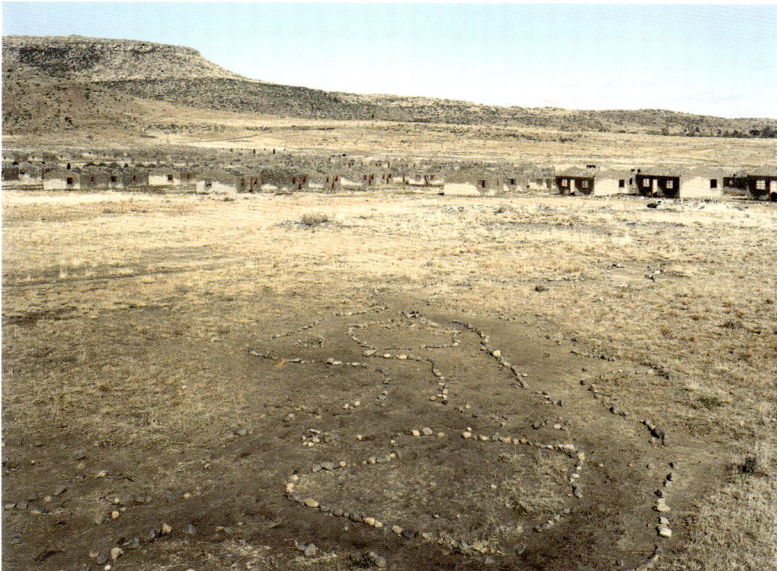

David Goldblatt, Remains of a children's game called *onopopi* and shells of incomplete
structures, part of a stalled housing plan. Kwezi-Naledi, Lady Grey, Eastern Cape, South Africa,
August 5, 2006 Courtesy Goodman Gallery, Cape Town

John Pawson

I normally think of photography as a tool, but
David Goldblatt's work proves that it can also be
art. This picture has hung in my office ever since
I bought it from the Marian Goodman Gallery
in Paris six years ago. I still find myself looking
at it every day. Of course there is the link with
South Africa—my wife, Catherine, was born
in Johannesburg—but the picture also perfectly
captures the desolation of the half-built,
which has particular resonance for an architect.
The juxtaposition of the abandoned structures
with the remains of a children's game only adds
to the poignancy. Goldblatt has a way of allowing
the viewer to make an emotional connection with
a subject without ever weakening that connection
with sentiment.

**John Pawson received the 2012 Casa Clima
Award, honoring sustainable design, for his
Casa delle Bottere, in Italy's Veneto region.
Last year, the Pinakothek der Moderne
in Munich devoted an exhibition to his work,
which included the architect's photographs.**

Denise Scott Brown

This vintage view is from the collection of
postcards we assembled while gathering
information for urban and architectural projects.
Steve Izenour found it. He was our assistant at
the time, a young architect who had worked with
us on our study *Learning from Las Vegas*.

He, Robert Venturi, and I shared an interest in
Miami Beach and a love for its Deco architecture,
so in the 1970s, when we began our study of South
Beach, Steve ordered postcards from catalogs and
found others in local tourist shops. We used them
as historical source material and as a basis for
drawings. The Breakwater Hotel, which probably
dates from the early 1940s, is one of my favorites.
Its depiction shows the complete Miami Beach
iconography: umbrellas, palm trees, blue sky,
blue sea, and the grand old hotel in the colors
of its time—mainly white, with a little orange
and turquoise. Today, the Deco District is known
as "SoBe," a chic international watering spot.
But I remember the social mix when we worked
there: retired Jewish New Yorkers, Cuban
refugees, hibernating Canadians, Venezuelans
on buying trips. It triggered nostalgia for a similar
but distant beach, Muizenberg, of my childhood
in South Africa.

**Denise Scott Brown was a cofounder, with her
husband Robert Venturi, of the architecture
firm VSBA. Among her writings are: *Learning
from Las Vegas* (co-authored with Venturi and
Steven Izenour, 1972) and *Having Words* (2009).
Her pioneering study of the Miami Beach Deco
District helped initiate the preservation and
development of its hotels and apartments.
She is currently working on a retrospective
exhibition of her photographs of everyday
American architecture of the 1960s.**

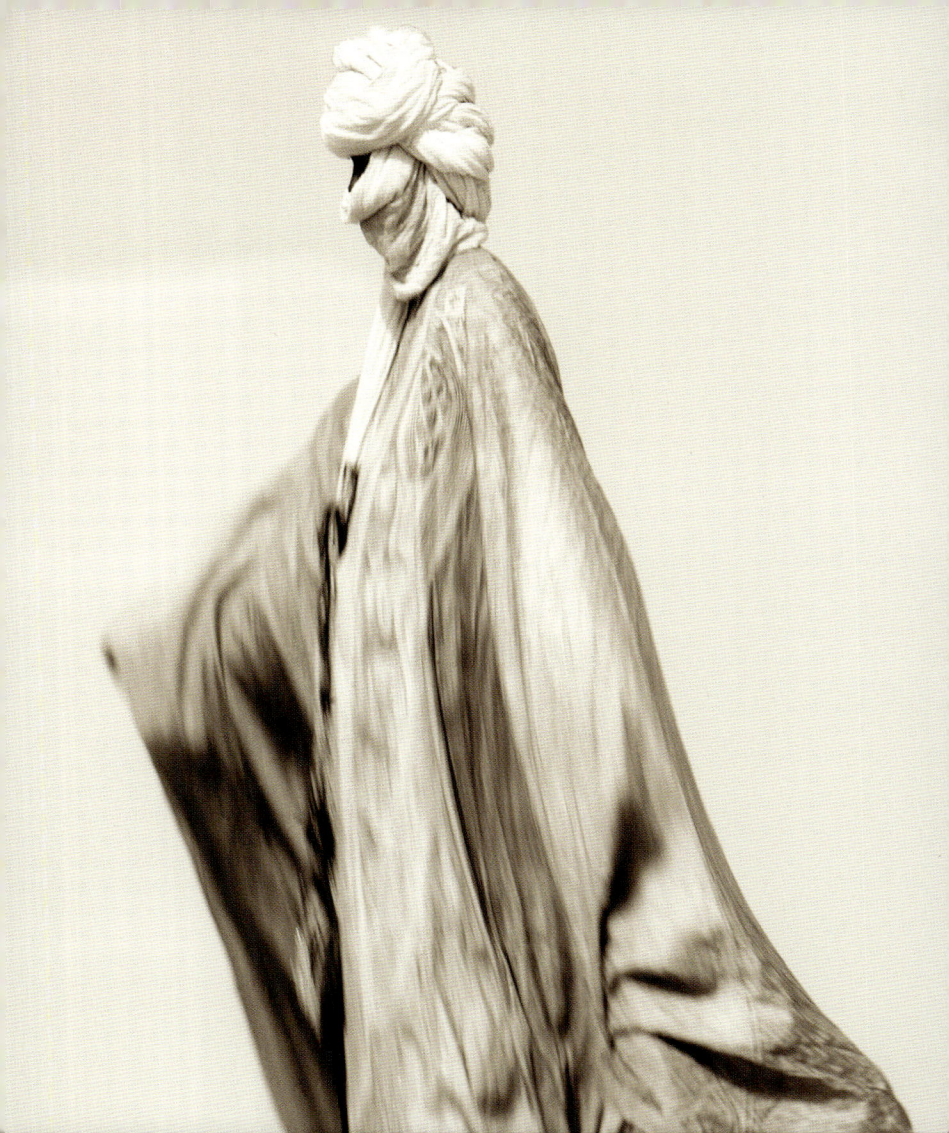

Elisabeth Sunday

GRACE

May 2nd - July 6th, 2013

Autographed Book Available:
GRACE: $50.00

Image: Elisabeth Sunday, Nobleman, Tuareg Man, Mali, 2007, Platinum Print, 24 x 20 in.

145 EAST 57TH STREET, 3RD FLOOR, NEW YORK, NY 10022
TEL 212.223.1059 FAX 212.223.1937
info@throckmorton-nyc.com www.throckmorton-nyc.com

Studio Visit
Photographers at Work

John Divola at his Riverside workplace
Jonathan Griffin

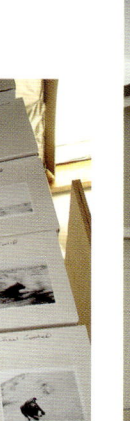

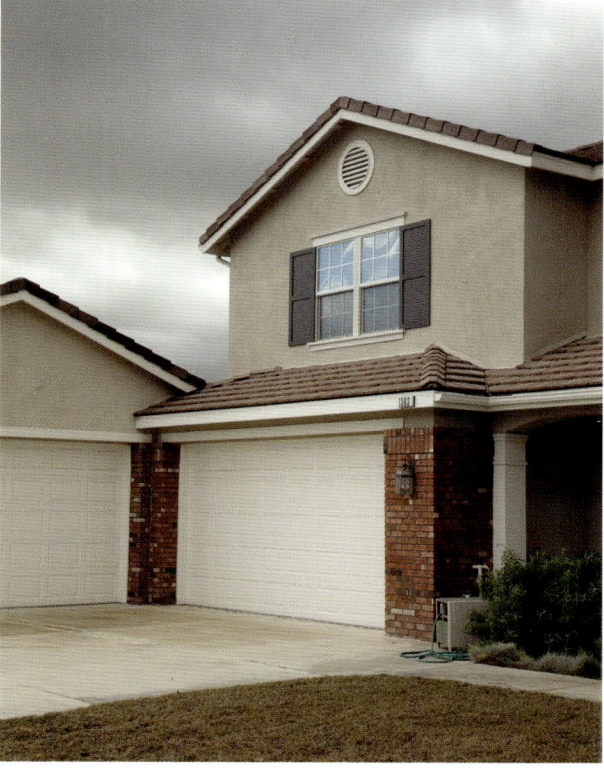

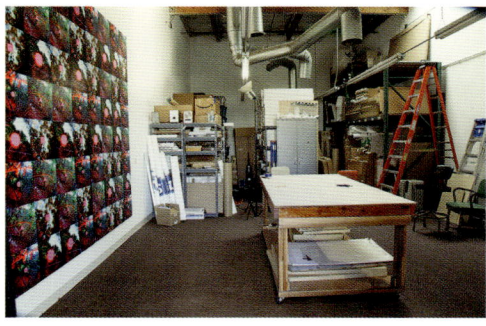

In the distance, a soaring elevated freeway intersection frames a wide-screen view of the San Gabriel mountains. The dissonance is typical of Southern California: awesome nature matched by equally awesome urban development. Despite the seemingly endless sprawl, it is rare in the Los Angeles basin that one cannot see out of it to the wilderness beyond.

Down below the traffic lies a quiet industrial development—rows of identical roller-doored units off a street with young trees and clipped lawns. In one of these units John Divola stores the bulk of his archive, which spans five decades, in metal shelves, with a table and empty walls at the front for viewing work. Two doors down, weightlifters have rented a unit as a gym. To his knowledge, he is the only artist on the block.

It is, perhaps, an unlikely place to find an artist's studio. The town of Riverside, where Divola has lived for over a decade and worked since 1988, is situated sixty or so miles east of Los Angeles, in the heart of the Inland Empire. It is a comfortable, suburban place—maybe even a little bland. Divola admits that most of his artist colleagues and students at the University of California Riverside, where he is a distinguished professor, choose to commute from Los Angeles.

What brought him to Riverside? Partly, perhaps, the same qualities that he cites for choosing the studio: "Being here is a practical consideration—it's very inexpensive, convenient, clean, and air conditioned." I point out that the area is not dissimilar to the San Fernando Valley, which he documented in an eponymous series of photographs from 1971–73, made at the outset of his career. In those images, I suggest, there was a sense of sociopolitical criticality, of the photographer's estrangement from the outwardly conventional suburban environment in which he had grown up.

"That's a misinterpretation," he says. "Even though I was to some extent alienated, especially by the war in Vietnam, I never had a desire to get away from it. It was what I was. And actually, one of the reasons my work changed after that was that your reading of that work was everybody's reading of that work—that it was critical. It wasn't. That was *my* landscape, and I was moving through that landscape, and I wanted to bring back an index of my engagement with it."

This widespread misreading of Divola's position as an artist has dogged him throughout his career, and it has to a great extent shaped his subsequent work. Putting himself in the picture, implicating himself in the situations that he photographs, is for him a central strategy. After the *San Fernando Valley* series he made *Vandalism* (1973–75), black-and-white images of derelict houses featuring spray-painted marks that, it becomes clear, were made by Divola himself. He is the vandal—or one of them.

In *Los Angeles International Airport Noise Abatement Zone* (1975) he photographed evidence of forced entry into empty houses marked for demolition. Was it the artist himself who had caused the damage? Additional photographs taken inside some of the houses suggest it probably was. In certain images from his *Zuma* series

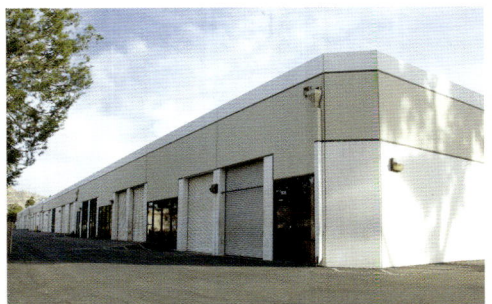

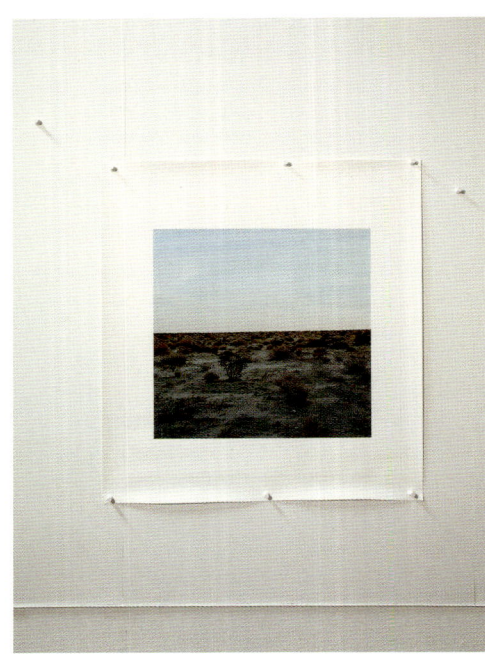

(1977–78), shot in an oceanfront house in Malibu, the camera flash pins objects such as a newspaper in midair, thrown into the frame by the unseen photographer.

Divola talks about himself as a "specter" haunting his pictures. He feels this especially strongly when he looks back at early photographs and tries to recognize himself in them. Retrospection has occupied him a great deal recently—not least because he is currently preparing for a three-museum exhibition in California this October. The Santa Barbara Museum of Art, the Los Angeles County Museum of Art, and the Pomona College Museum of Art will mount coinciding but separate exhibitions of his work, none of which, Divola insists, is a retrospective.

He also found himself reflecting on his photographs from the 1970s while scanning old prints for his book *Three Acts*, published by Aperture in 2006. Revisiting these images prompted him to look once again for abandoned houses in which he could make photographs—this time with far more advanced technology.

Divola's *Dark Star* series, from 2008, was shot largely in an empty house fifteen miles inland from Riverside, at the eastern edge of the megalopolis that stretches all the way to the Pacific Ocean. Large discs of black spray paint recollect the mysterious markings he had made in *Vandalism*. In the same house, Divola made the more recent series *Theodore Street* (2008–12) using

an ultra-high-resolution method of photography called Gigapan. Between 40 and 120 separate photographs are stitched together by software to make a picture that can be printed at large scale without losing detail. Divola says his early prints are small only because, printed any larger, the raw materiality of his subject—scraps of plywood, shattered glass—would have been overwhelmed by the grain and fuzz of the photograph. In prints up to five by ten feet, some of which will be shown in Santa Barbara, Divola physically enters the scene and conceals himself among the details. There is plenty of space for the artist to get lost.

Divola doesn't actually make art in his studio. His "indoor practice," as he calls it, is taken up with managing his archive, logistical challenges that he likens to Napoleon marching through Russia ("because it's hard to move forward when you're looking after the stuff in the rear"). The studio also gives him space to assess prints, old and new, some of which, such as his unfinished multipart work *Malibu Progressions*, from 1984, he is revisiting now that he has large inkjet printers at his disposal.

The real work, however, is done out in the field. "The beauty of photography, or conventional photography, is that it draws you out into the world, it draws you into an engagement with present reality," says Divola. And with that, we're out the door.

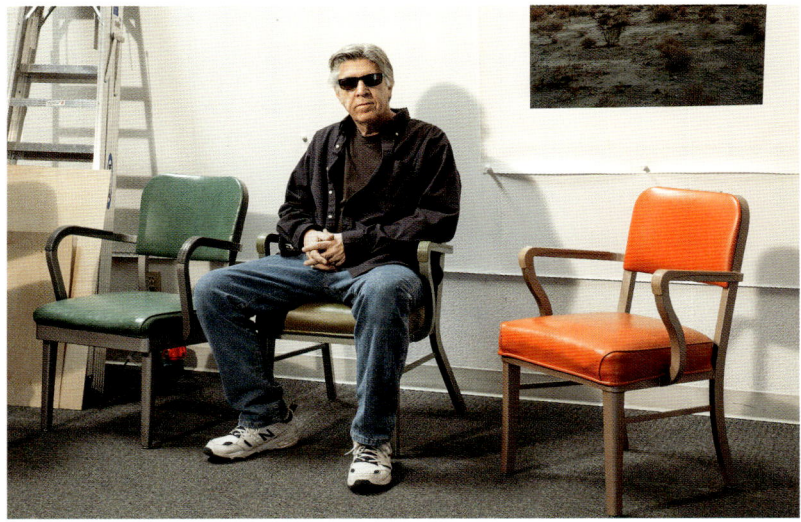

Bottom: self-portrait
All photographs by
John Divola, 2013

Jonathan Griffin is a contributing editor for *Frieze* living in Los Angeles.

Katie Paterson,
History of Darkness,
2010 and ongoing
Courtesy Ingleby Gallery,
Edinburgh, 2011

How close is distraction to discovery? From the mundane to the cosmic, Brian Dillon considers perspective, observation, and enlightenment found at the periphery.

**Attention! Photography and
Sidelong Discovery**
Brian Dillon

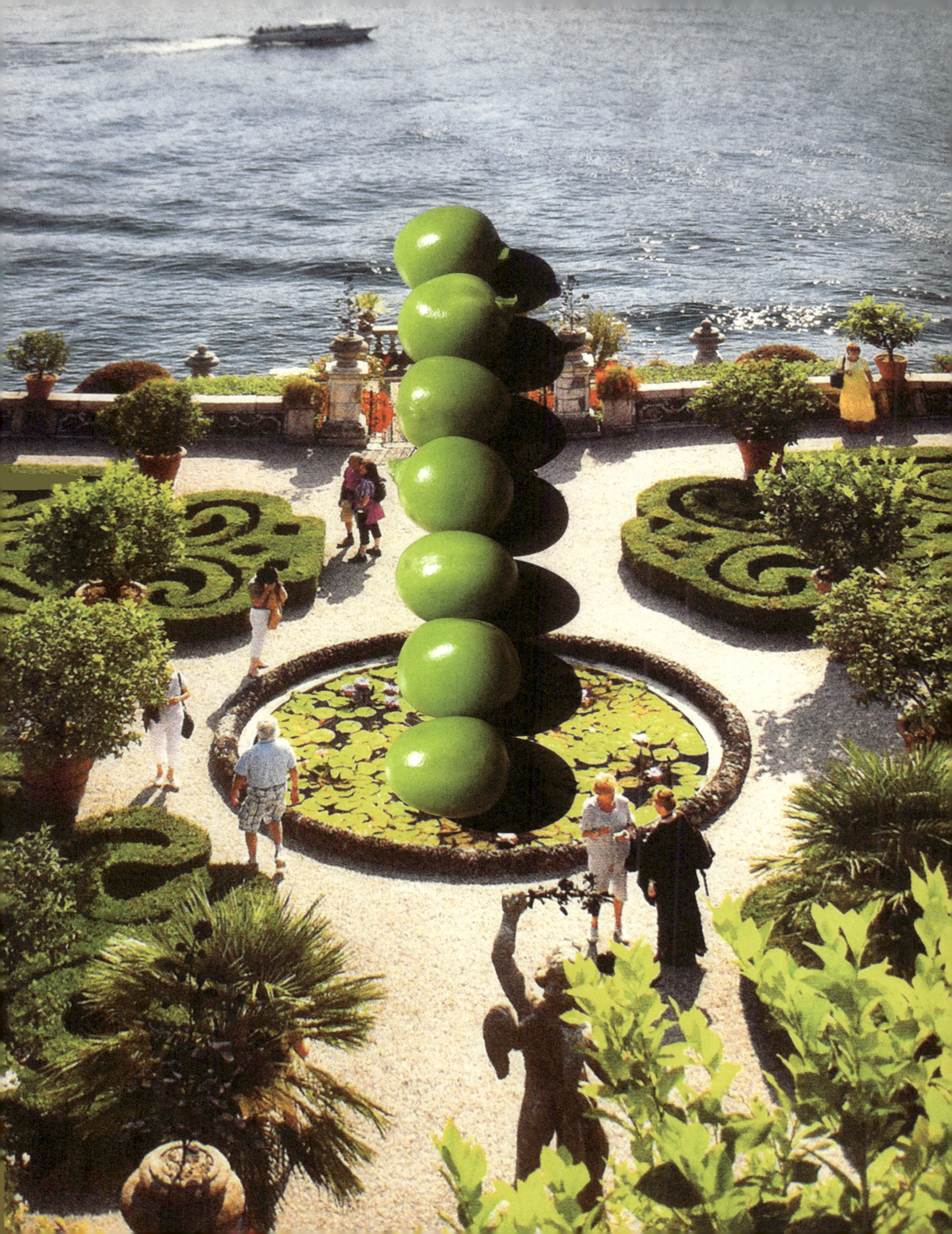

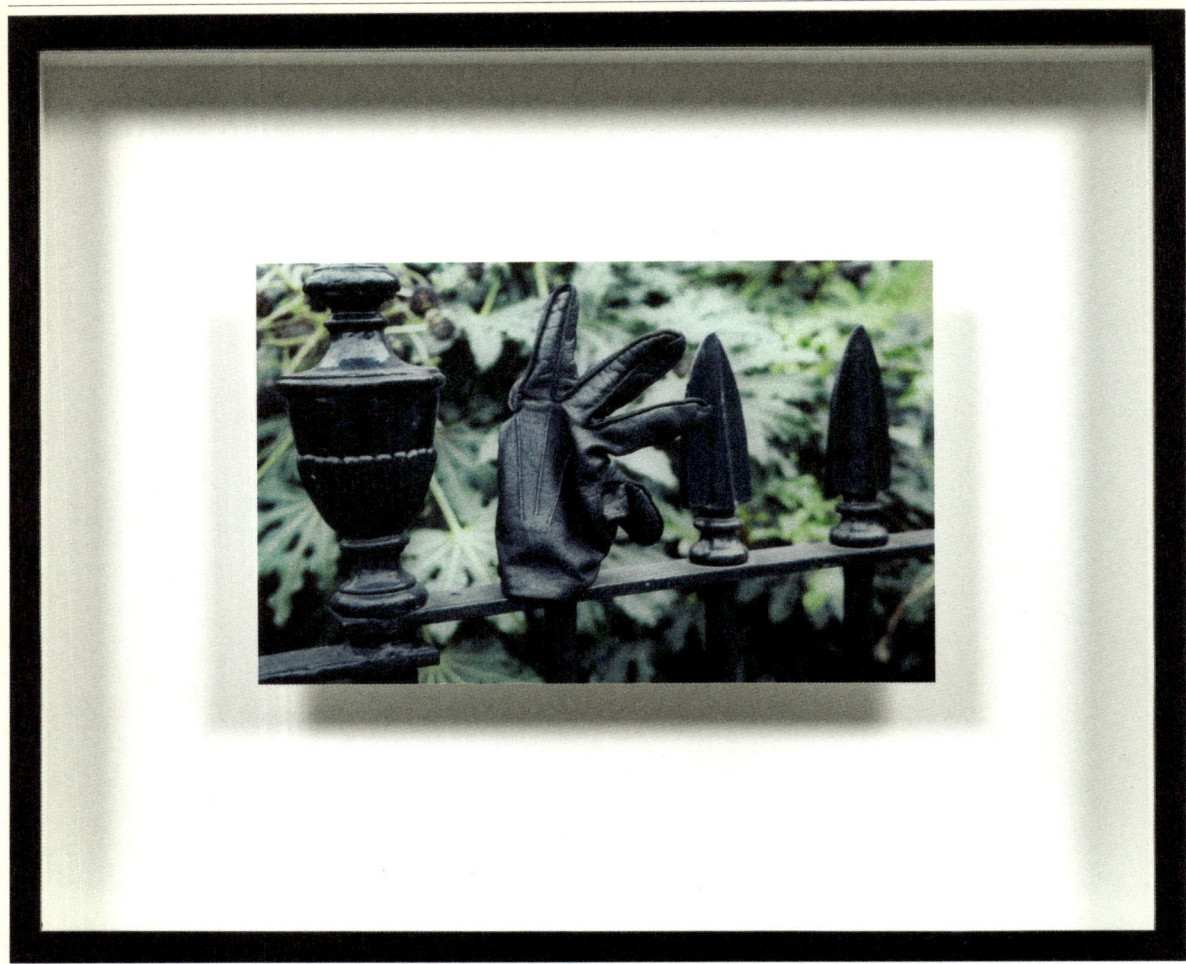

Richard Wentworth,
London, 1994. Making
Do and Getting By, 1999
Courtesy the artist and
Lisson Gallery, London

Curiosity is an oddly ambivalent word that historically has pointed almost as frequently to a condition of ruinous distraction as to a state of intense and productive concentration or to an urge to discover. To be curious or to be interested in curiosities is to be charmed by details, trifles, niceties, or subtleties, and to disregard fundamentals. Distraction has its uses, however, as the history of detective fiction tells us. In Edgar Allan Poe's "The Purloined Letter" (1845) the stolen object fails to reveal itself to the most sedulous searches; the suspect's apartment is investigated long and hard, the walls and carpets peered at through microscopes, the furniture probed with needles. The very cobblestones in the courtyard are prised apart, to no avail. At length, Poe's detective Dupin discovers the thing, tattered but undisguised, on a letter rack in the rooms of the minister who has stolen it. Dupin's distracted, sidelong mode of attention has won out over the prefect of police and his zealous and methodical program of close inspection.

Poe's prototypical sleuth springs easily to mind when considering the role of curiosity in photography, past and present. And once we have thought of Poe it's a safe bet that somebody will invoke Walter Benjamin's comment about the photograph looking increasingly, in the twentieth century, like the scene of a crime. This last is a conceit that does not apply only to photography's evidentiary potential: it's of a piece with the idea that the photographer sees more intensely into the heart of things, but also reminds us of all the lures and feints that he or she might employ to frustrate that assumption. The melodrama of appearance and reality conditions much of our thinking about photography and what it discovers about the world. But there's another sort of photographic curiosity, something like Dupin's state of oblique diversion or attention to the humblest, most fleeting scraps of the made world and their abject, slapstick, sometimes delicate poetry.

Richard Wentworth,
London, 1977. Making
Do and Getting By, **1977**
Courtesy the artist and
Lisson Gallery, London

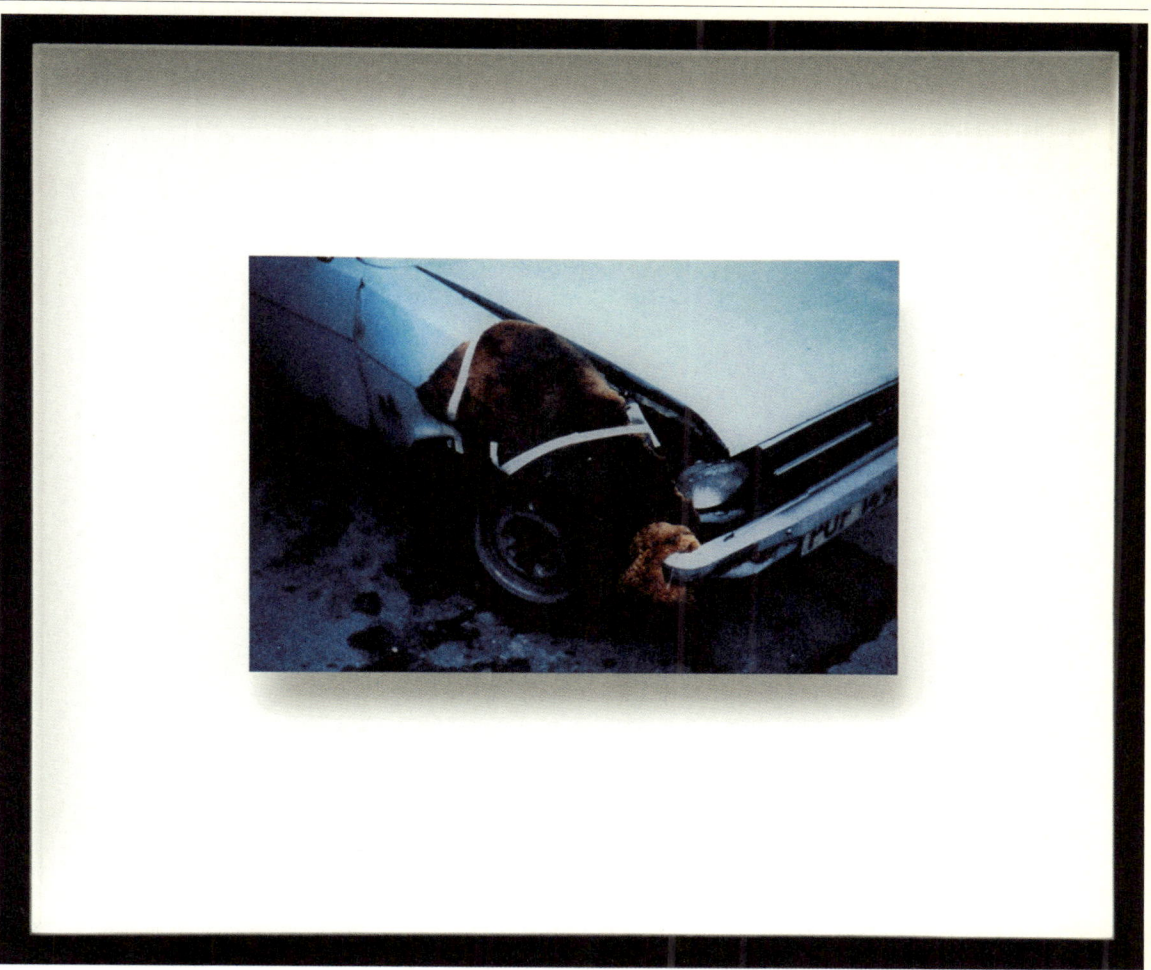

Consider *Making Do and Getting By*, the photographic series that British sculptor Richard Wentworth has been producing since the 1970s, and which amounts at this point to an archive of found semi-sculptural interventions in the fabric of the everyday. Many of them (as in Poe's tale) involve scraps of paper slotted or crammed into slits and crevices. There are napkins and newspapers jammed under café tables, bits of cardboard or tape holding things together, or nearly. Wentworth is fascinated by how the ordinary world around us has been made—step into a London street with him and he will spin a narrative out of the history of manhole covers—but also by the materials we append to our surroundings by way of repair or warning or inadvertent decoration. *Making Do and Getting By* includes numerous curbside assemblages designed to keep drivers out of parking spaces: hulking agglomerations of old gates and busted chairs, or sparse but informative settings of bricks and broken plaster balusters. Elsewhere, the stuff superadded starts to assume the form and substance of its support, of a surface or structure that now serves as temporary storage: discarded paper cups seem to sprout like spring buds from the pipe they've been jammed behind; scribbled notes on somebody's palm bleed into the hand's lines; and a lost leather glove stuck on black metal railings takes on the spiny structure of the railings and the foliage in the background. Wentworth alights time and again on those moments when forms and substances transmute into each other, and the most incongruous additions seem organic outgrowths of ordinary infrastructures.

There's something of Wentworth's capacity for simply noticing things in Nina Katchadourian's photographs; the two artists share a knack for spotting ephemera crushed in the street: a driver's license plate (Wentworth) or an old music cassette (Katchadourian) so completely flattened by traffic

The melodrama of appearance and reality conditions much of our thinking about photography and what it discovers about the world.

that it has become a mere phantom stain on the asphalt. In fact, Katchadourian, whose hugely various work includes sound, video, installation, and performance, has described her art as precisely a process of noticing—of paying more attention to the world than the rest of us do. Her skewed sense of curiosity is to be seen, for example, in her long-running series *Sorted Books*, begun twenty years ago, in which the titles of books in a given library compose scurrilous or touching found poems, jokes, and legends: in one tellingly summarizing image from 1996, two volumes have come together to say: "*What Is Art?/Close Observation.*"

It's a tendency that finds some of its keenest, and funniest, expression in Katchadourian's *Seat Assignment*: a series of photographs—latterly also video and sound—made entirely in flight, with her camera phone. A subset of this series found unexpected celebrity in 2011 when her group of *Self-Portraits in the Flemish Style* were taken up by mainstream media outlets such as the *New Yorker* and even Oprah Winfrey's website. (In March 2010, she spontaneously tricked herself up in an airplane bathroom, using tissue and paper toilet-seat covers, as a figure out of Flemish portraiture; many more such images followed.) But the admittedly hilarious Flemish pictures are just one small part of a much larger corpus of curious improvisations. In more recent images, for example, two small figures train a telescope on a night sky dominated by a salt or sugar constellation, and ectoplasmic clouds obscure photographed faces. The series has begun to splinter into more subseries—*Landscapes*, *High-Altitude Spirit Photography*, *Creatures*, *Athletics*, *Disasters*, even *Top Doctors in America*—all made with in-flight magazines, airplane food, and the crude lighting effects available at Katchadourian's aisle seat.

The comic register broached by Wentworth and Katchadourian feels light, almost frivolous, but it has something profound to say about the effort and pleasure involved in breaking habits of looking or not looking, of paying a new sort of attention. (I suspect that part of the appeal of *Seat Assignment* is in our envy that Katchadourian is the one person on the plane not bored senseless.) One version, philosophically speaking, of that process is summed up in Ludwig Wittgenstein's definition of the aim of his discipline as "to show the fly the way out of the fly-bottle." The aphorism ghosts British artist Jeremy Millar's 2012 photograph of a fly on Wittgenstein's grave in Cambridge, England. No doubt Millar, whose videos, photographs, and installations frequently address modes of museological or archival looking, knows that Wittgenstein's fly is an ambiguous creature: natural curiosity has got the insect into trouble in the first place, and it takes some rigor and self-control to crawl back out to the other side of the glass.

The curious photographic impulse I'm trying to corral here is also capable of a kind of metaphysical facetiousness. All the works I've mentioned are as much about the boundaries of our native curiosity, the constraints in which we improvise our existence, as they are about acts of extreme concentration and discovery. There's a cosmically scaled version of that comedy of ambition and overreach in Katie Paterson's *History of Darkness*: a "lifelong project" (as she calls it) in which the Scottish artist is amassing images of darkness, sourced globally from observatories and laboratories and transferred to 35mm slides, that show vacant black fragments of the night sky or of deepest, emptiest space. The slides are exhibited in a box that allows them to be taken out and examined, and each is labeled with a date and location in the heavens; an offshoot of the project (with the same title) involves large-scale photographic prints, similarly void. We know or suspect, of course, that there

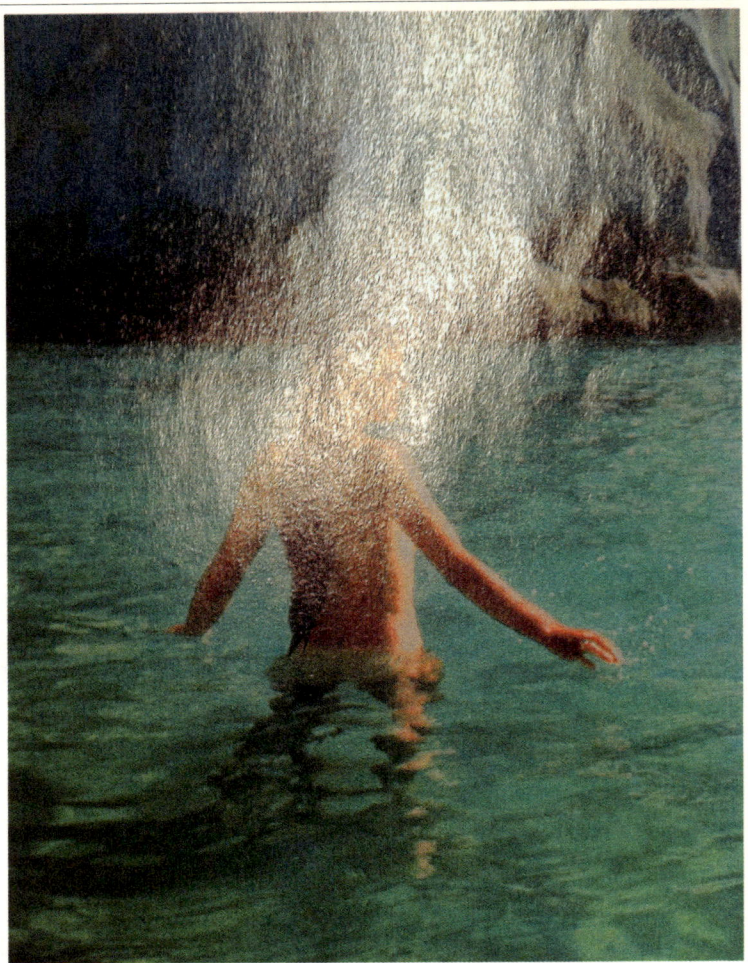

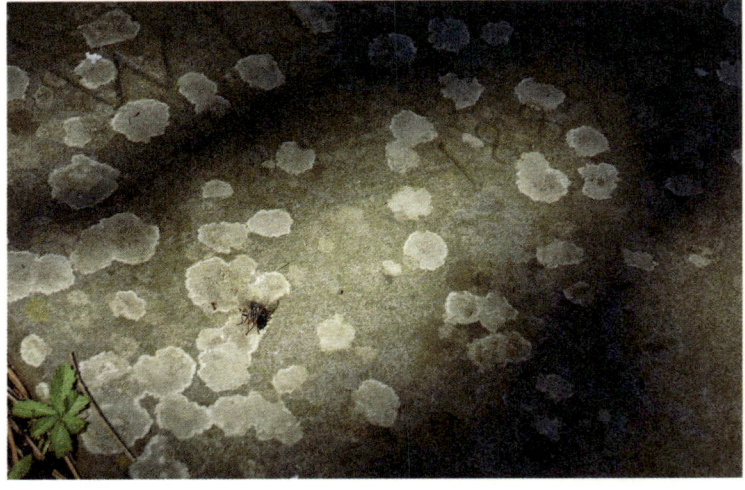

Top:
Nina Katchadourian,
Bather, from *High-Altitude Spirit Photography*, part of the series *Seat Assignment*, 2010 and ongoing
Courtesy the artist and Catharine Clark Gallery, San Francisco

Bottom:
Jeremy Millar, *Fly on Wittgenstein's Grave*, 2012
Courtesy the artist

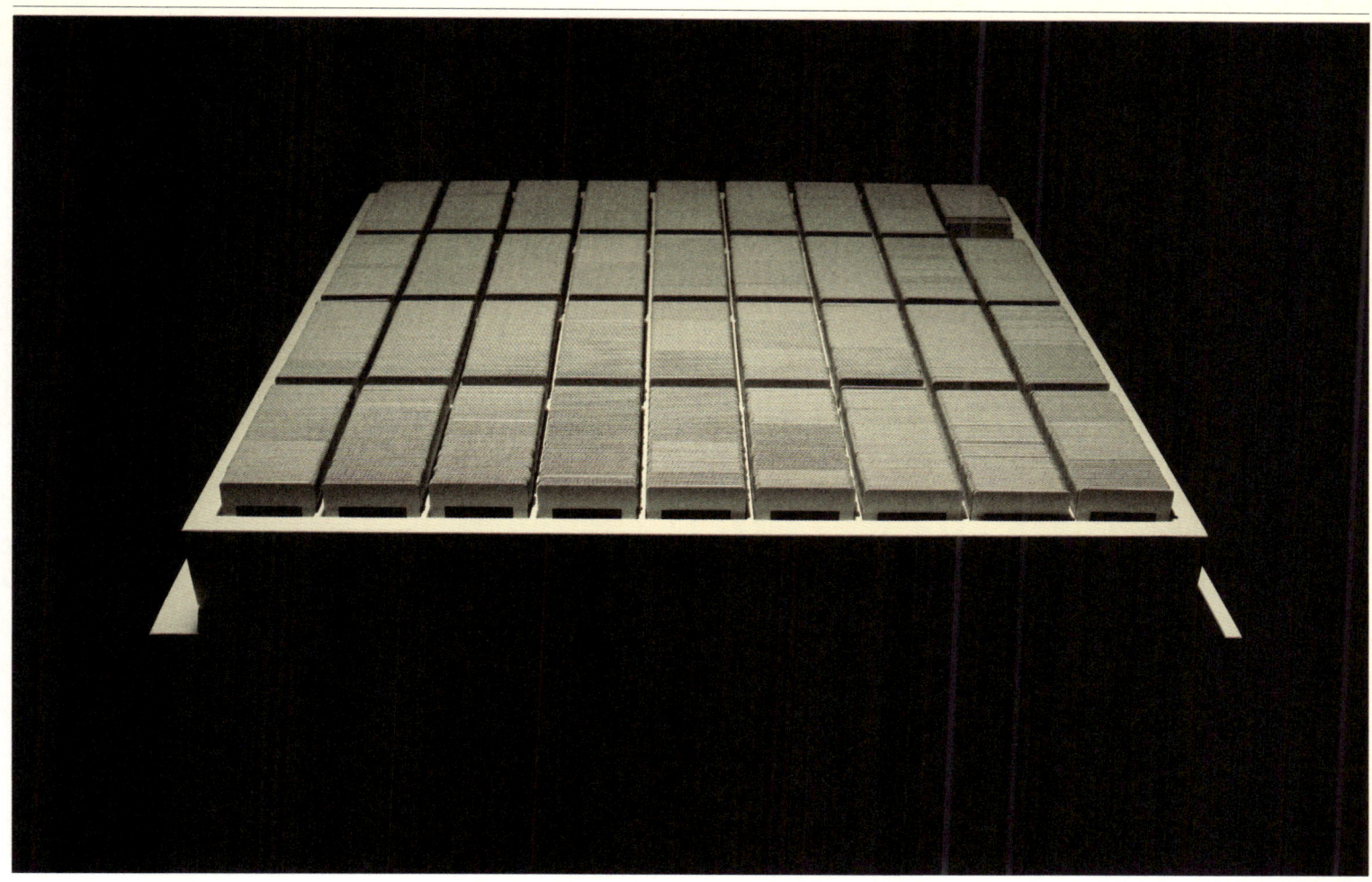

is something beyond or behind the darkness shown there, but even the most prying look will not disclose it as we hold each slide to the light. It's a lesson in the infinitude of human curiosity and its attendant hubris.

History of Darkness is just one of several of Paterson's works that essay a cosmically laconic take on astrophysical discovery and the protocols of its recording. A 2007 work, *Earth-Moon-Earth*, involved translating the first movement of Beethoven's "Moonlight" Sonata into Morse-code radio signals and bouncing it off the moon; in the gallery a player piano performed the piece—somewhat degraded during the transmission—as it returned to Earth. For *The Dying Star Letters*—like *History of Darkness*, a continuing project—Paterson is sent an email each time scientists note that a star has expired; she then writes a letter of condolence, directed for instance to a staff member at the gallery where the work is on display: "I'm sorry to inform you of the death of the star SN2011kd." The piece composes an index of disappearances, the light winking out as previous discoveries vanish into the void.

As Poe's Dupin tells us in another story, "Murders in the Rue Morgue" (1841), the best way to catch sight of a heavenly body is to catch it off guard by looking a little to the side—"it is possible to make even Venus herself vanish from the firmament by a scrutiny too sustained, too concentrated, or too direct." An excess of application, in other words, may result paradoxically in a *failure* of attention, and the cure is an oblique curiosity, a faith in peripheral vision. (What is Paterson's *History of Darkness* if not an archive of all that's off to the side?) It's an essential lesson, especially in an era when we like to guiltily accuse ourselves of regular failures of attention, dispersed as our minds supposedly are among digital distractions. The history of curiosity reminds us that accidents will happen, and instructs its contemporary adepts how to be waiting when they do.

Katie Paterson,
History of Darkness,
2010 and ongoing.
Installation view, BALTIC
Centre for Contemporary
Art, Gateshead, UK, 2010
© Katie Paterson and
courtesy the artist and
James Cohan Gallery,
New York and Shanghai,
and Haunch of Venison,
London

Brian Dillon is UK editor of *Cabinet* magazine and teaches critical writing at the Royal College of Art. A collection of his essays, *Objects in This Mirror*, will be published by Sternberg Press in May 2013.

Curiosity: Art & the Pleasures of Knowing, a Hayward Touring exhibition conceived in association with *Cabinet*, will be presented at Turner Contemporary, Margate, England, May 25–September 15, 2013. The exhibition will travel to Norwich Castle Museum & Art Gallery (September 28, 2013–January 5, 2014) and then to de Appel, Amsterdam (June–August, 2014).

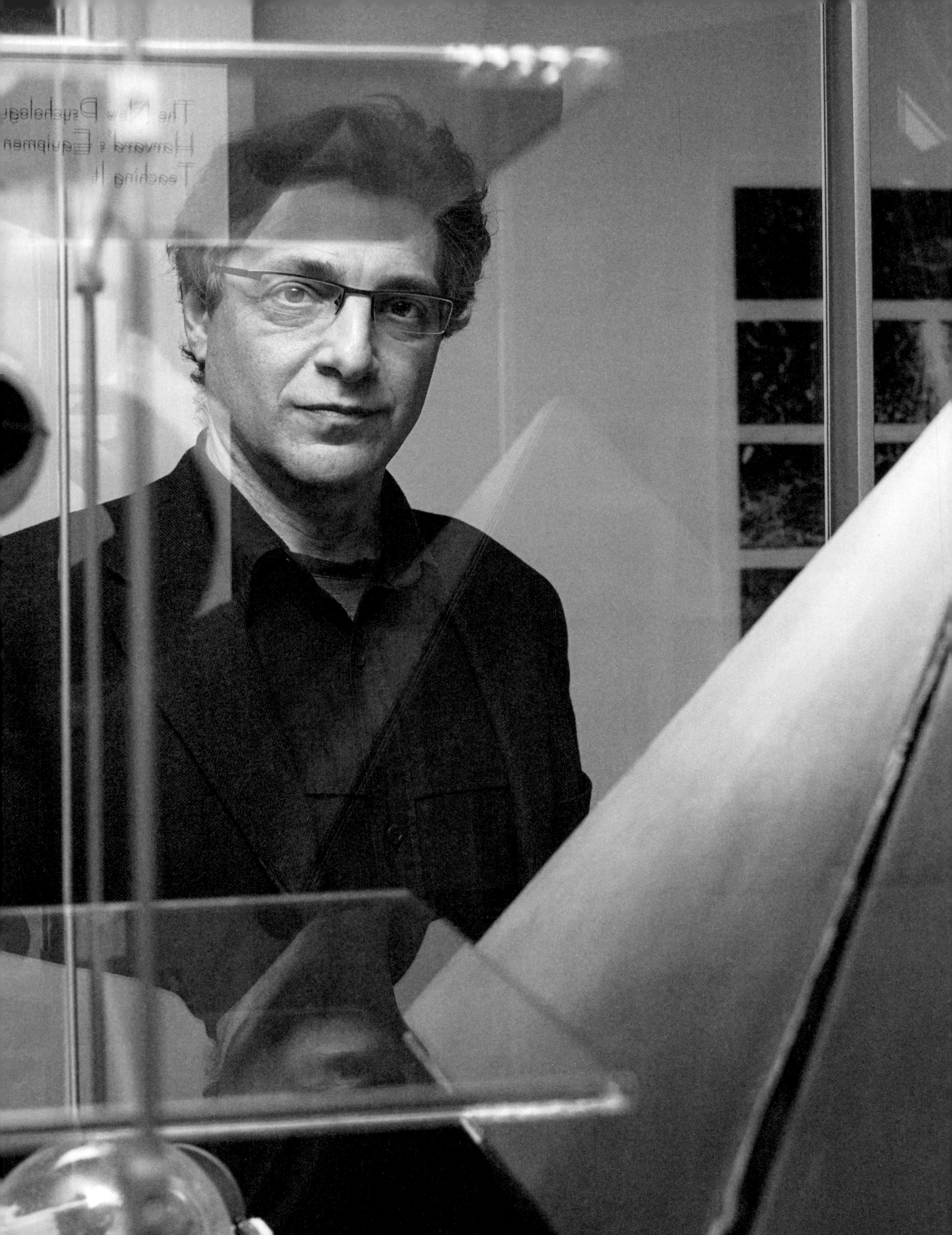

What is observation? What is objectivity? What counts as "right depiction"? Are images today now *doing* more than showing? What does the future of imaging hold?

Peter Galison, one of the world's leading historians of science, has written widely on how visual representation shapes our understanding of the world. Trevor Paglen is an artist whose work with photography has explored governmental secrecy and the limits of seeing. For his most recent project, *The Last Pictures*, Paglen worked with a group of scientists to create a disc of images marking our historical moment; the project culminated in last year's launch of a satellite (carrying the disc) that will remain in Earth's orbit perpetually. The following conversation took place at Aperture's office earlier this year.

The Lives of Images
Peter Galison in conversation
with Trevor Paglen

Opposite:
Photograph of Peter Galison
by Matthew Monteith,
January 2013

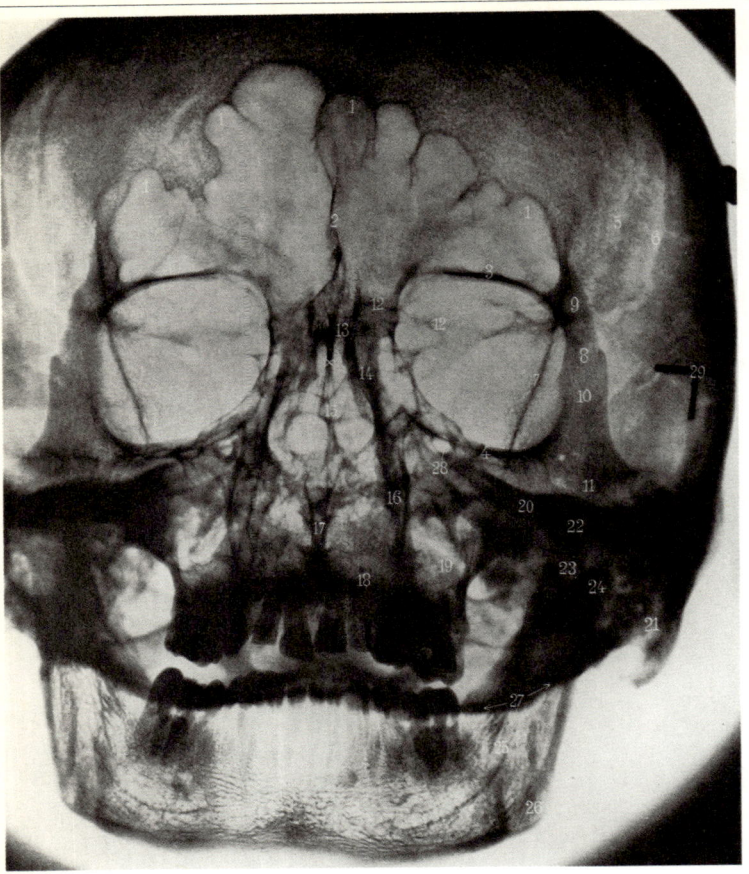

Rudolf Grashey, X-ray of skull, from *Atlas typischer Röntgenbilder vom normalen Menschen* (Atlas of typical X-rays of a normal person), 6th ed. (Lehmann, 1939)

It seems that we're moving away from thinking about images in terms of representation and toward thinking about their creation as part of a networked process, guided by political or economic "scripts" embedded in the algorithms controlling these image-making networks.

Trevor Paglen: **A number of historians have pointed out that over the last few hundred years, vision has taken on a much more prominent role as a purveyor of truth in Western thought. When Galileo saw and then claimed that the moon was craggy and pockmarked, it was heresy. His contemporaries held that the moon was smooth, because Aristotelian physics said as much. The idea of sight being a privileged path to knowledge, the argument goes, is a relatively recent occurrence, but we are living at a time when vision is absolutely central to how we understand and manipulate the world. Do you think this is true: does it all go back to Galileo's telescope?**

Peter Galison: Seeing has been important to science for a very long time, certainly back into the medieval and Renaissance eras. But what counts as seeing, *systematic* seeing, natural-philosophical or scientific seeing, does change. My view is that the scientific category, the scientific self, and what counts as vision are very closely allied. I think that since the scientific self is constantly in mutation, vision also alters in radical ways. So when we say that Galileo observes a ball on an inclined plane, or that the 2,500 physicists of the ATLAS collaboration observe the Higgs boson at CERN [the European Organization for Nuclear Research], we mean radically different things. It is crucial to understand what's changing about the phrase "we see"—who (or what) the seeing subject is.

TP: **One of the things you discuss in your book *Objectivity* is the relationships among seeing images, representation, and knowledge. You use the history of scientific atlases to understand the changing relationship between vision and knowledge, how different models of "ideal" vision were developed and discarded over a relatively brief period between the eighteenth and twentieth centuries. The reason for these continually changing ideals has to do with the fact that they all seemed limited. All of them fell flat in various ways. Can you outline briefly the argument of that book?**

PG: Within the sciences and medicine, there are volumes of systematically collected images that define the basic working objects of a domain of inquiry. There are atlases of clouds, there are atlases of skulls, there are atlases of hands, of brains, of elementary particles, of crystals—there are atlases of almost any object category you can think of. Historically, they were used to categorize and organize our encounter with nature. These atlases were not, in general, decorative volumes. They were often printed on archival paper with special kinds of bindings. They were considered to be a lasting legacy of knowledge. This kind of object goes back to the eighteenth century and in some instances earlier. So these picture books give us a window onto science and medicine that allows us to look at changing ideas of representation, sight, and right depiction. What do we want from our scientific images?

In the eighteenth century, the most appropriate scientist to draw or depict the world was a kind of sage, or a genius, who could part the curtains of experience and draw the basic forms of objects as they should be—to see the platonic forms, if you will, that lay behind any particular oak or clover or cloud. In the nineteenth century, there was a different ideal of what the scientist should be. Not a genius or sage, but rather a kind of trained, self-restrained worker. The workers of the era were supposed to know enough to help keep the machines running, but weren't going to interfere and, say, customize a bullet or a fork that was coming off of the metal presses of the time. You didn't want somebody making by hand his or her particular

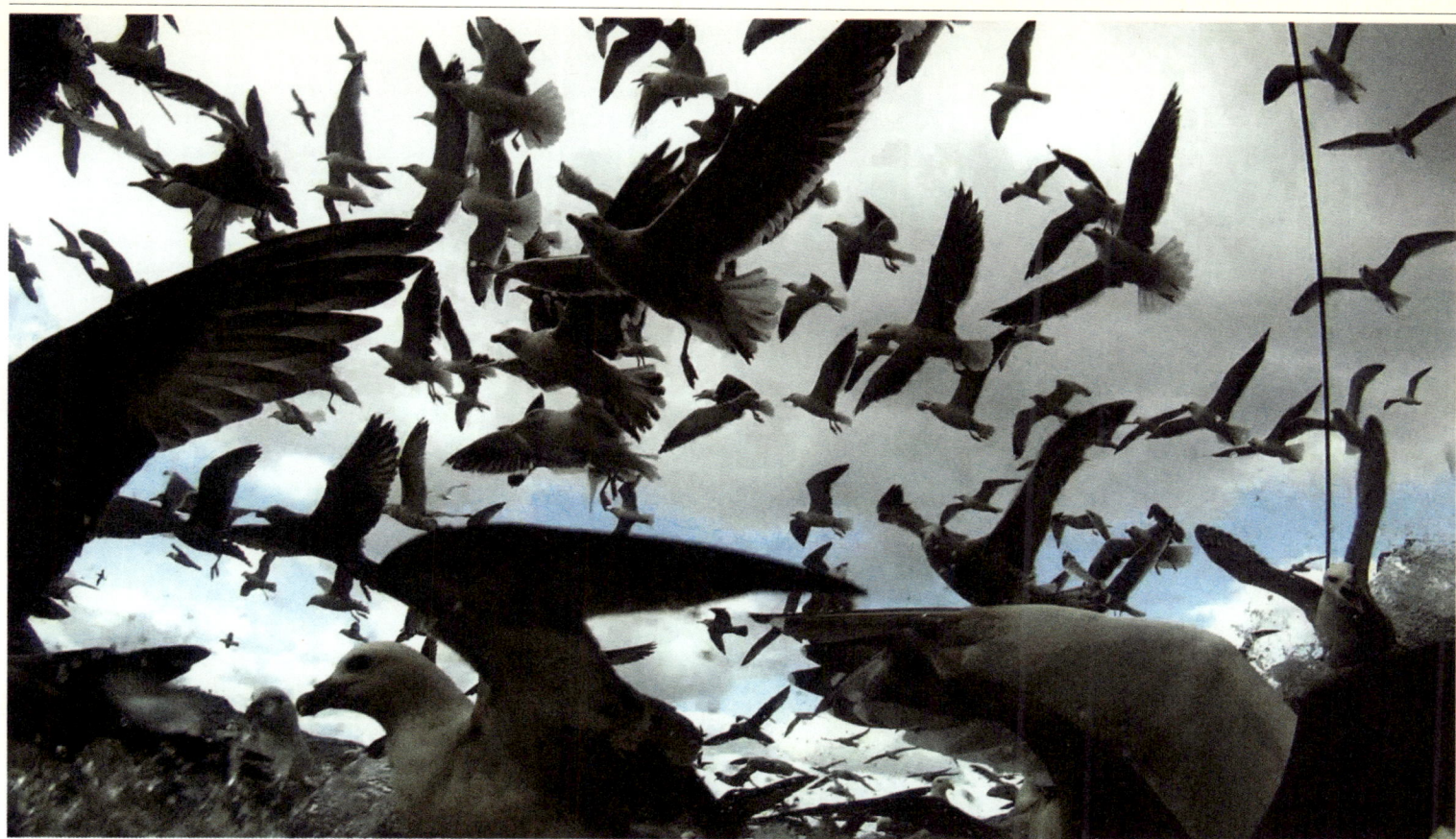

Still from the film *Leviathan*
(dir. Lucien Castaing-Taylor
and Véréna Paravel), 2012
Courtesy Cinema Guild

idea of what an ideal item should be. In fact, there emerged in the machine age an aesthetic fascination with the identical quality of machine-produced objects.

And so it was for the scientists, too. Mid-to-late-nineteenth-century scientists didn't want to know what you or I or somebody else *thought* a clover should look like. They wanted to see an image of a specific clover with as much fidelity as possible to the actual object. They wanted by any means possible to transfer a particular entity—a skull or a skeleton, whatever it was—to the page. You say: "Well, does that have to be chemical-based photography?" No. It could be tracing. It could be inking a leaf and then pressing it onto a piece of paper. There were many other mechanical modes of transfer. "Mechanical" back then meant any process that did not involve personal intervention.

Once chemical-based photography entered the scene, it became part of this desire for mechanical objectivity, but chemical photography did not cause the turn to objective depiction. In fact, when photographs were first used in science, people would, for example, take several pictures of a cell and then cut out different pieces and glue them together to make the ideal form of the cell. So you actually see analog photography being pulled into the ideal of representation that was characteristic of the *eighteenth* century.

Then, in the twentieth century, you have a third epoch of "right depiction." There emerges the persona of a trained expert, one who doesn't think: "I am a genius like Goethe, and I can improve the image to its ideal form." Nor: "I am a faithful technician of supreme self-restraint." Instead, he or she says: "I have been trained in such a careful way, I have apprenticed myself to the craft so fastidiously, that I will know if an artifact being produced by the machine needs correction." When the first magnetic-resonance machines were used to make images, doctors did a lot of unnecessary surgery on people's backs because those who were using the machines didn't really understand the method: you might think somebody needed back surgery who *didn't* need it. That was a situation where you wanted a trained observer who would say: "Oh, that distortion in the backbone, that's not real." Depiction by the trained expert is not a slavish adherence to the mechanically produced image. Nor is the expert declaiming: "I know the true form of a back." The expert says: "I know this machine; I've worked with this machine; I've apprenticed myself to its functions, and I know that under certain conditions you get this distortion." So you have a trained observer—not a genius, not a self-abnegating worker, but a trained worker—who begins to produce images that are corrected in this way, with expert knowledge—an expertly produced image.

TP: **What you alluded to just now is a move away from a representational paradigm altogether. You're talking about practices in which seeing and doing are the same thing.**

PG: In the current moment, there is another kind of image making that's become very important, that isn't any of the ones we've talked about: neither an ideal, nor a mechanical, nor an expert-altered image. The surgeon, the electronics fabricator, or somebody working with toxic materials—they are all using the image to *manipulate* something. I think that images actively used as part of manipulation mean we are no longer concerned with *re*-presentation, but rather with *presentation*. Images are a part of the primary intervention into the world. In that world, which is more engineering or surgery or sampling, the fundamental question is not, as with the classic from particle physics: "Does this exist?" Instead, it's: "Does our evidence demonstrate to a reasonable probability that there are particles of the type that we've described?"

We are no longer wondering if our re-presentation of the thing matches something out there. Today, more and more, we want images that do things. An evidentiary image is no longer sufficient for many scientists. We want images that help us organize information, that are accessible, that may not be a copy of something "out there" at all. Taking the data from CERN and mapping it in novel mathematical-physical spaces, or using false

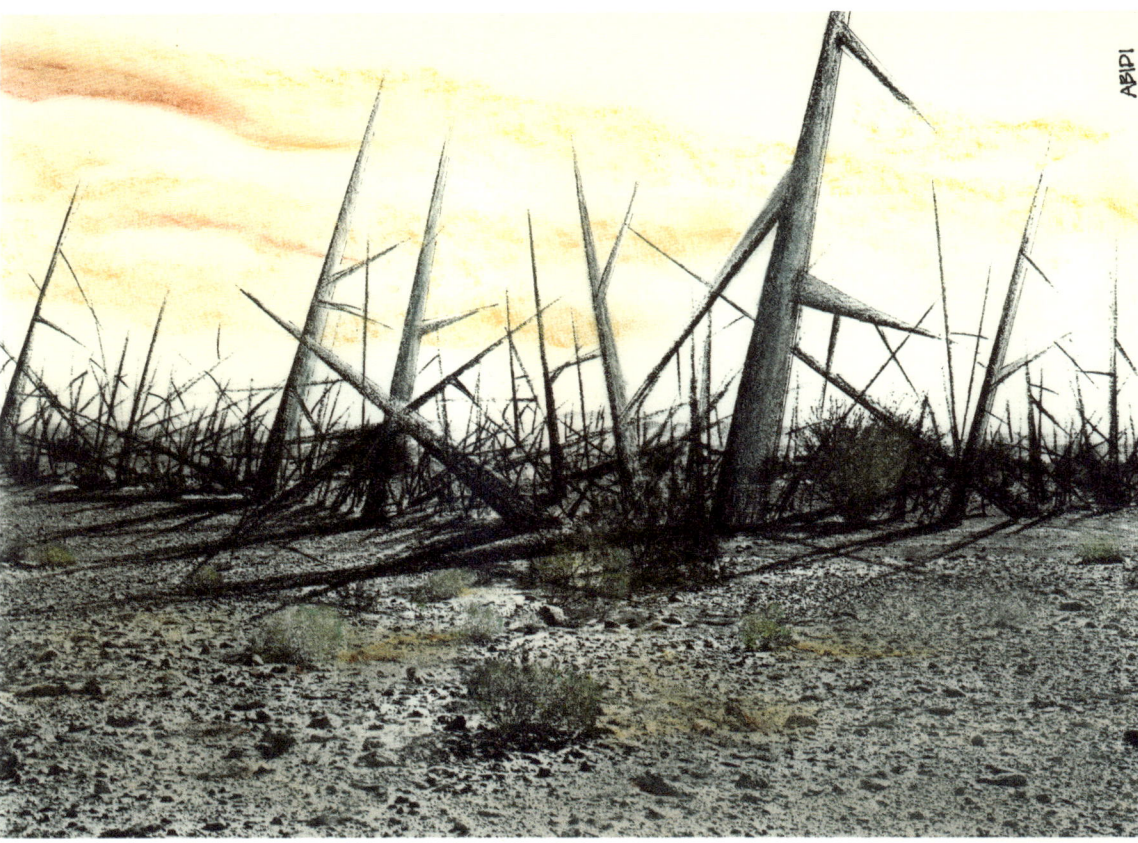

"Landscape of Thorns," concept by Michael Brill, art by Safdar Abidi, from *Expert Judgement on Markers to Deter Inadvertent Human Intrusion into the Waste Isolation Pilot Plant*, Sandia National Laboratories report, SAND92-1382/ UC-721
Courtesy Mike Brill Archive

colors in astronomy to demonstrate heat, are simple examples. But, more than that, images become tools, like a video-monitor image used by a distant doctor to conduct tele-surgery. When images are there to cut, fold, connect, or manufacture, their purpose is to help us do things beyond the classical task of categorizing and confirming.

TP: **We've both spent a lot of time considering extreme-case studies of what images can do, and what sorts of information they can and cannot transmit. I'm thinking here of the effort to design warning signs for the distant future at the WIPP [Waste Isolation Pilot Plant] site in New Mexico, which are meant to warn future generations that radioactive waste is buried there. I'm also thinking about the collection of images attached to the *Voyager* space probes in the 1970s, which were meant to explain something about life on Earth to extraterrestrials. Both of these are collections of images that are meant to work outside of history; the idea underlying them is that images are able to transmit information and even instructions across vast amount of time, and in the case of *Voyager*, even across planets and species. What do you make of these very strange uses of images?**

PG: I am in the midst of writing and making a film about nuclear waste. I'm working on it with my longtime collaborator Robb Moss. We're interested, for example, in the only licensed, operational underground nuclear-waste repository in the world —an astonishing site located in southeastern New Mexico, near the city of Carlsbad. The repository is located in a five-hundred-million-year-old bedded salt layer, about two thousand feet underground. As a condition for opening this radiological storage site, Congress demanded that the Environmental Protection Agency stipulate that people should be warned, for a period of ten thousand years, against inadvertent intrusion into the site. The Department of Energy then had to ask: How can you mark the plutonium-infested in a *legible* way? They brought in materials scientists, semioticians, linguists, and scientific illustrators like Jon Lomberg, who worked on marking the "Golden Record" [the phonographic record of selections from Earth's culture, sent up with the *Voyager* spacecraft]. The SETI [Search for Extraterrestrial Intelligence] founding fathers, including Carl Sagan and Frank Drake, were brought in, too. Warn four hundred future generations? Necessary and impossible.

In marking the WIPP site there was a fundamental split of opinion. One group said: "Make the best *universal* images." Spiky things, for example, would communicate danger of harm to the far future. Images of the human form will communicate with whatever human civilization succeeds us ten thousand years from now. Facial expressions of disgust, for example, seem to cut across cultures and times, according to certain ethnographers and ethnologists.

That universalism was disputed by others on the team. The anti-universalists said: "If you try to make something so abstracted from the specificity of culture and history, it becomes a kind of abstract art that won't communicate worth a damn." The future might see these images as art or religion or just about anything. Suppose, the skeptics said, you have a sequence of images of somebody—like a graphic novel—going toward a cask of stuff, opening it up and falling down. Well, what if you read them backwards? Then it's someone cured from being sick: the radiologically "cured" victim looks as happy as a clam after exposure. Even today, people read from right to left, down to up, and up to down. So it's very hard to know how to make a universal sequence. In fact, they took some of the images and showed them

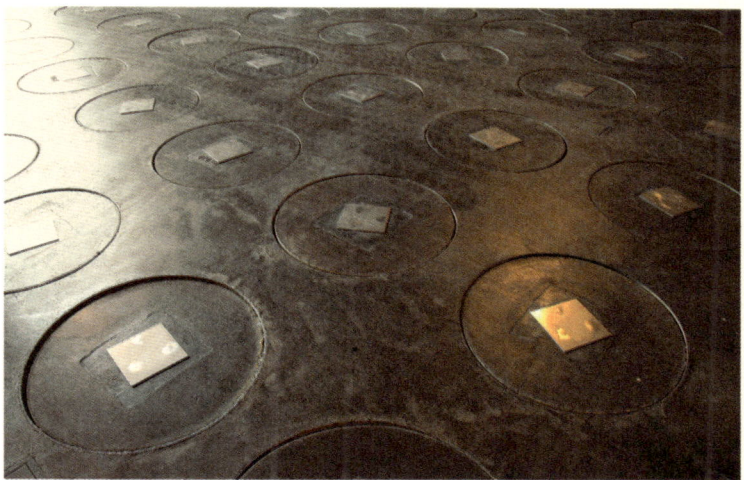

Buried canisters of classified high-level nuclear waste at the Savannah River Site
Photograph by Peter Galison

Images become tools, like a video-monitor image used by a distant doctor to conduct tele-surgery. When images are there to cut, fold, connect, manufacture, their purpose is to help us do things beyond the classical task of categorizing and confirming.

to residents of Carlsbad, who misinterpreted them—just spitting distance from the site of the waste.

The anti-universalists said: "Look, we decoded the Rosetta Stone. Put down in stone our science, our verbal warnings. Use different languages accepted by the U.N. Put it in Arabic and Hebrew, in English, German, and French, put it in Hopi and Navajo. With enough context, enough length, enough variations in the way you express it, people in the future will be clever enough to decrypt it. They will decode it the way we cracked the Rosetta Stone. Forget the dream of universal images."

This battle runs deeply, and I think that it appears in debate about the status of the image in art, and representation, and mimesis. Should art imitate life or not? What's the role of painting? The idea of abstraction in photography, in film, in painting and sculpture is something that is not just fought in the moment of high modernism. It's fought again and again, because it's deeply rooted in the contradictory desires that we have for images, and for what we want them to do in the world.

TP: **To bring things back to the present day, and to the near-term future of photography and image making, I want to pick up your comments about images becoming more about processes than distinct things we look at and learn from. Here is an example of what I mean. Last year, information about a system called TrapWire became public. TrapWire is meant to involve networks of surveillance cameras around "high-value" sites all over the country. The network would be able to link, for example, a camera in a Las Vegas casino to one at Heathrow Airport to another on Wall Street, all of which are linked to centralized law-enforcement and intelligence databases. The imagery is constantly monitored by algorithms designed to look for "suspicious" behavior, such as people taking pictures. It seems to me that whether or not this particular system works, this is a vision of the near future. It seems that we're moving away from thinking about images in terms of representation and toward thinking about their creation as part of a networked process, guided by political or economic "scripts" embedded in the algorithms controlling these image-making networks. If we look at Facebook's facial-recognition and search technologies, or at Instagram, we see similar things going on, but in a commercial context.**

PG: Well, what is it that the digital really does? There are many ways in which the digital is shaped by the legacy of analog photography and film. Both for political reasons and aesthetic reasons, what's really important is the fact that digital is small, cheap, and searchable. The combination of these three features is dramatic. It means that your smartphone does facial recognition—no longer is that an inaccessible and futuristic piece of the state-security apparatus. It's ubiquitous.

Aesthetically, this can mean a kind of decentering, a vision of the world that is not directly human. It also means that cameras are everywhere, and you're not even aware of them. There's an interesting film by a colleague and friend, Lucien Castaing-Taylor, working with Véréna Paravel, called *Leviathan* (2012), filmed on fishing boats in the North Atlantic. A lot of the film would have been completely unimaginable just a generation ago. They use little high-resolution digital cameras to achieve points of view that would previously have been impossible: amidst the pile of dead fish, or underwater as the tank is being filled, or looking back at the front of the boat. These are not impossible camera angles, but they're *nonhuman* points of view. I think that is interesting. Looking at the Mars rover pictures, we're still trying to imagine that we are there. What's shocking about some of these new kinds of images,

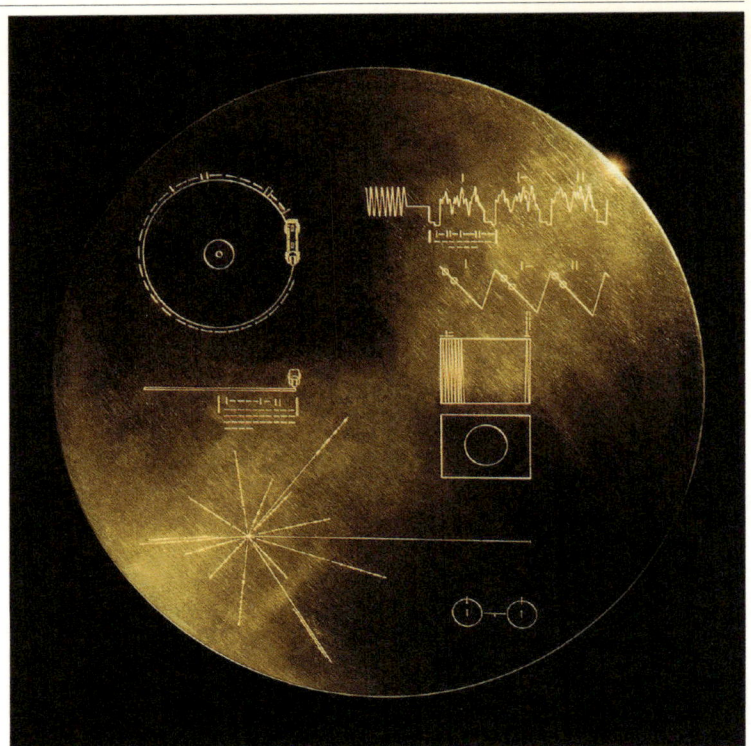

View of the inscriptions on the "Golden Record," a twelve-inch gold-plated copper phonographic disc containing sounds and images selected to portray the diversity of life and culture on Earth, carried into outer space by the Voyager 1 and 2 missions, launched in 1977
Courtesy NASA/JPL-Caltech

The searchable, cheap image, the archives of our digital lives—these will, I am sure, transform our way of life and our concepts of power.

aesthetically speaking, is that they put you where you couldn't or wouldn't ever be: the dead fish's POV.

In the early days of security cameras, people would make maps depicting how you could walk through Manhattan to avoid them. Today that would be a fool's errand. It's meaningless. The digital technology not only makes these cameras tiny, cheap, and ubiquitous, it also makes the results searchable, combinable with other kinds of sources—the whole is archiveable for the indefinite future. This archive of ubiquitous imagery raises privacy concerns, of course.

The final thing I want to say about the politics of this is that a lot of my work—and your work, too, Trevor—has been about state power. I think it is important to consider state power, because actions by the government are in our name, and we pay for them. But it may well be that the real threat to privacy, the real power of image-based surveillance, is tipping toward the private sector. Secretive as governments might be, corporations can be even more so.

There are incredibly powerful tools to mine data from images, and facial recognition is just the beginning of that. How people move, where they are, what they buy, what they search for, who they contact, what they say over lines of communication … all this is the new frontier of privacy, surveillance, and control. The image is an integral part of this new matrix of power, and I think that we don't really understand where it is going or what it will become. The searchable, cheap image, the archives of our digital lives—these will, I am sure, transform our way of life and our concepts of power.

TP: **We can invert that line of thinking when we consider certain kinds of scientific imaging. As those technologies advance, a number of scientists are beginning to think of the images they produce as works of art.**

PG: Yes. If images become tools, it's easier to see them as stepping-stones to other things. For me, the fundamental separation between art and science is not an eternal characteristic of science. The split happened in a historical moment. If you said to Leonardo da Vinci—pardon me, historians—"Are your studies of turbulent water art or science?" he would reply (so I imagine): "You're crazy! What are you talking about? I don't even recognize this choice." But in the nineteenth century, you begin to have the idea of an objective image and of a scientist who is defined by being self-restrained, followed by the idea of maximal detachment from the image. At that moment, Charles Baudelaire criticized photography, saying (approximately): "You know, this isn't really part of art because it's insufficiently modulated by the person who says he's an artist." In that sense, Baudelaire and late-nineteenth-century scientists are saying the same thing, except they come to opposite conclusions. What they agree on is that art is defined by intervention and science is defined by lack of intervention.

I believe the trunk split, at that point, into two branches. But in many ways the branches are coming back together again in our moment. People in the art world aren't frightened, in the way they once were, of having a scientific dimension to what they do. It's not destabilizing for Matthew Ritchie to collaborate with scientists, nor is it a professional disqualification for scientists to work with artists.

TP: **That's a great point. I think photographers in particular would do well to abandon some of the preconceived notions we all have of what photography is, or should be. The relationship between a photograph and what it may**

or may not represent out in the world is something we should continually question.

PG: For a long time, photography has been understood as part of everyday practice in a way that particle physics isn't—and, for that matter, even sculpture isn't. The popular notion of photography, this idea that it represents something *as it was*, lingers. Ansel Adams spent his whole life trying to tell people: "No! If you go to Yosemite's Half Dome, you can snap all the pictures you like and still wonder—'Why can't I make my image look like an Ansel Adams?'" Adams was anything but secretive about his work. He said repeatedly how *fashioned* his images were, and even demonstrated many of his steps along the way: "This is what it takes." He was proud of his modulation of the images, never embarrassed by it.

TP: **In the darkroom, Adams worked like a kind of painter.**

PG: Yes. But I think something of the old conception of photography is still with us. The high and low are never radically disjunct, and I think the fascination with what I call, in a more technical sense, the "subjective image," the idea of a re-presentation with a minimum of intervention, lingers in the background of popular understanding about what a photograph is or should be. Even though it was perfectly obvious during the nineteenth century that if you made a long exposure (as photographers were obliged to do), moving people disappeared. Photographs are not and never were mimetic representations—and yet this poetic epistemology never seems to die.

We want it to be so, even though we know perfectly well it's not! And Photoshop has exponentially increased the number of people who know it's not—Photoshop is everywhere. It's on your phone and it's in your computer, and everybody has the experience of Photoshopping somebody into a group picture, so that the photographer can be in the image. We know! And yet we still have this idea, this *ideal*, this nearly indestructible belief in the mimetic photograph. We're only slowly arriving at a moment when the manipulated image is part of our perception. Not just in worried newsrooms and anxious scientific-journal headquarters —not (or not just) in the sense of a dreaded onslaught of fraud.

I don't mean manipulation as the devil's intervention. I mean manipulation in the centuries-old sense of the hand being able to intervene, and that images are part of the flux of our way of interacting with the world. I think the rest of the twenty-first century will be characterized by this shift. Not just in arcane branches of science, but in every part of people's visual encounter with the world. Where we come out of that, where that leads—I don't know. I can't wait to see.

Trevor Paglen is an artist, writer, and scholar working across multiple disciplines in a variety of media. Among his books are *Torture Taxi* (Melville House, 2006), *Blank Spots on the Map* (Dutton, 2009), and *I Could Tell You But Then You Would Have to Be Destroyed by Me* (Melville House, 2010). His most recent book is *The Last Pictures* (University of California Press, 2012).

Paglen's book *Invisible: Covert Operations and Classified Landscapes* was published by Aperture in 2010.

Peter Galison is the Pellegrino University Professor at Harvard University. His work explores the relation between material circumstances and abstract theories of physics. Among his books are *How Experiments End* (University of Chicago Press, 1987); *Image and Logic* (University of Chicago Press, 1997); *Einstein's Clocks, Poincaré's Maps* (Norton, 2003); and (with Lorraine Daston) *Objectivity* (Zone, 2007). His film with Robb Moss, *Secrecy*, premiered at the 2008 Sundance Film Festival; they are currently completing a feature documentary on nuclear waste, *Containment*.

In a time when the world and its phenomena have been photographed many times over, what can we learn by revisiting the early days of photography, when strange, dramatic, and novel images served as both evidence and entertainment?

Marvels and Spectacles:
Photographic Exploration and the "First Glimpse"
Jennifer Tucker

Opposite:
Gabriel Loppé, *The Eiffel Tower Struck by Lightning*, ca. 1890
© RMN-Grand Palais/ Art Resource, New York

A century and half ago, James Glaisher, astronomer, meteorologist, and longtime president of the Royal Photographic Society, made a series of balloon ascents from London, recording measurements in the upper atmosphere. Although gas leaks from the balloon fogged his plates and spoiled his photographic efforts, Glaisher's vivid accounts of his experience (published with illustrations in his 1871 book *Travels in the Air*) raised both scientific and popular interest in what might be seen if cameras were taken into new places or situations.

The history of photographing marvels—both natural and artificial—is made up not only of images. While early photographs of microbes, solar eclipses, the lunar surface, fleeting meteorological events, biological specimens, faraway landscapes, and the like today have much value as objects of research and as aesthetic wonders, they also have a story to tell about the making, display, and sensationalizing of "first glimpses" for mass audiences. Like the Eiffel Tower and other feats of Victorian engineering, dramatic "first glimpse" photographs of the period provoked questions and deliberations about the new technologies used to achieve them: Did they bring new understanding? Could they be trusted? How far—and by whom —was their impact felt? And was there a line between knowledge and entertainment, between science and show?

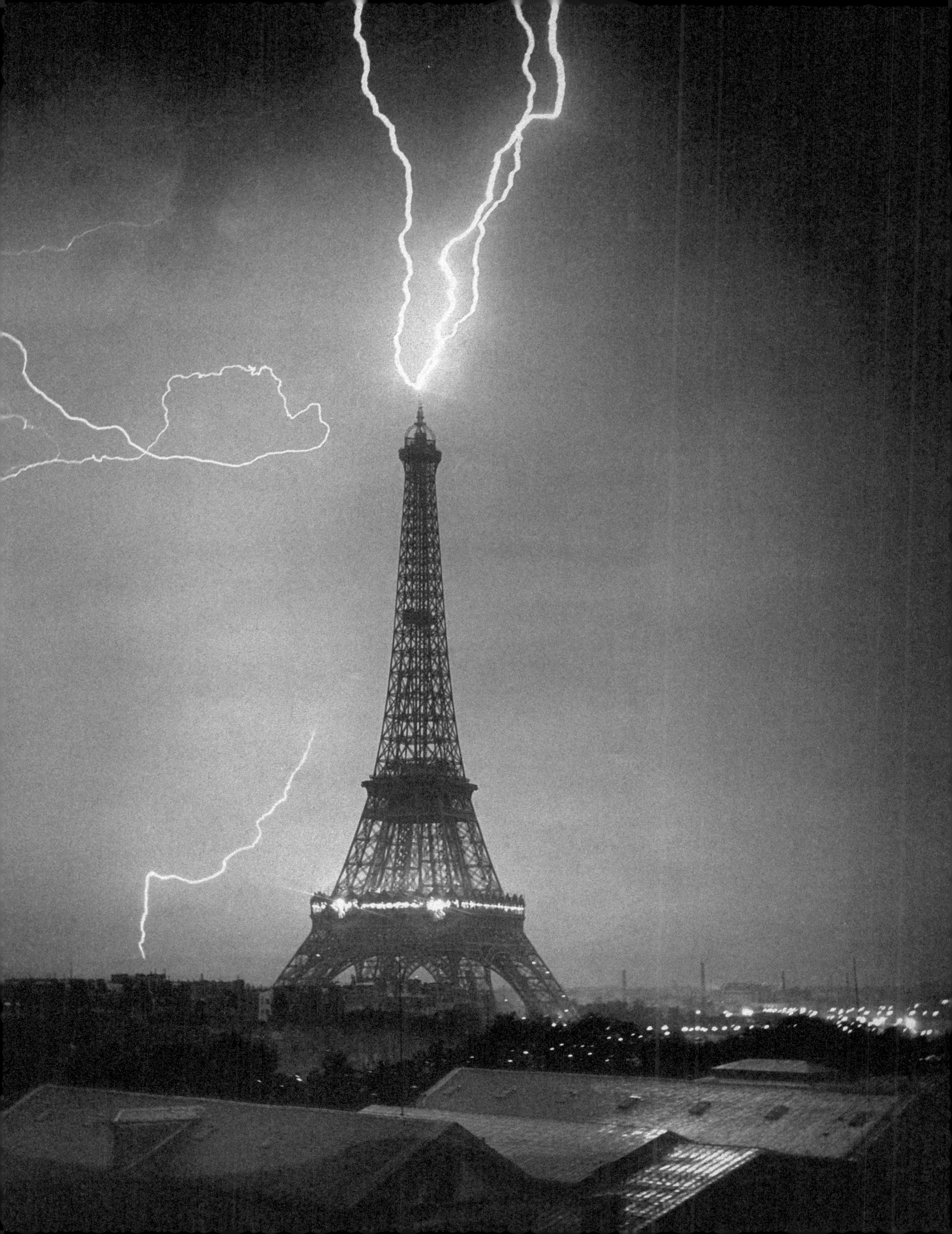

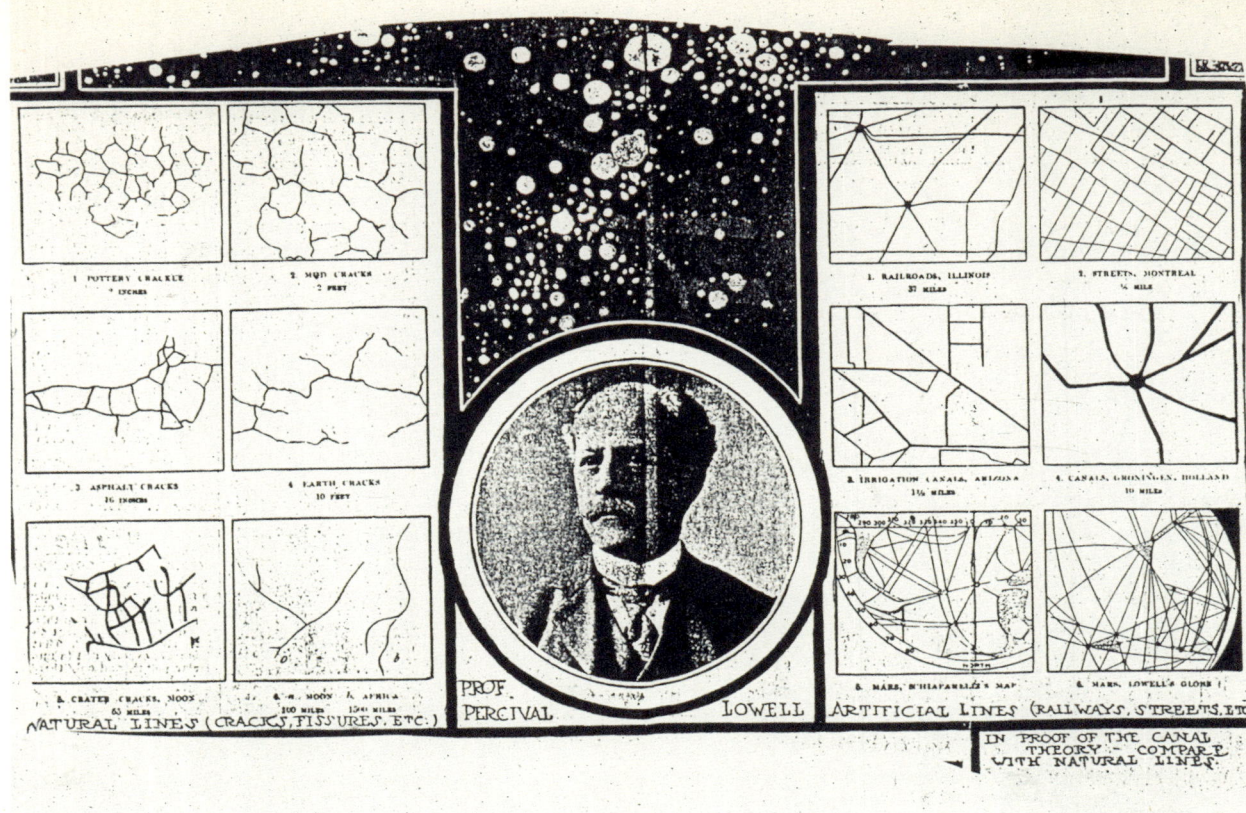

Professor Percival Lowell, with illustrations contrasting "natural" cracks (geological formations) and "artificial" cracks (railroad tracks and canals). From "Will the New Year Solve the Riddle of Mars?," *New York Herald*, December 30, 1906
Press Clippings Collection, Lowell Observatory Archives, Flagstaff, Arizona

Many described the emergent roles of photography in terms of social types: *witness, detective, spy*. Photographs were often referred to as *curiosities* and *specimens*— to be collected and exchanged like interesting rocks or botanical samples.

Photography in the nineteenth century offered a new way of seeing the world, and of sharing unprecedented views with myriad others. Beginning in the 1850s, exploratory expeditions were often accompanied by photographers, and by 1900 virtually every national museum, observatory, and hospital in Western Europe had its photographic operator. Optimists proposed the creation of national archives throughout the world, to house thousands of photographic images, from visual chronicles of scientific travels to records documenting the progress of diseases. Photographs from afar were praised for bringing "to our own fireside pictures from every land" —which came to the public at first in books, and later in magazines and newspapers, as well as in lantern slide shows, popular-science demonstrations, and World's Fairs and similar expositions.

And along with the wonders it brought home to the fireside, the technical phenomenon of photography was of course an attraction in itself. At London's National Gallery of Practical Science, Blending Instruction with Amusement (also known as the Adelaide Gallery), photography and its products were touted as "useful and beautiful" tools. The Gallery was a well-known public venue where inventors could demonstrate their work to patrons and audiences and appear before the public as respectable "men of science." It was a labyrinth of spaces containing working laboratories, lecture halls, a Loom and Lithographic Press Room, a Microscope Room (housing a "Grand Oxy-Hydrogen Microscope"), and at its center a massive Long Room that featured a seventy-foot canal for demonstrating models of paddle-driven steamboats. Associated with optical phenomena from the start, the Adelaide Gallery was also the workplace of French photographer Antoine Claudet, one of the first daguerreotype portraitists in England, who operated a rooftop studio here from 1841 to 1851. The arcade and streets surrounding the Gallery were filled with fashionable shops and vendors competing for attention, displaying everything from waxworks, sculpture, and painting to optical implements showing panoramas, dioramas, and dissolving views.

The landmark Great Exhibition of the Works of Industry of All Nations, held at the Crystal Palace outside London in 1851, was the first in a series of World's Fairs that brought together for public amazement the latest products of art, science, and manufacturing, from kitchen appliances and reaping machines to the famous Koh-i-Noor diamond and the world's first voting machine. Visited by more than six million people, the exposition also incorporated the first large international exhibition of photography, a display that included French and English calotypes, American daguerreotypes (Mathew Brady received an award for his), Frederick Scott Archer's revolutionary wet-plate process, John Whipple's daguerreotype of the moon, and stereo-daguerreotypes that are said to have fascinated Queen Victoria—and sparked a craze for stereoscopic viewing.

The imagery being produced by new visual technologies allowed unprecedented insight into scientific endeavors, and as such it required a vibrant new vocabulary. The French chemist J. L. Gay-Lussac remarked in 1839: "It is certain that through Monsieur Daguerre's invention physics is today in possession of … a new instrument which will … furnish the nucleus around which new researches and new discoveries will be made." Astronomer, chemist, and experimental photographer John Herschel dubbed photography a "joint work of nature and art," while Englishman William Crookes, a chemist and physicist, as well as editor of *The Photographic News*, praised it as nothing less than a "moral agent." Critics of the medium, on the other hand, saw in photography a "cheapening of taste" and the "decline" of modesty and other values. Elsewhere, photography's various uses were likened to a kind of domestic service: *The Photographic News* reported in 1882 that, forty years after its invention, the camera was not just an "upper-servant" but rather a "maid of all work" (the reference was to dry gelatin-plate photography, which no longer had to be developed on the spot or by technical experts). Others described the emergent roles of photography in terms of social types: *witness*, *detective*, *spy*. Photographs were often referred to as *curiosities* and *specimens* —to be collected and exchanged like interesting rocks or botanical samples.

As laypeople came to terms with this complicated new medium, scientific advancements found in it a perfect conduit to the public eye. Across the professional and amateur sciences, from astronomy and microscopy to medicine and physiology, practitioners sought ways to engage the public as spectators, patrons, and in some cases (in the field sciences, in particular) collectors and correspondents. Gabriel Loppé's photograph from around 1890 of lightning striking the Eiffel Tower provided a perfect touch-point for the public's fascination with technology, spectacle, and displays of Nature's awesome power. One of hundreds of photographs used for a taxonomic project by the Royal Meteorological Society to record different types of atmospheric electricity, the photograph was immensely popular, and—like many scientific photographs of the time—could not be precisely classified as either "art" or "science."

The visual "spectacularization" of scientific projects took various forms, depending on the discipline, but most scientists understood that financial support for their work depended upon an appealing public profile—a profile that in turn relied largely upon photographs and other images. Popular-science lectures, attended by crowds of interested middle-class spectators, might be enlivened with images projected from a "magic lantern." Scientists and laypeople alike kept albums of images of scientific and natural wonders for display to friends and colleagues, as did one researcher who accompanied the H.M.S. *Challenger*'s 1872–76 exploratory expedition. For this extraordinary voyage,

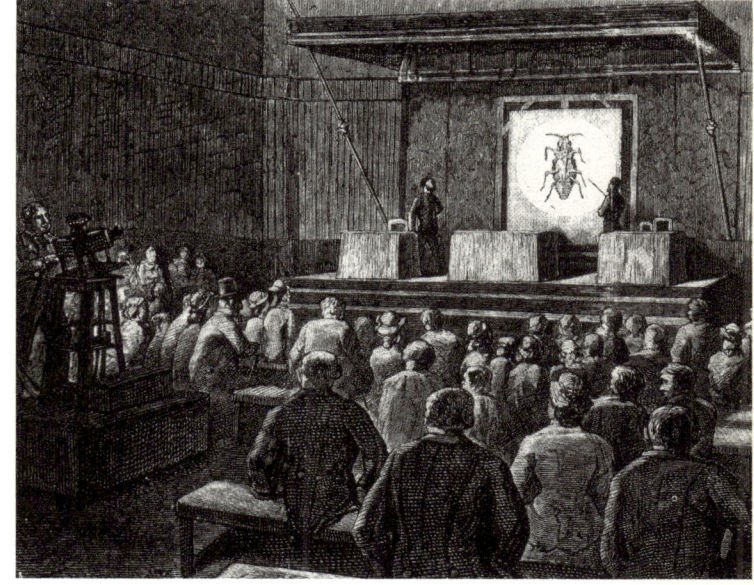

Popular-science lecture about microscopic images, using a "magic lantern" projector, ca. 1870. Reproduced in Leslie Pearce Williams's *Album of Science: The Nineteenth Century* (Scribner, 1978)

a British Royal Navy ship was refitted for scientific work: guns were removed to make space for laboratories, dredging operations, and specimens of more than four thousand species. During their four-year adventure—encompassing the Cape Verde Islands, Hong Kong, the Cape of Good Hope, Australia, New Zealand, and Japan—the expedition's scientists made discoveries that laid the foundations of oceanography. They also made photographic records of a gamut of subjects, from the botanical to the ethnographic to the astronomical: one page shows a scientist seated with local inhabitants during one of the *Challenger*'s stops, with solar eclipse photographs pasted below. The ship's photographer had his own darkroom onboard; the *Challenger* expedition seems to have been the first to use this relatively new technology. The British public was keenly interested in the voyage, and the press kept them apprised— though with drawings and engravings far more than with photographs (only after the ship's return to England were some of the many photographs published).

Salons and other meetings of the scientific literati offered forums for "first glimpse" images within the academic community. One photomicrograph of bacteria by Victorian microscopist Andrew Pringle, from around 1890, shows us how scientific photography occasionally borrowed aesthetic conceits from other areas of photographic practice: in this case the "portrait frame," used popularly for commercial photographs. Pringle was a member of the Royal Microscopical Society as well as an expert photographer; his images of bacteria and other microscopic phenomena were circulated in scientific atlases, textbooks, and prints. Microbiologist Edgar Crookshank's striking image of bacteria magnified twenty-five hundred times was published in his 1887 book *Photographs of Bacteria*—the first text in English devoted solely to photographs of bacteria.

The press naturally played an important role both in bringing such images to the public and in deploying photography as a forceful tool in convincing readers of the veracity of certain scientific—and sometimes unorthodox—theories. In 1905 the first photographic pictures of Mars were made at the Lowell Observatory in Flagstaff, Arizona. Percival Lowell, an American astronomer—and a believer in life on Mars—felt that his photographs revealed a network of canals, thus providing "objective proof" that there was intelligent life on the planet. (He later referred to the images as "doubt-killing bullets from the planet of war.") But even with this photographic "proof" in hand, Lowell had to get the images out to the world in order to get his message across. The original photographs were small and the canals difficult to discern in them; mechanical reproduction in print would pose serious challenges. To overcome this hurdle, Lowell followed a path well trod by entertainers, science popularizers, and tradespeople alike: he toted his original photographs of Mars from place to place, making them available for public inspection at natural-history museums and scientific societies throughout the United States and Europe. His efforts were wildly successful; indeed, it seems that the maverick scientist himself was sometimes of more interest to audiences than his canals: the December 30, 1906, *New York Herald* shows "Professor Percival Lowell" as the central image, framed on either side by illustrations contrasting "natural" and "artificial" planetary fissures.

Lowell's campaign hit its mark, at least for a moment. In 1907 the editors of the *Wall Street Journal* asked readers: "What has been in your opinion the most extraordinary event of the [past] twelve months?" As the paper reported, it was "not the financial panic which is occupying our minds" (it had been a bad year for the stock market), but rather "the proof afforded by astronomical observations … that conscious, intelligent life exists upon the planet Mars."

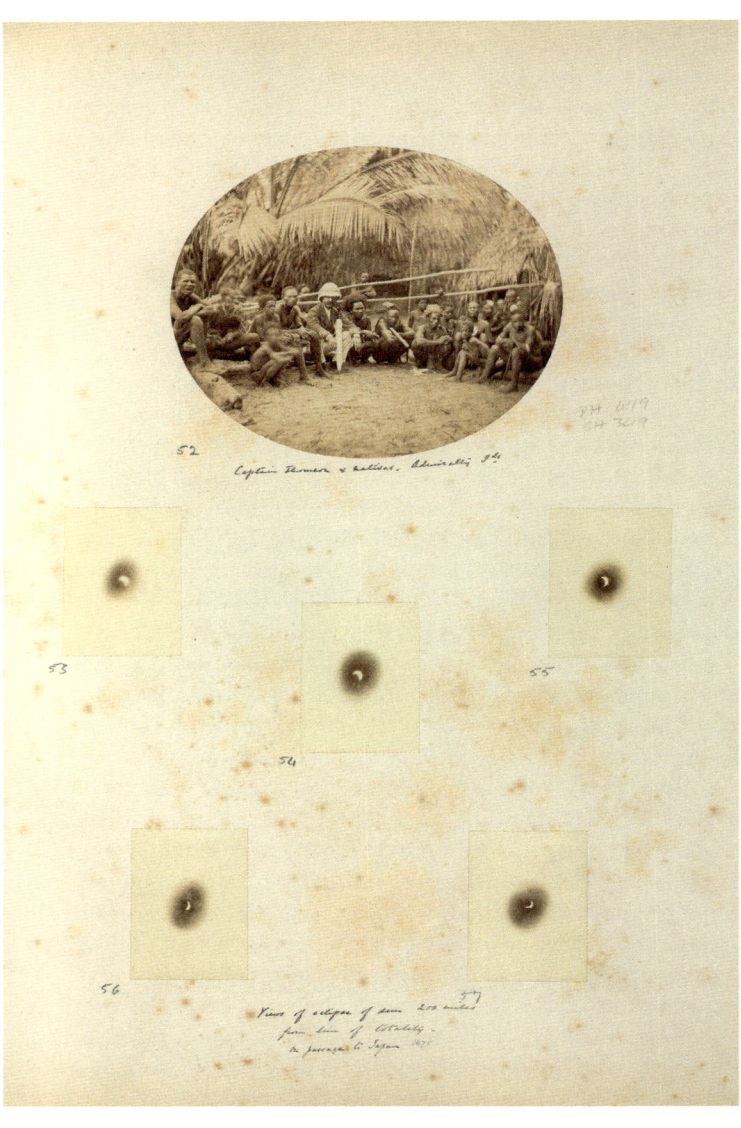

Photographs of a solar eclipse pasted below a group portrait (titled *Captain Thompson with Natives, Admiralty Islands*), showing a scientist seated with inhabitants of the South Pacific Admiralty Islands, made during the expedition of the H.M.S. *Challenger*, 1872–76, from an album of photographs belonging to Alfred Carpenter, a lieutenant who traveled on the *Challenger*
Courtesy Picture Library, The Natural History Museum, London

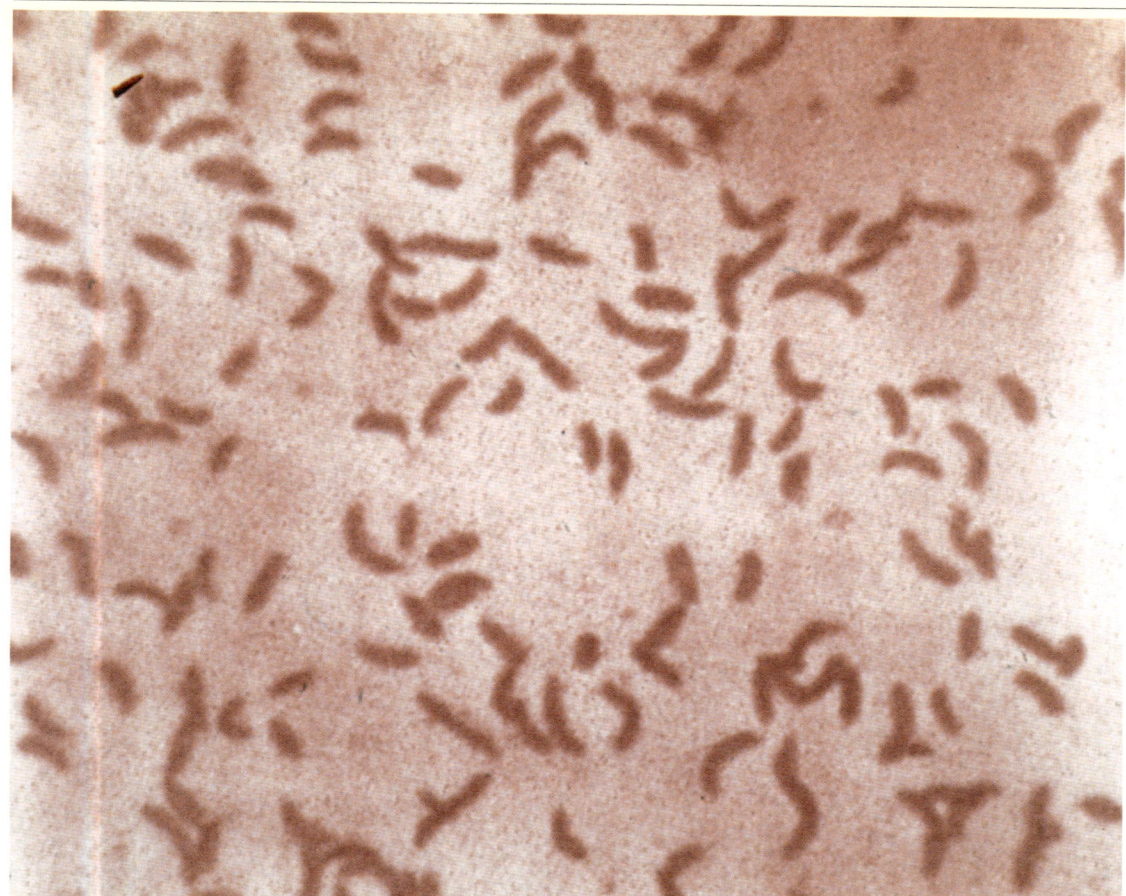

Comma-bacilli, stained with fuchsine. Enlargement (2,500 times) from a photographic negative. Plate from Edgar Crookshank's *Photography of Bacteria* (London: H. K. Lewis, 1887)

Percival Lowell, an American astronomer—and a believer in life on Mars—felt that his photographs revealed a network of canals, thus providing "objective proof" that there was intelligent life on the planet. (He later referred to the images as "doubt-killing bullets from the planet of war.")

Such was the power of the photographic image in that era of spectacle—a power that was sometimes compounded by tabloid rhetoric. NASA's 2012 Mars photographs, by contrast, came nowhere near to trumping the world's economic news or other headlines for public attention—despite assurances from the press that we had never before seen anything like this: "*Curiosity* Rover Snaps 1st Photos of Mars at Night" (NBC News) and "NASA Reveals Stunning New Images from Mars *Curiosity*" (in London's *Daily Mail*). In our age of image inundation, there is perhaps no longer such a thing as a "first glimpse"—or if it exists, the public's interest in it is quickly diverted.

It has been often observed that the impact of photography in the nineteenth century was in many ways as revolutionary to the public mind as the advent of the Internet has been for today's generations. And the questions raised back in the era of mechanical reproduction pertain in new ways now: Do new technologies bring new understanding? Can they be trusted? How far—and by whom—is their impact felt? Is there a line between knowledge and entertainment, between science and show? To these questions we may add another: Are we capable still of experiencing the exhilarating shock of amazement that once accompanied images of discovery?

Jennifer Tucker is an associate professor in the History Department and Science in Society Program at Wesleyan University in Middletown, Connecticut, and the author of *Nature Exposed: Photography as Eyewitness in Victorian Science* (Johns Hopkins University Press, 2006; reissued this year in paperback and as an ebook).

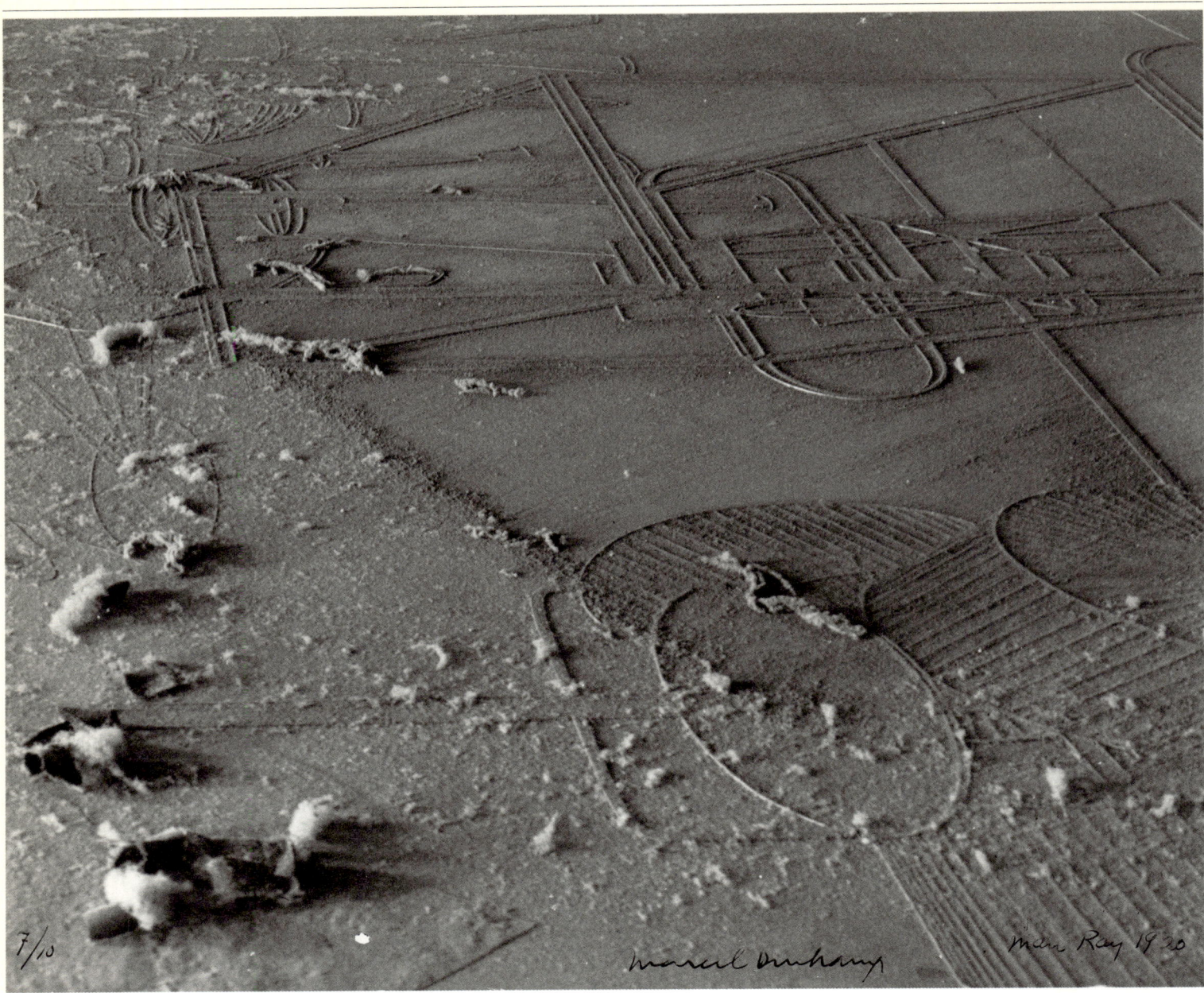

Man Ray, *Élevage de poussière/ Dust Breeding*, 1920
© Metropolitan Museum of Art/Art Resource, New York/Artists Rights Society, New York

What on Earth?
Photography's Alien Landscapes
David Campany

**Opposite, top:
Frederick Sommer,
*Arizona Landscape
(Bagdad)*, 1943**

**Opposite, bottom:
Frederick Sommer,
Arizona Landscape, 1945**
Both photographs ©
Frederick & Frances Sommer
Foundation

What happens when the Earth begins to look extraterrestrial, when we look at a photograph and can't determine what we're looking at?

Between 1943 and 1945 Frederick Sommer made several photographs of the Sonoran Desert near his home in Arizona. They depict bone-dry hillsides without horizons, strewn evenly with rocks and dotted with cacti. Shot in black and white with a large-format camera, they oscillate for the eye between flatness and the receding space of incidental detail. There are no traces of human presence, and even the vantage point where Sommer placed his camera offers us little mastery.

Photography is usually a matter of projecting three dimensions onto two, via an aperture. It is a medium of distances and perspectives. This means that making sense of it is never just a matter of recognizing what is depicted: it also involves knowing *from where* it has been depicted. An unorthodox vantage point may render abstract even the most optically clear photograph. Likewise an apparently abstract photograph may cohere once we know its point of view. The more one looks at Sommer's landscapes the more disconcerting they become, both as pictures and as records of the world. With a poet's economy he spoke of each image as a *constellation*, a word that might suggest something prosaic, like a gathering or an assembly. In astronomy a constellation is an arbitrary formation of stars perceived as a figure or design. It's the seeking of pattern that turns the chaos into order.

Sommer's photographs are as carefully composed as any, yet they ruffle our composure. We might say they are composed to show the essentially uncomposed, unnervingly brute fact of nature from which we are alienated by our very capacity to contemplate it. These are not landscapes fashioned to reflect back our wishes, our dominion, or even our physical scale. They are alien.

In 1944 two of Sommer's desert photographs appeared in the American Surrealist journal *VVV*, spread over two pages. At first glance they seemed to resemble a pair of stereoscopic images, promising the clarity of a third dimension. But each is quite singular; in fact, their pairing only doubles their individual disturbances. In 1962 a similar layout appeared in an issue of *Aperture* magazine dedicated to Sommer's work. These were the only landscapes amid the still lifes and collages for which he is best known, but they are just as ambiguous. Surrealist photography tended to explore claustrophobic spaces as metaphors for the darkly malleable space of the unconscious. For Sommer the great outdoors and its blinding light were just as unfathomable, their beauty always a little disturbing.

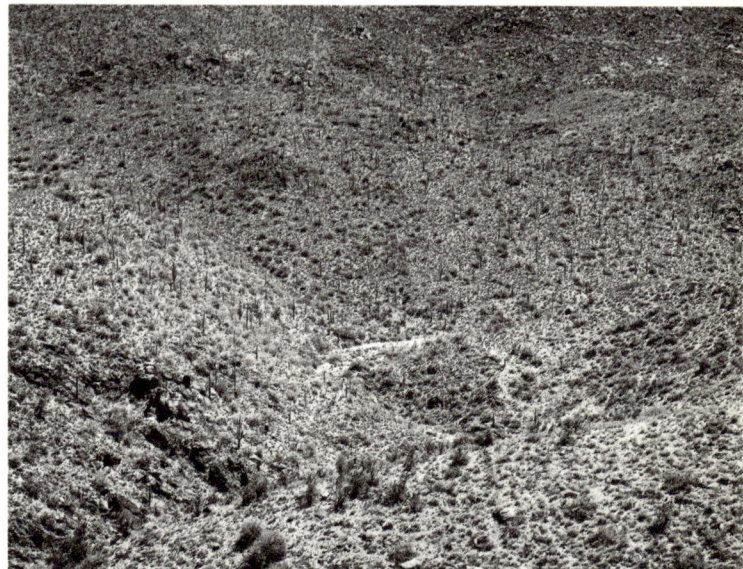

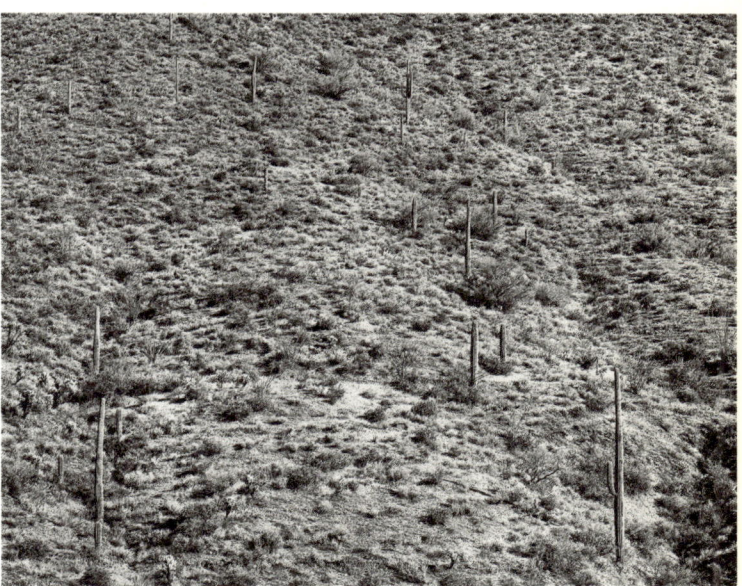

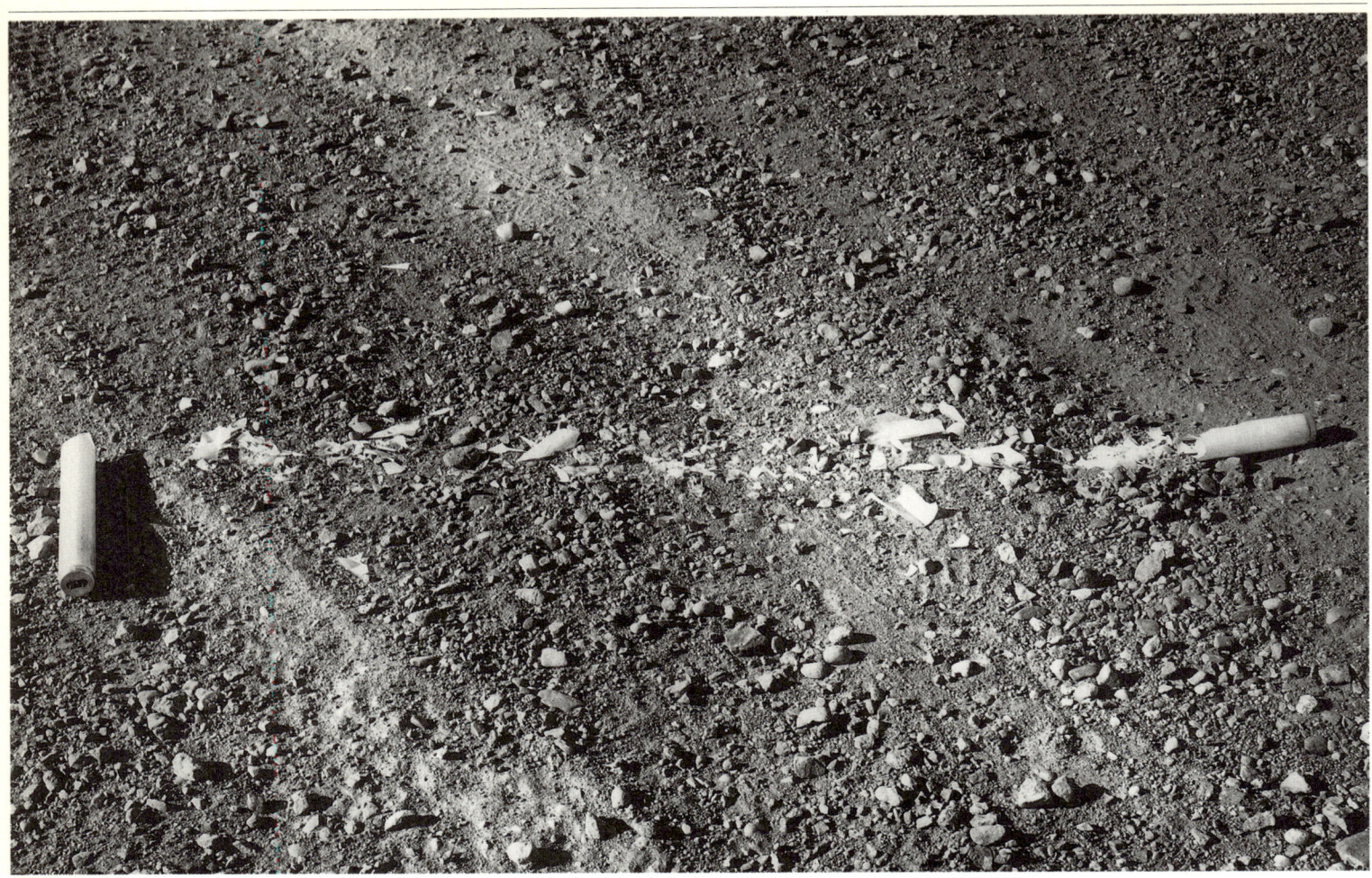

Lewis Baltz, *Fluorescent Tube* (from *Nevada*), 1977
© Lewis Baltz and courtesy Galerie Thomas Zander, Cologne

Today cameraless darkroom prints and other forms of nonfigurative photography are enjoying a revival in art, but such work often misses the more unsettling idea that the world *itself* is essentially abstract.

What happens when we look at a photograph but cannot figure out what it is of? Never mind what it *means*, just what it is *of*? Most images aim to be easy, so this is not something we face often. But those moments when our basic recognition is challenged may tell us a lot about the ways in which habits of seeing shape the pleasure and knowledge offered by photographs.

In the realm of photography particularly, *abstraction* is a fraught term that tends to be tamed by opposing it to *figuration*. But they are inseparable, one haunting the other, and forcing them apart does not help us to understand the medium. Indeed, their separation has led to great confusion about everything from the real and realism to form and formalism. These ideas may be explored through two types of image that seem at first to be furthest from abstraction: the landscape photograph and the forensic photograph.

There are certain images that play both roles, or seem to. In 1922 the Parisian journal *Littérature* published an image attributed to Man Ray with a caption suggesting it was a landscape viewed from an airplane. The new perspectives of aerial-intelligence photography had entered the popular imagination in the years following World War I. But Man Ray's photograph was not a landscape at all. It was a close-range study of dust accumulating on a sheet of glass for what was to become Marcel Duchamp's sculpture *La Mariée mise à nu par ses célibataires, même/The Bride Stripped Bare by Her Bachelors, Even*, also known as the *Large Glass* (1915–23). Man Ray cropped the image to leave no marginal evidence that this was Duchamp's Manhattan studio. Only later was the photograph given its familiar title: *Élevage de poussière*, or *Dust Breeding*.

While Sommer's purist landscapes are now regarded as supreme modernist pictures, Man Ray's splicing of photography with sculpture, process, and performance anticipated the

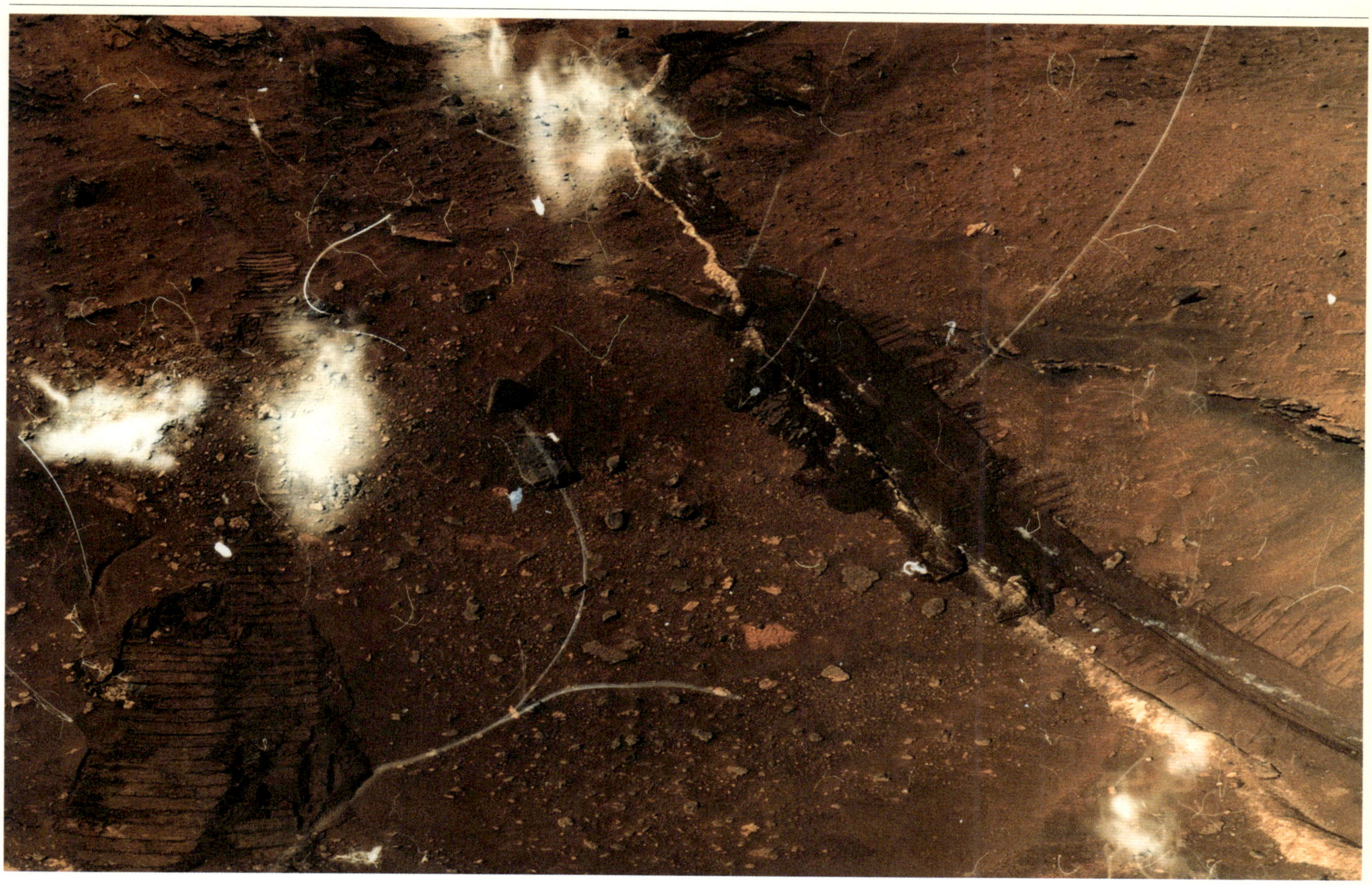

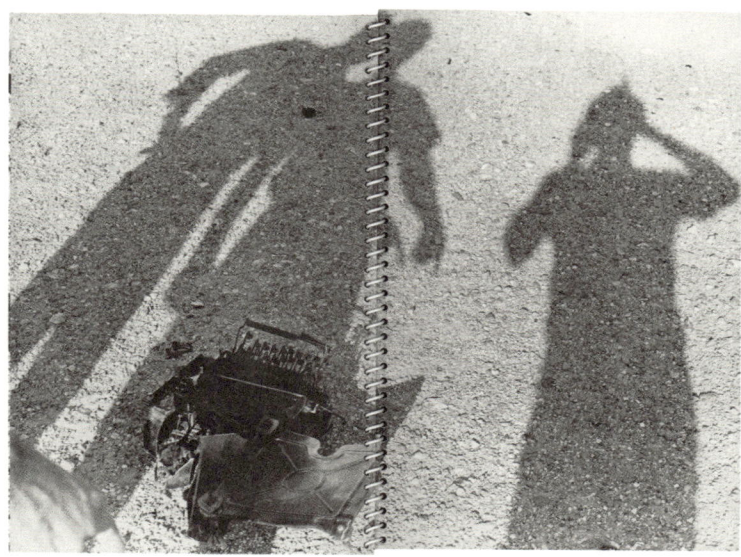

Top:
**Eva Stenram, *Per Pulverem
Ad Astra B.2*, 2007**
Courtesy the artist; source
image courtesy NASA/
JPL-Caltech

Bottom:
**Ed Ruscha, from
Royal Road Test, 1967**
© Ed Ruscha, Patrick
Blackwell, Mason Williams,
and courtesy Gagosian
Gallery

mixing of media that came to dominate art in the second half of the twentieth century. Both artists pushed photography toward abstraction while retaining a "forensic" interest in detail. Surfaces bearing traces are viewed obliquely: a downward tilt of vision turns incidental marks into signs for interpretation. The camera surveys a plane that appears as a code to be deciphered, or a mystery to be solved.

Although its form is quite specific, the applications of this type of image are broad. Indeed it is extraordinary just how often it occurred in the art of the late 1960s and into the 1970s, a period characterized by an interest in traces and evidence. Lewis Baltz's topographic projects, such as *Nevada* (1977), for example, pored over details of bulldozed landscapes being converted into suburbs. Larry Sultan and Mike Mandel's book *Evidence* (1977) was a comic humiliation of the functional photograph: visiting various archives in police departments, fire stations, and industrial laboratories, they removed images from their contextual dossiers and left them adrift on white pages. The book's enigmatic opening shot shows a floor covered in some kind of dust and footsteps. Similarly perplexing pictures also found their way into the work of Ed Ruscha, and into the documentation of Land art and performance art, particularly that of Richard Long, Robert Smithson, Ana Mendieta, and Gordon Matta-Clark. In a period of art that is thought to have broken with any notion of "style," this essentially forensic image form was pervasive.

While these investigations into the evidential image were going on, a remote camera landed on the surface of Mars. The art historian Ernst Gombrich saw its first image beamed back to Earth, reproduced in *Time* magazine. In his 1980 essay "Standards of Truth: The Arrested Image and the Moving Eye," he suggested:

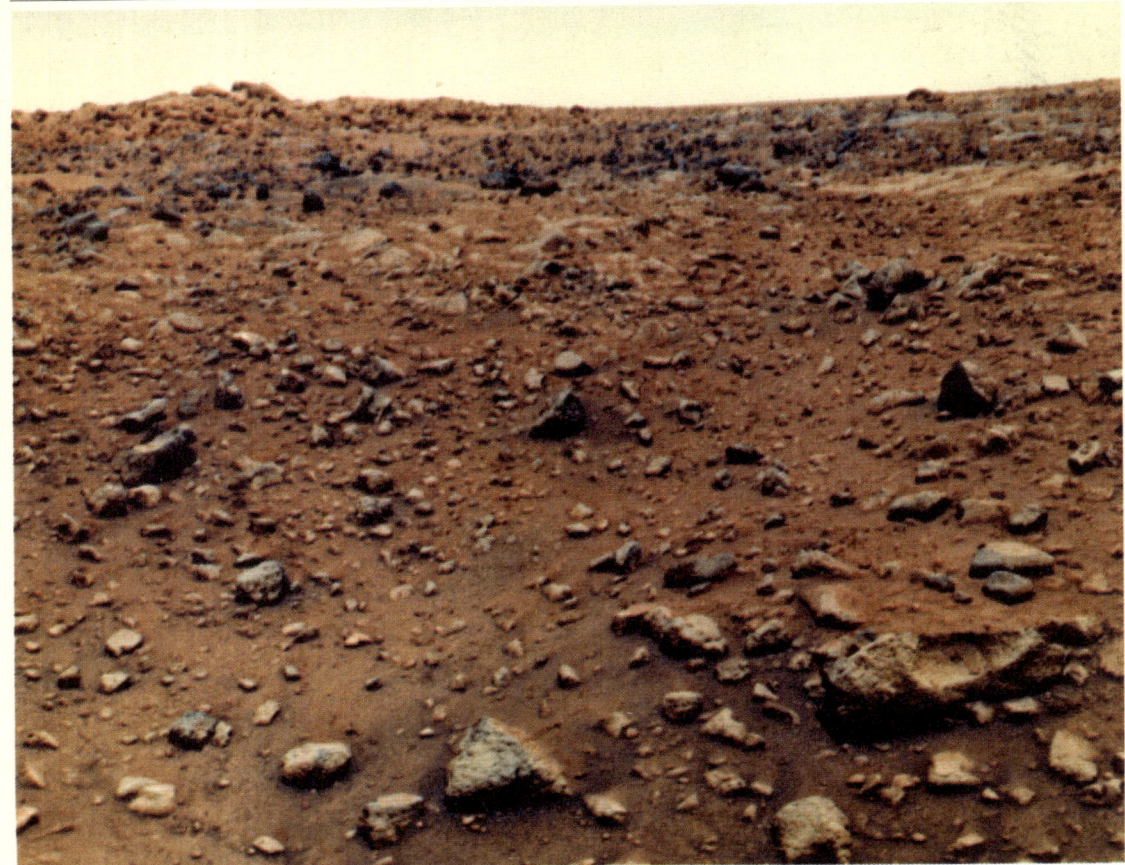

We cannot really tell the size of the boulders or ridges which are visible on the picture from Mars unless we know their distance, and vice versa, though for proximate objects there may be additional information through such clues as texture or "grain"—assuming that we guess correctly at their composition. An arrested image [Gombrich means an optically-derived image] *might thus be compared to a single equation with two variables such as* $n=x/y$. *We can calculate the size of an object if we know the distance and the distance if we know its size, to know both we would have to have additional information.*

One wonders if Gombrich, ever the analyst of realism, was making a droll reversal of the old question of whether photography is transparent enough to be understood by Martians. Although they looked uncannily familiar to many viewers, the Mars images demanded a great deal of specialized knowledge to be understood. Similarly, the views offered by aerial photographs of our own planet may require trained professionals to extract their data. This is one aspect of photography's complicated relation to abstraction. Today, cameraless darkroom prints and other forms of nonfigurative photography are enjoying a revival in art, but such work often misses the unsettling idea that the world *itself* is essentially abstract. It always demands the imposition of conventions of seeing and the skilled vigilance of interpretation. In the series *Per Pulverem Ad Astra* (2007), by the artist Eva Stenram, these two versions of abstraction— figurative and nonfigurative—are wittily compounded. Stenram downloaded from the Internet some of NASA's 1976 pictures of Mars and converted them into negatives that were then left to gather dust before being printed. The already uncertain landscapes are now seen through puffs of whiteness that could be cosmic—or plain domestic.

Clearly one can trace a line from Stenram's pictures back to *Dust Breeding*, but the quiet influence of Man Ray's photograph has extended into some unlikely domains as well. In 1970 it

was included as a keynote image in the catalog of the New York Museum of Modern Art's *Information*, its first major survey show of Conceptual art. Two decades on, it inspired French photographer Sophie Ristelhueber, whose work focuses on traces of war and violence, to make one of the most troubling projects of recent decades. In early 1991 Saddam Hussein's army of Iraqi conscripts was being bombed out of Kuwait. Ristelhueber saw an aerial photograph of the incident, again in *Time* magazine, which prompted her to visit the Kuwaiti desert herself. But it was the ambiguous *Dust Breeding* that provided the form. In the newspaper *Le Monde* (September 27–28, 1992), she stated:

By shifting from the air to the ground, I sought to destroy any notion of scale as in Man Ray and Marcel Duchamp's Élevage de poussière. It's a picture which fascinates me and which I kept in my mind throughout the time I was working [in Kuwait]. *The constant shift between the infinitely big and the infinitely small may disorientate the spectator. But it is a good illustration of our relationship to the world: we have at our disposal modern techniques for seeing everything, apprehending everything, yet we see nothing.*

Before turning to photography Ristelhueber studied literature, with a keen interest in the writer Alain Robbe-Grillet, who was stretching literature to the point where description becomes abstract. In Robbe-Grillet's careful accounts of surfaces, objects, and places, everything is crystal clear, and yet their precise significance is elusive. Rejecting what he called "the archaic myth of depth," Robbe-Grillet dramatized the tension between fact and meaning. This is from his 1959 novel *Dans le labyrinthe/ In the Labyrinth*:

The fine dust that dulls the shine of the horizontal planes, the varnished tabletop, the polished parquet, the marble of the mantelpiece and that of the chest of drawers, the cracked marble

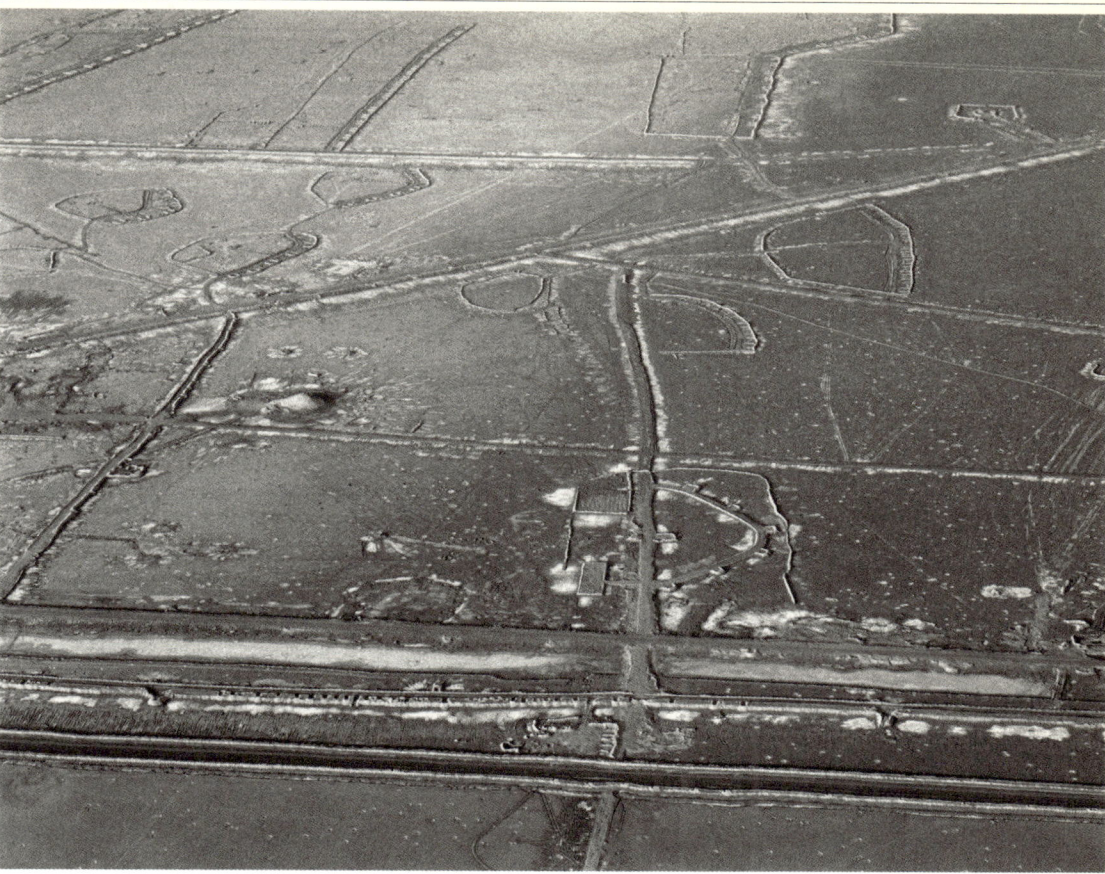

Sophie Ristelhueber,
*À cause de l'élevage
de poussière* (Because
of the dust breeding),
1991–2007
© Sophie Ristelhueber/
ADAGP, Paris

*of the chest of drawers, the only dust here comes from the room
itself: from the gaps in the parquet possibly, or from the bed,
or the curtains, or the ashes in the fireplace. On the varnished
tabletop the dust has marked the place occupied for a while—
for a few hours, a few days, minutes, weeks—by small objects
since removed, the bases of which are clearly outlined for a while
longer, a circle, a square, a rectangle, other less simple forms,
some of them partly overlapping, already blurred or half-erased
as if by the flick of a rag.*

Details simply "are." Their value is a matter of human
projection. Ristelhueber saw connections between this and the
camera's indifferent mode of recording. Titled *Fait* (meaning both
fact and *done*), her Kuwait project comprises seventy-two color
and black-and-white images. In a further play on the enigma
of scale, it is exhibited as a monumental grid but published as a
modest little book. A final image, left out of the series, stands alone,
titled *À cause de l'élevage de poussière*: *Because of the dust breeding.*

This is what we might call the politics of abstraction. Habits
of seeing are estranged strategically in the hope of opening
up a space to think differently (about warfare, about landscape,
about photography, about vision). It is a risky strategy, always
provisional and contingent upon the cultural norms that are
being challenged. How to discuss abstraction as a principle of
modern social, industrial, and political life, while avoiding empty
formalism? How to address the systemic rationalizing of the
world's appearance without turning it into mere pattern? How
to "interpret" such imagery without resorting to extrapolation?

So many contemporary landscape photographers walk
these lines, from Robert Adams and Richard Misrach to Andreas
Gursky and Edward Burtynsky. But it's not a matter of making
politically correct images. The viewer has a responsibility, too,
to avoid the easy options of reveling in abstraction for its own
sake or denouncing photographers for their lack of engagement.
It is a matter of what the musician John Cage, who was also deeply
affected by Man Ray's dust image, called "response ability."

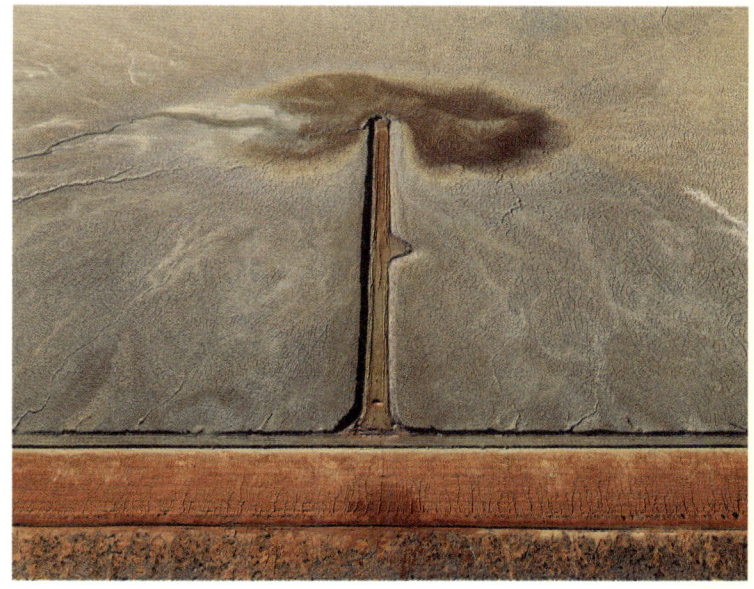

Edward Burtynsky,
Tailings #1, Kalgoorlie,
Western Australia, 2007
© Edward Burtynsky,
courtesy Nicholas Metivier
Gallery, Toronto, and
Howard Greenberg Gallery
& Bryce Wolkowitz, New York

David Campany's latest books are
Walker Evans: The Magazine Work
(Steidl, 2013) and *Gasoline* (MACK,
2013). He is currently curating major
shows of the work of Victor Burgin
and Mark Neville.

Campany's *The Open Road:
Photographic Road Trips Across America*
will be published by Aperture in May 2014.

How is color perceived? How is it replicated with photography? What happens when science and art come together in a photographic image? For photographers from William Henry Fox Talbot, Berenice Abbott, and Hiroshi Sugimoto to a little-known research scientist creating color film for Kodak in the 1930s, the mysterious properties of color as rendered through photography continue to transfix, perplex, and dazzle.

Curious about Color
Kelley Wilder

In the 1930s Kodak research scientist Edwin E. Jelley photographed a particularly beautiful experiment—in color. Using a polarizing light microscope, he was investigating the interference patterns of crystals. These patterns—which occur in light, sound, and surface-water when two or more waves intersect and form new waves as a result—are vibrantly colorful when viewed under polarizing light. Although interference patterns had been studied in this way since the nineteenth century, Jelley's images are among the few surviving photographs of the experiment to be made in color. What prompted him to make them? Jelley, one of a team of scientists working on the development of Kodak's color film and processes, may have been preparing a talk for Ward's Natural Science (a Rochester-based purveyor of science-education materials), or researching what are known as "newton rings" in the layers of color photographic paper, or he might have been studying the nature of the crystalline structures themselves—the end purpose of these photographs is unknown.

So-called conoscopic interference pattern experiments like this one have long played a part in investigations into the composition and action of light as it passes through minerals. Years before they were photographed, such experiments had been noted for their extreme beauty and vividness. A century before Jelley's photographs were made, William Henry Fox Talbot described to members of the Royal Society "rings of vivid color" he had observed in certain crystals seen through his polarizing light microscope. Talbot, like many of his colleagues, was interested in the relationship between light and materials, believing that link to be a key to understanding the chemical composition of both. Talbot's paper on this subject, "Further Observations on the Optical Phenomena of Crystals," was published in *Philosophical Transactions* in 1837, accompanied by a series of illustrations. In the 1850s Talbot rendered these interference patterns as photographs—as did William Crookes in the 1880s and other curious scientist-photographers over the years. By the 1930s, interference images were commonly used as illustrations of the wave theory of light.

Scientists have benefited greatly over the past century and a half from photography's capacities to illustrate, to alter and record what is observed, to make events appear slower or speed them up, to magnify, and to provide reliable images for collection and comparison. These are not, however, the sole reasons to make photographs and films of scientific matters. Researchers

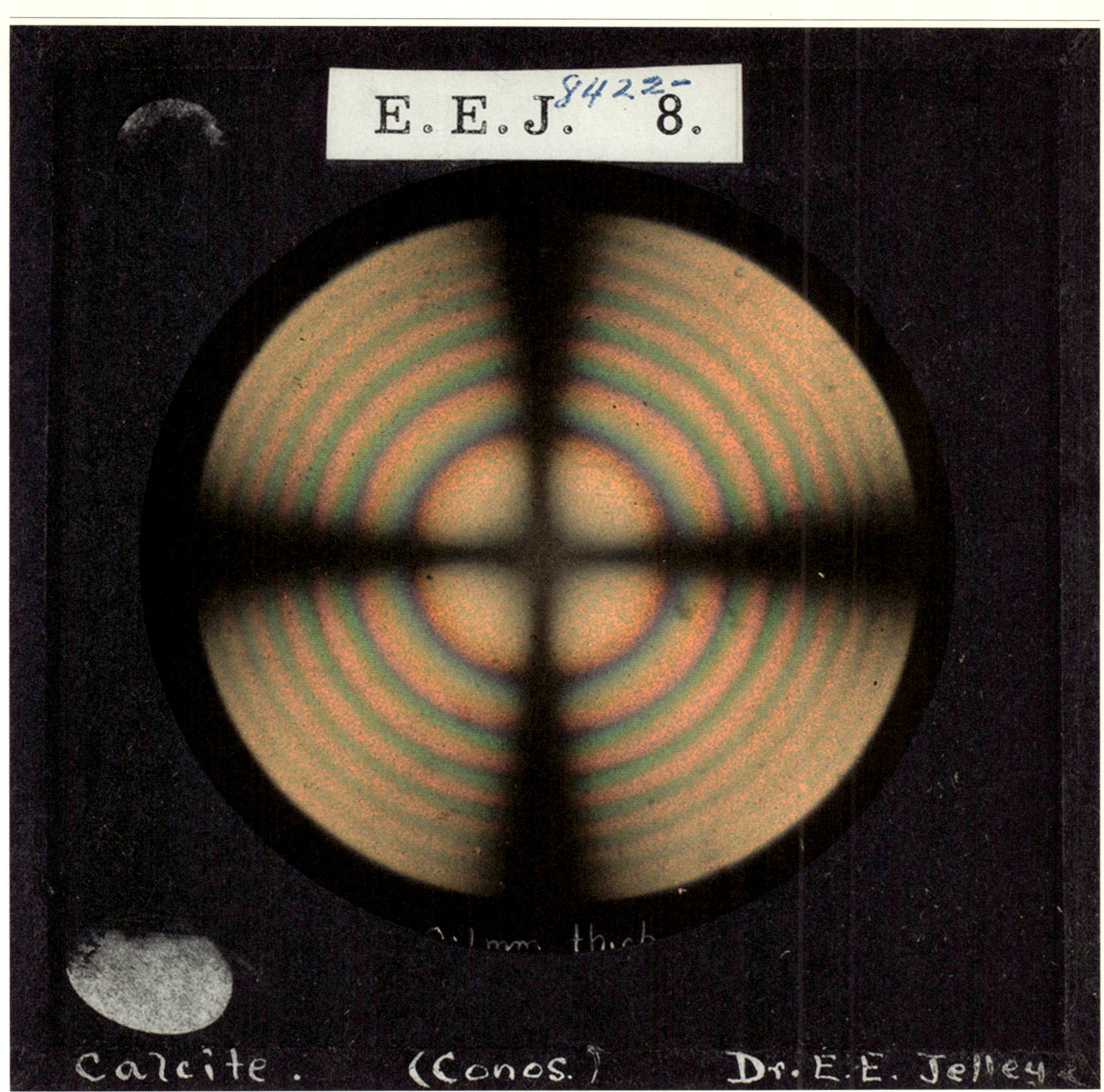

Edwin E. Jelley, Calcite
(Conos), 0.1 mm thick,
8.8 cm color plate,
screen (Autochrome)
process, ca. 1935
Courtesy George Eastman
House, International Museum
of Photography and Film,
Rochester, New York

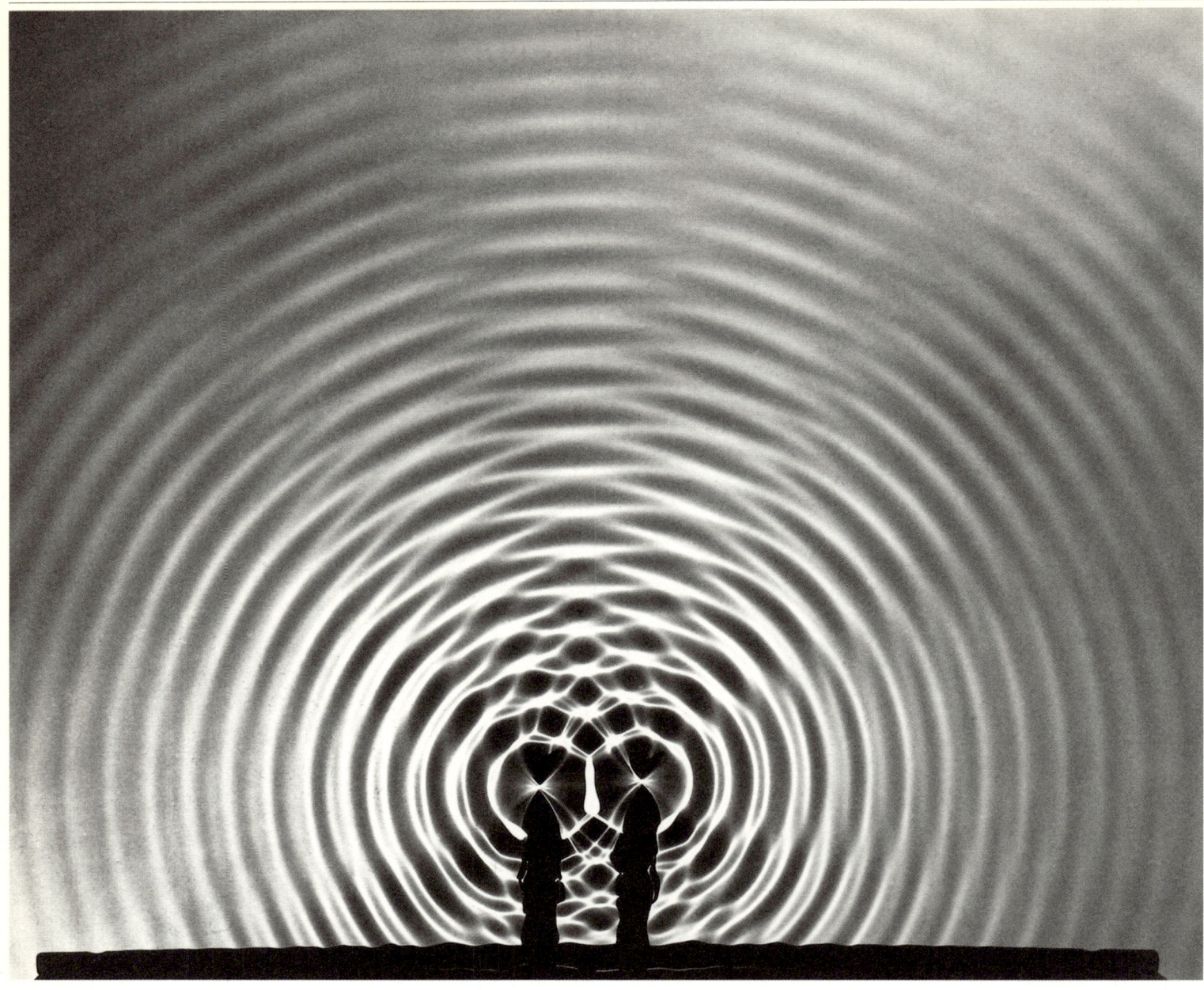

Berenice Abbott,
*Interference pattern
produced by two
interacting sets of circular
waves, ca. 1958*
© Commerce Graphics,
courtesy Howard Greenberg
Gallery, New York

(and increasingly the lay public) appreciate certain scientific subjects under study as being both appealing to the eye and elegant as illustrations of phenomena. So while scientific photographs have an important value as documentary data and as visual demonstrations of scientific theories, they have also found a home in exhibitions for general audiences. Consider, in recent years, such shows as *Beauty of Another Order* (National Gallery of Canada, Ottawa, 1997–98), *Wahr-Zeichen/Emblems* (Technische Sammlungen, Dresden, 2006–7), *Brought to Light* (San Francisco Museum of Modern Art, 2008–9), and 2012's *In the Blink of an Eye* (National Media Museum, Bradford, U.K.). These exhibitions, spotlighting scientific marvels from the microscopic to the astronomical in photographs both vintage and contemporary, have attracted crowds of curious viewers who may have no connection to scientific fields but who have an interest in the visual manifestation of scientific phenomena.

In Jelley's day, too, scientific and technical photographs were frequently featured in exhibitions for the general public. In the 1930s, each year brought showcases of the wondrous worlds revealed through the microscope, X-ray, or with the aid of high-speed photography. Jelley, who along with his work at Kodak was a member of the Royal Photographic Society, reviewed the 1934–35 edition of the Society's annual exhibition, which he dubbed a "Pageant of Science." He also cautioned that the public's enthusiasm for much-sensationalized "new discoveries" seemed to be outweighing the appreciation for the long-term progress of science (perhaps he had his own work with interference patterns in mind).

Photography is in many ways uniquely suited to serve as a medium between the realm of science and the general public. "There needs to be a friendly interpreter between science and the layman," Berenice Abbott wrote in 1939. "I believe photography can be this spokesman." Over the course of thirty years, Abbott made it her mission to create stunning, communicative images of scientific subjects. To help her toward this goal, she used stroboscopic techniques, freezing the motion of waves in a point of light. In 1942 she invented her signature macro-photographic technique called "Super Sight"—by projecting an image in a darkened room, she could focus it onto 16-by-20-inch sheet film. The detail of such large negatives lends the prints a sharpness rarely seen in scientific photographs, many of which are constrained by the size of the experimental apparatus.

Working with the Physical Science Study Committee at the Massachusetts Institute of Technology from 1958 to 1960, Abbott created some of the most memorable and widely disseminated photographs of the wave interference phenomenon. (Last year's monograph *Berenice Abbott: Documenting Science* focused on some of these images, as did the related exhibition at the MIT Museum.) Intriguingly, Abbott chose to produce her images of these vividly colored subjects in black and white—a decision that seems almost radical, given the intense interest in the depiction of scientific subjects in color, just two decades earlier.

As Abbott surely knew, colors can be both alluring and deceptive. The debate about what color is and how it can be perceived and reproduced stretches into the distant past. Artists and scientists alike—from J.M.W. Turner, Wassily Kandinsky, and Josef Albers to John Frederick William Herschel and James Clerk Maxwell—have been fascinated by both the human perception of colors and the ability of different light-sensitive substances to reproduce them. At Kodak and other film manufacturers, the first challenge to tinkerers and researchers like Jelley was to create a black-and-white film that was equally sensitive to all visible colors. The second was to make a photographic positive or negative/positive system that replicated natural colors as humans see them.

But human perception of color is hardly a quantifiable element, linked as it is to individual experience and emotion. Hiroshi Sugimoto has investigated this notion of the subjectivity of perception in his ongoing series *Colors of Shadow*. Sugimoto's visual meditation on the manifestations of colors of shadows —invoking Goethe's musings on color perception in his 1810 treatise *Zur Farbenlehre/Theory of Colors*—takes on the challenge of human perception and also addresses photography's manner of representing color on a material level. Whitewash, angles of incidence and reflection, and the quality of light on walls come into play, but Sugimoto's subject is also the way particular films are *made* to produce color. Kodachrome was well known for its warm red bias, and Ektachrome for blue. Each photographic palette, both analog and digital, contains its own patented foibles. Viewing one of Sugimoto's pieces from the series is a curious sensation: the longer the work is in sight, the greater the number of colors that seem to appear. It isn't only the color of a shadow that we see, but also the subtle colors built into the photographic surface by the manufacturer.

These distinctions and leanings in hue were the subject of close study in the 1930s, when Kodak and other manufacturers were honing in on the chromatic qualities with which each would soon become associated. It was a period of intense competition in the area of color photography. Kodachrome

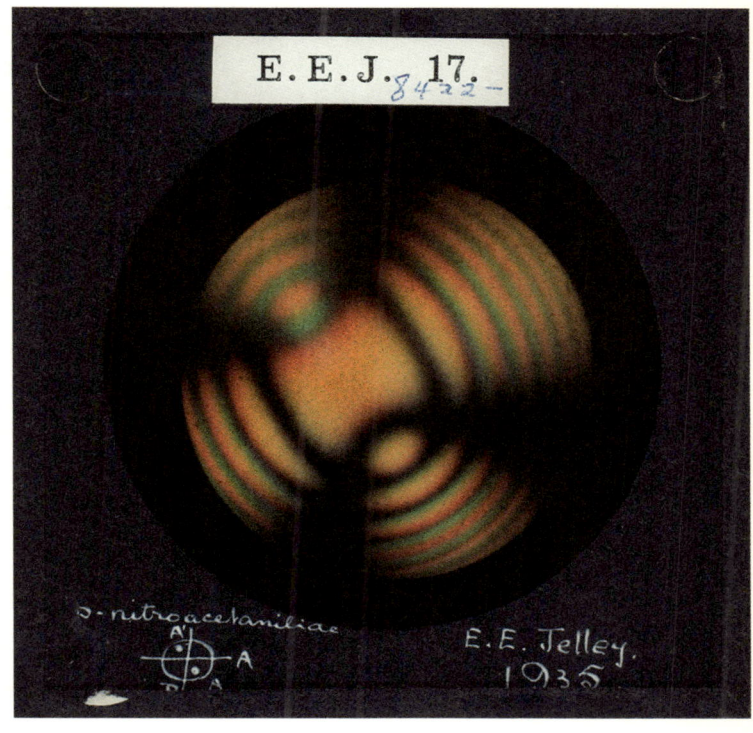

Edwin E. Jelley, 0-nitroacetanilide, 8.8 cm color plate, screen (Autochrome) process, ca. 1935
Courtesy George Eastman House, International Museum of Photography and Film, Rochester, New York

Human perception of color is hardly a quantifiable element, linked as it is to individual experience and emotion.

was released commercially in 1935, signaling the gradual replacement of the additive process of Autochrome by the subtractive process of reversal film (the Autochrome plate, which had been launched in 1907 by Lumière, was discontinued in the 1930s). Shows like the 1937 *First International Exhibit of Scientific and Applied Photography*, by the Photographic Society of America, showcased a range of now-obscure color processes —Vivex, Wash-off Relief, Dufay Color, Defender Chromotone, and early Kodachrome—each with a characteristic palette that reproduced colored phenomena with sometimes slight, sometimes extreme differences. Eastman Kodak showed a great number of prints in the exhibition, in categories ranging from high-speed photography to atomic physics and astronomy— as well as several entries using polarized light to study crystals and metals.

The potentials inherent in these new color processes would have a far-reaching impact, as would the myriad other new photographic technologies that were becoming widely available during this period. Unconventional photographic forms flourished, many of them playing a part in what László Moholy-Nagy termed "Neues Sehen" or New Vision. Much in the minds of Bauhaus and New Bauhaus proponents, these ideas referred in part to the unprecedented perspectives photography offered into the wonders of nature. Moholy-Nagy advised readers of his influential treatise *The New Vision* to use "nature as a constructional model," and to seek "prototypes in nature." While New Vision photography was initially and primarily focused on form in black and white, Moholy-Nagy himself produced a body of color work in 1934 and continued to experiment with new color techniques, as well as with the properties of light, until his death in 1946. (A selection of his color images was exhibited at the Bauhaus-Archiv in Berlin in 2006, accompanied by the publication *László Moholy-Nagy: Color in Transparency*.) György Kepes, Moholy-Nagy's colleague and cofounder of the New Bauhaus in Chicago, headed the school's "Light and Color" workshops. Kepes would follow Moholy-Nagy's lead with the landmark 1956 exhibition and publication *The New Landscape in Art and Science*, in which modernist works of art were juxtaposed with scientific images. Kepes, who later founded the Center for Advanced Visual Studies at MIT, also experimented with color processes and avant-garde techniques. His many visual investigations into the interactions of art and science were witnessed in the 2010 exhibition *The Pleasure of Light* at Budapest's Ludwig Museum (a two-person exhibition featuring the work of Kepes and Frank J. Malina), which included photographs, photograms, and works in other media focusing on light as a dynamic and visually compelling subject.

Berenice Abbott observed in 1939: "There is an essential unity between photography, science's child, and science, the parent." As the abundance of recent exhibitions and publications on the subject shows, there continues to be a keen interest in the visual properties of science—an aspect that has been explored by both artists and scientists since the early days of photography. The advances in color processes, helped along by the likes of Edwin E. Jelley and his colleagues in the 1930s, have allowed scientific phenomena to be experienced in all their visual splendor.

Kelley Wilder is Reader in Photographic History at the Photographic History Research Centre, De Montfort University, Leicester, U.K. She is the author of *Photography and Science* (Reaktion, 2009).

Pictures

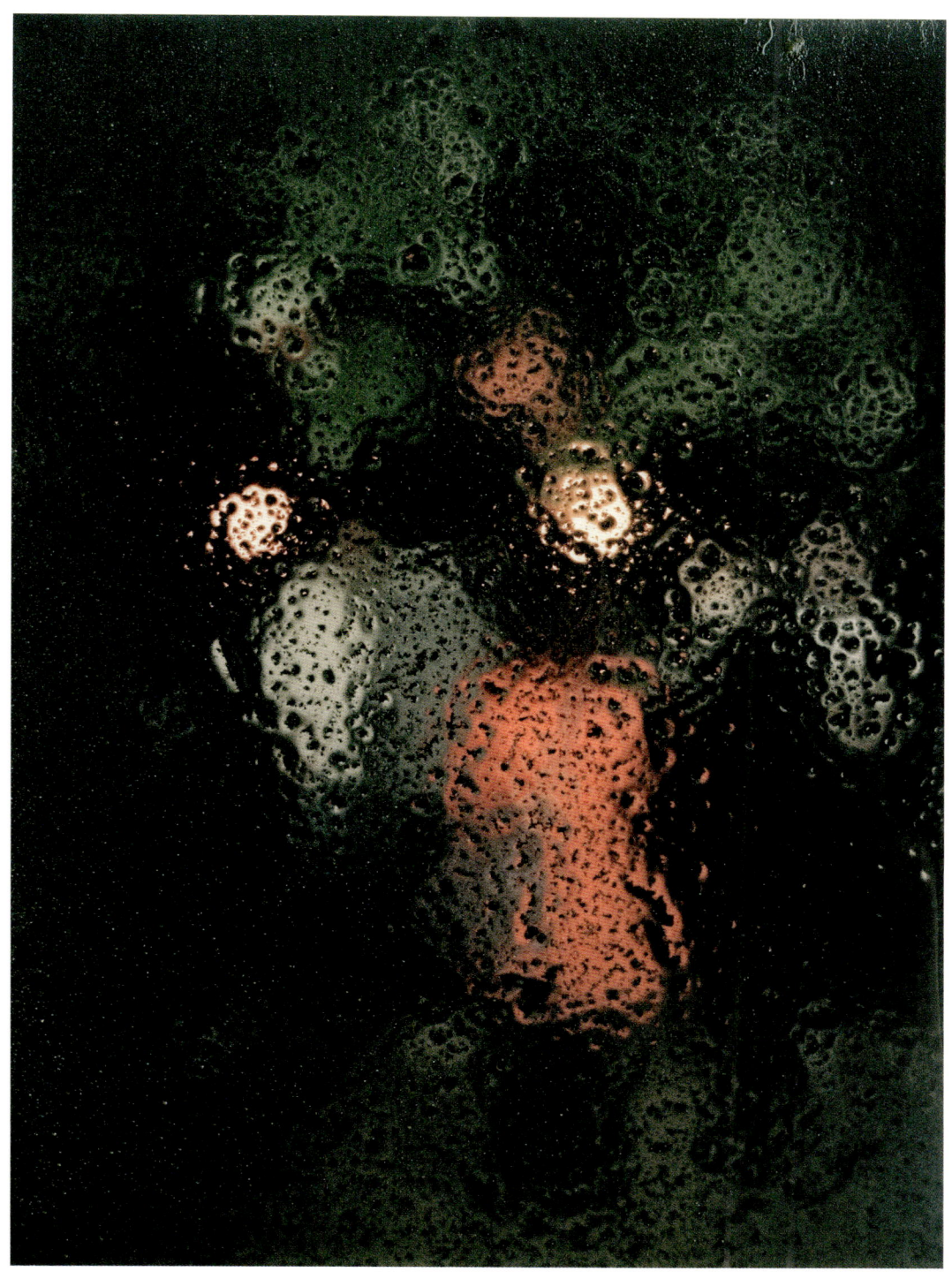

In 2012 the prolific and inventive British photographer Stephen Gill was commissioned to make a photographic response to the postindustrial town of Dudelange, Luxembourg, once a center of European steel manufacturing. For this project he focused on a heavily polluted pond that had been used to cool the steel mill's furnaces, drawing visual parallels between the microscopic life in the water and the human life in the nearby town. Of this micro-macro approach, Gill writes: "I became committed to the idea of attempting to bridge these two apparently disparate worlds—so physically close yet so different in scale." With this goal in view, Gill visited the University of Luxembourg, where he made use of a medical microscope to examine single drops of water to better understand the existence teeming below the pond's murky surface. His images reveal a minuscule ecosystem —diatoms and other creatures—a sign that the abused pond may be coming back to life. Aboveground, everyday existence carries on as well, in pubs and cafés and on the streets. Seen through Gill's watery lens, the residents appear to be caught in a strange dreamscape.

—The Editors

Stephen Gill

Coexistence

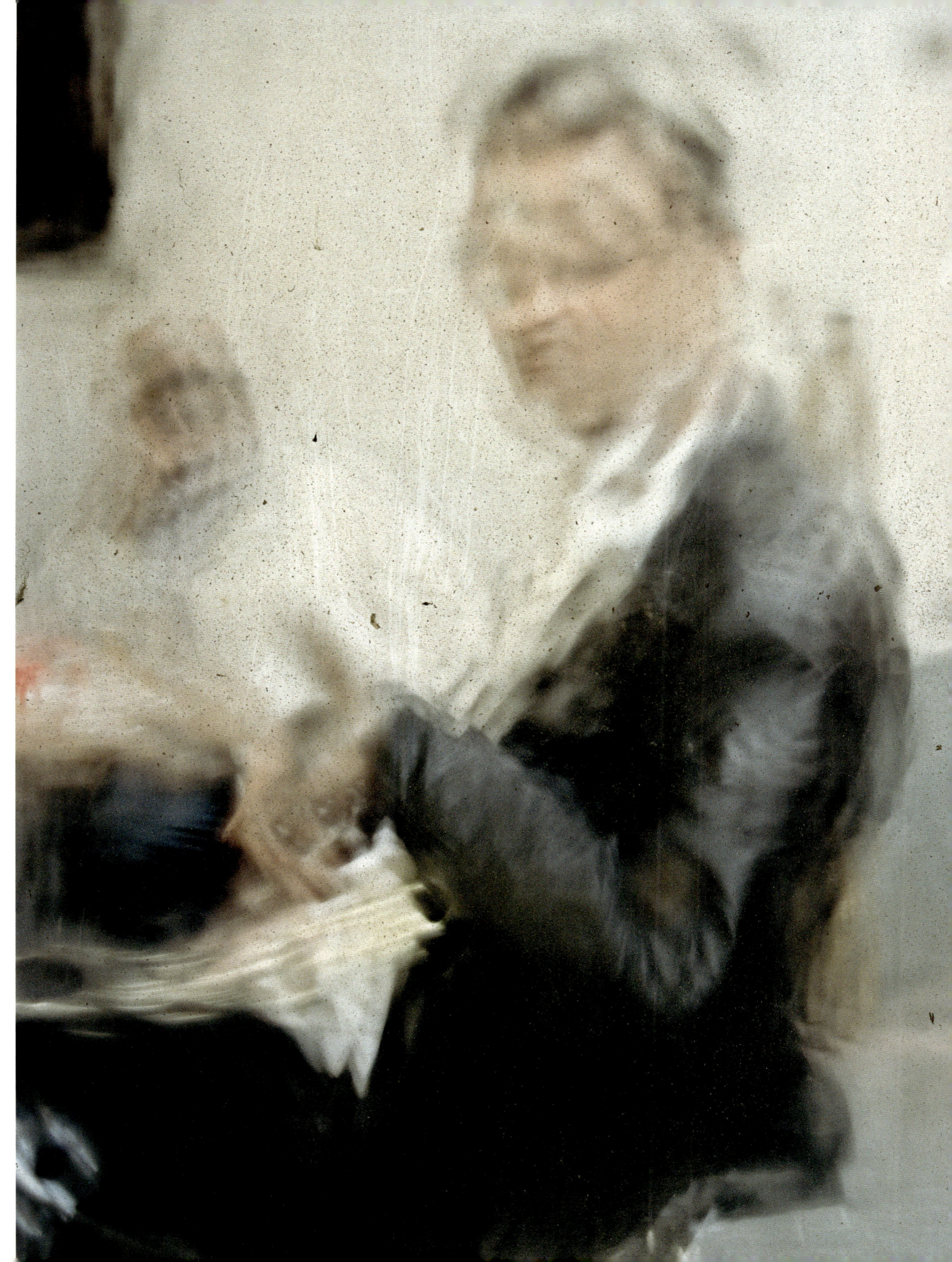

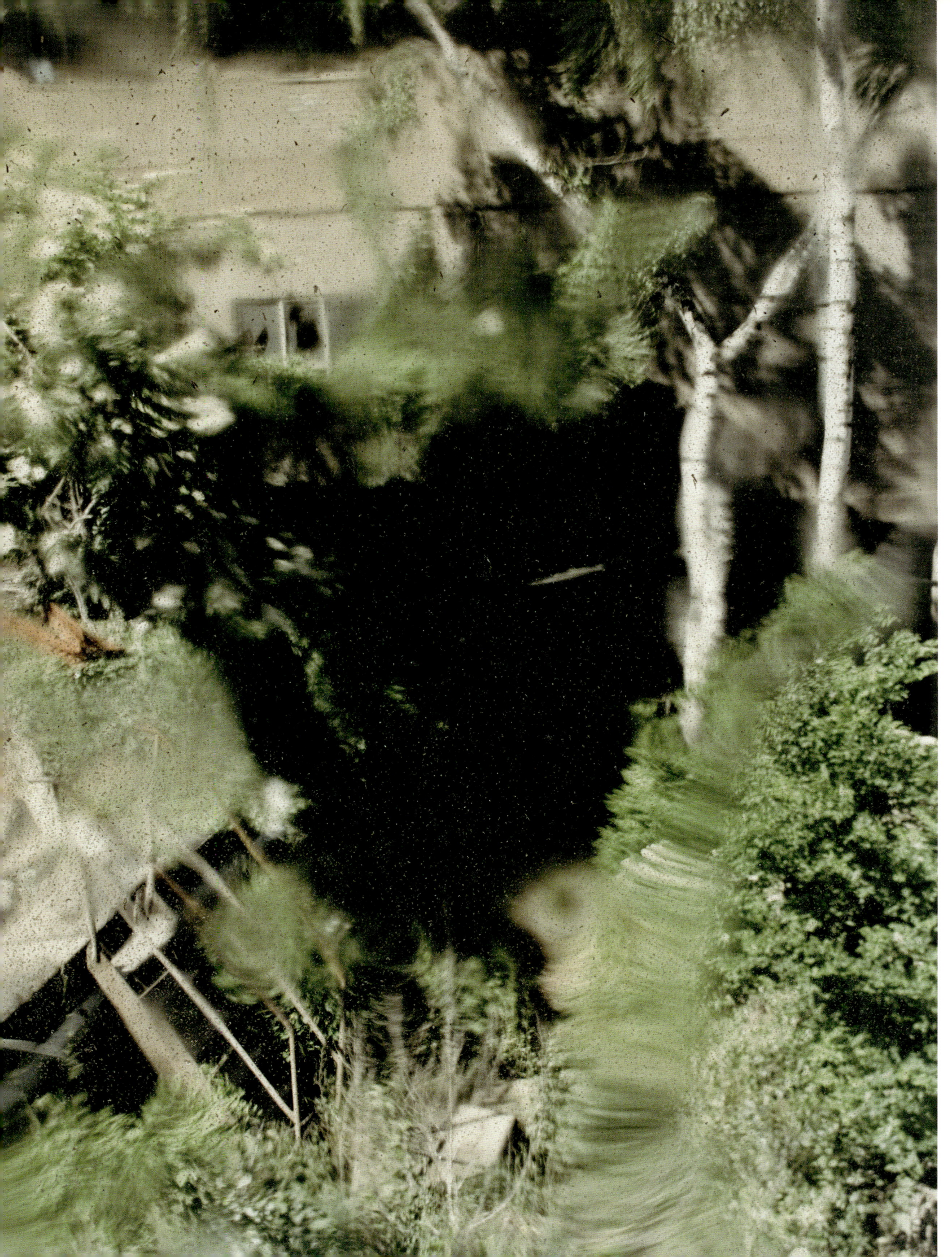

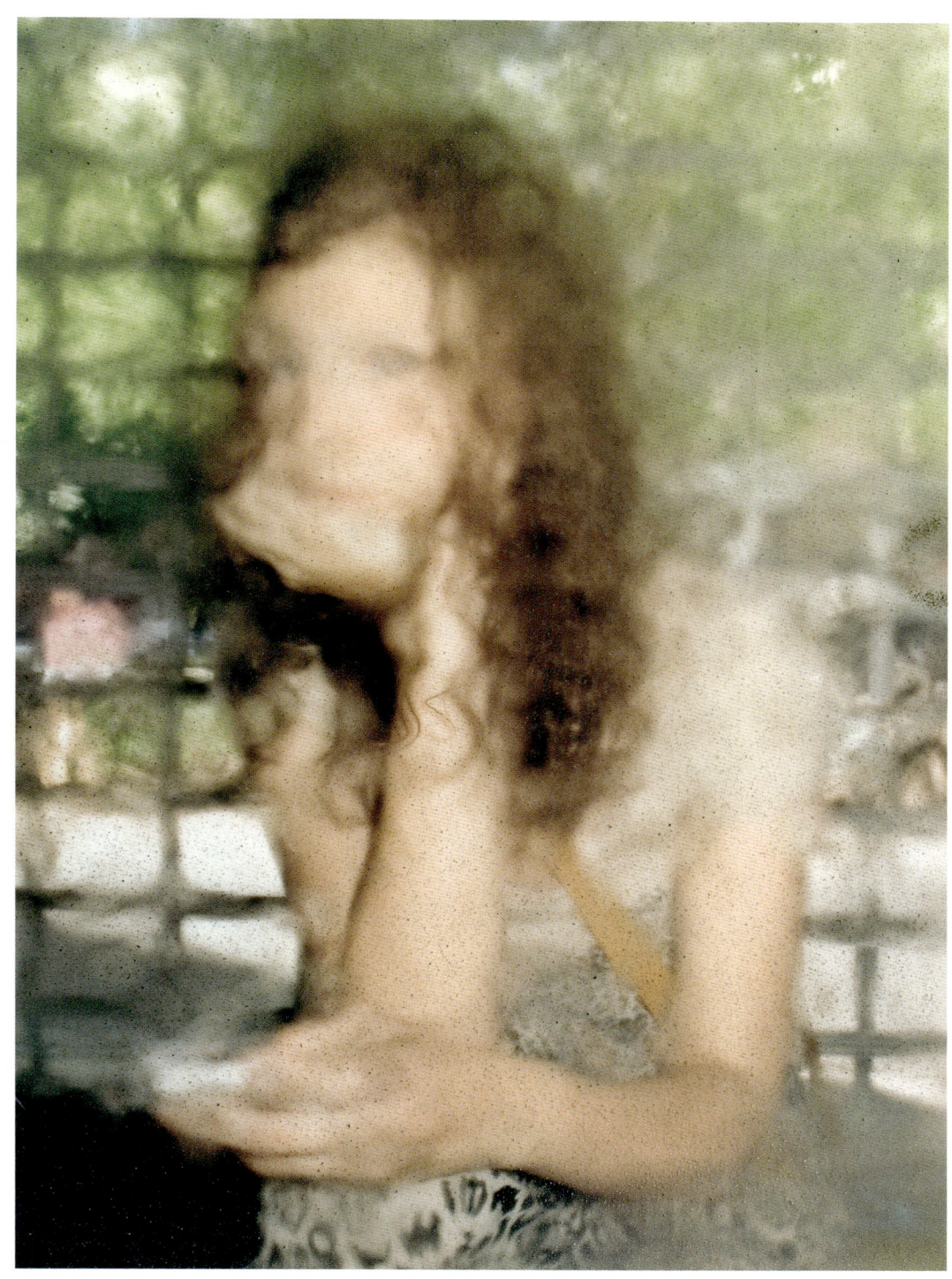

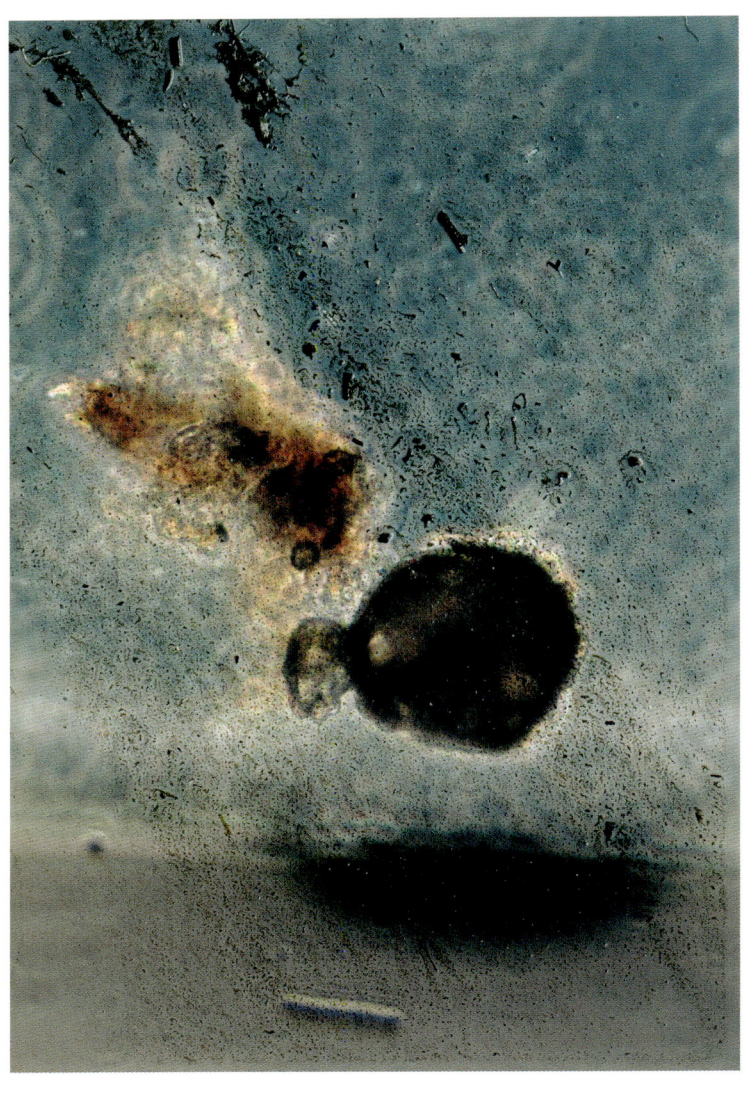
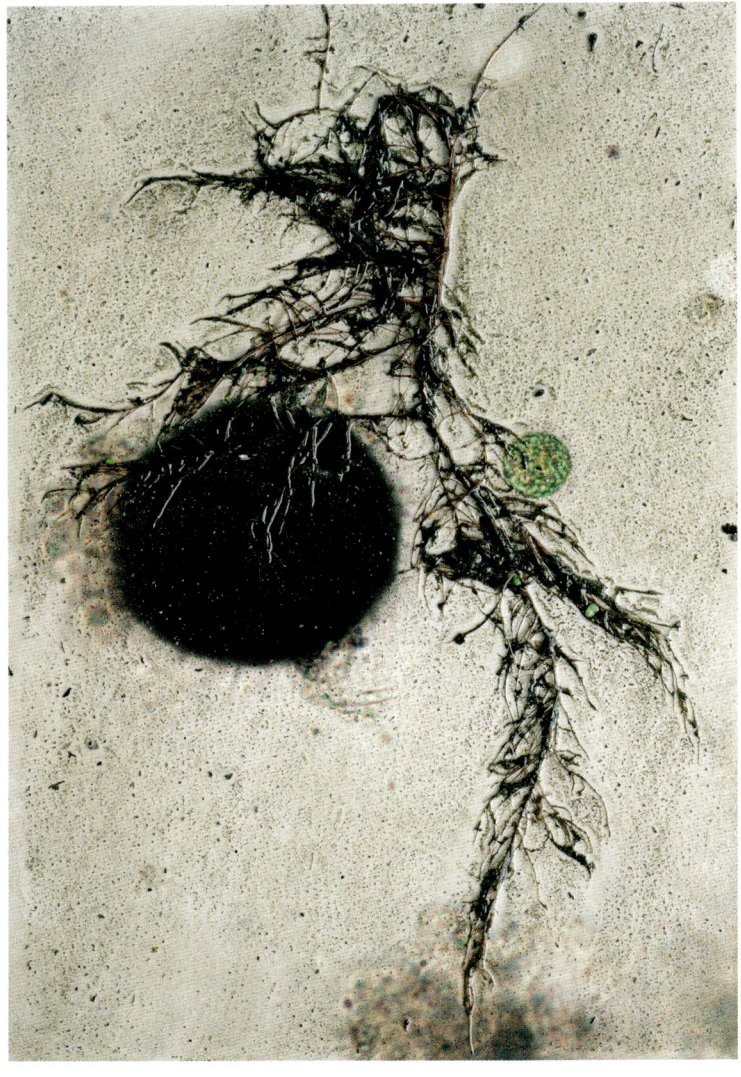

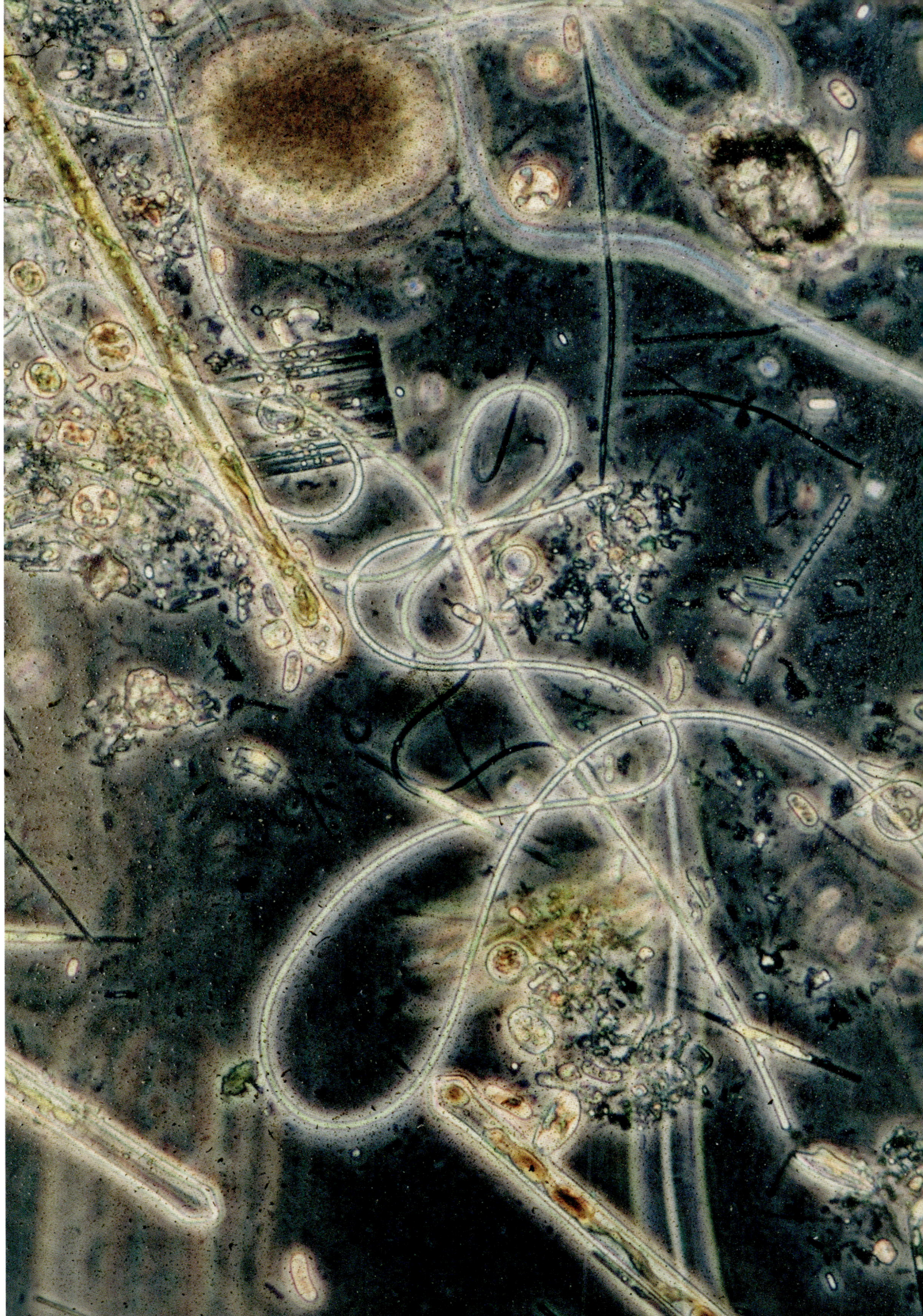

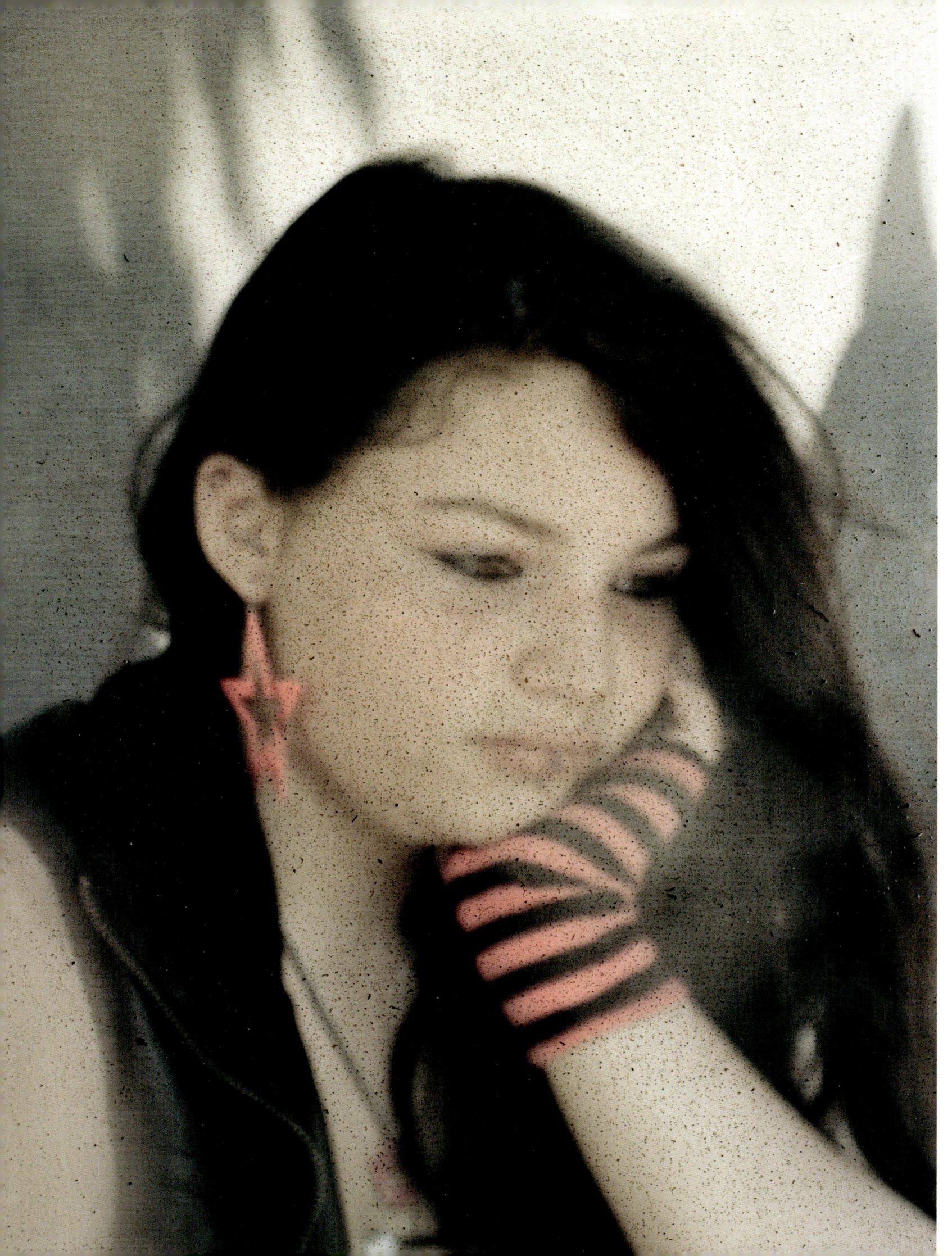

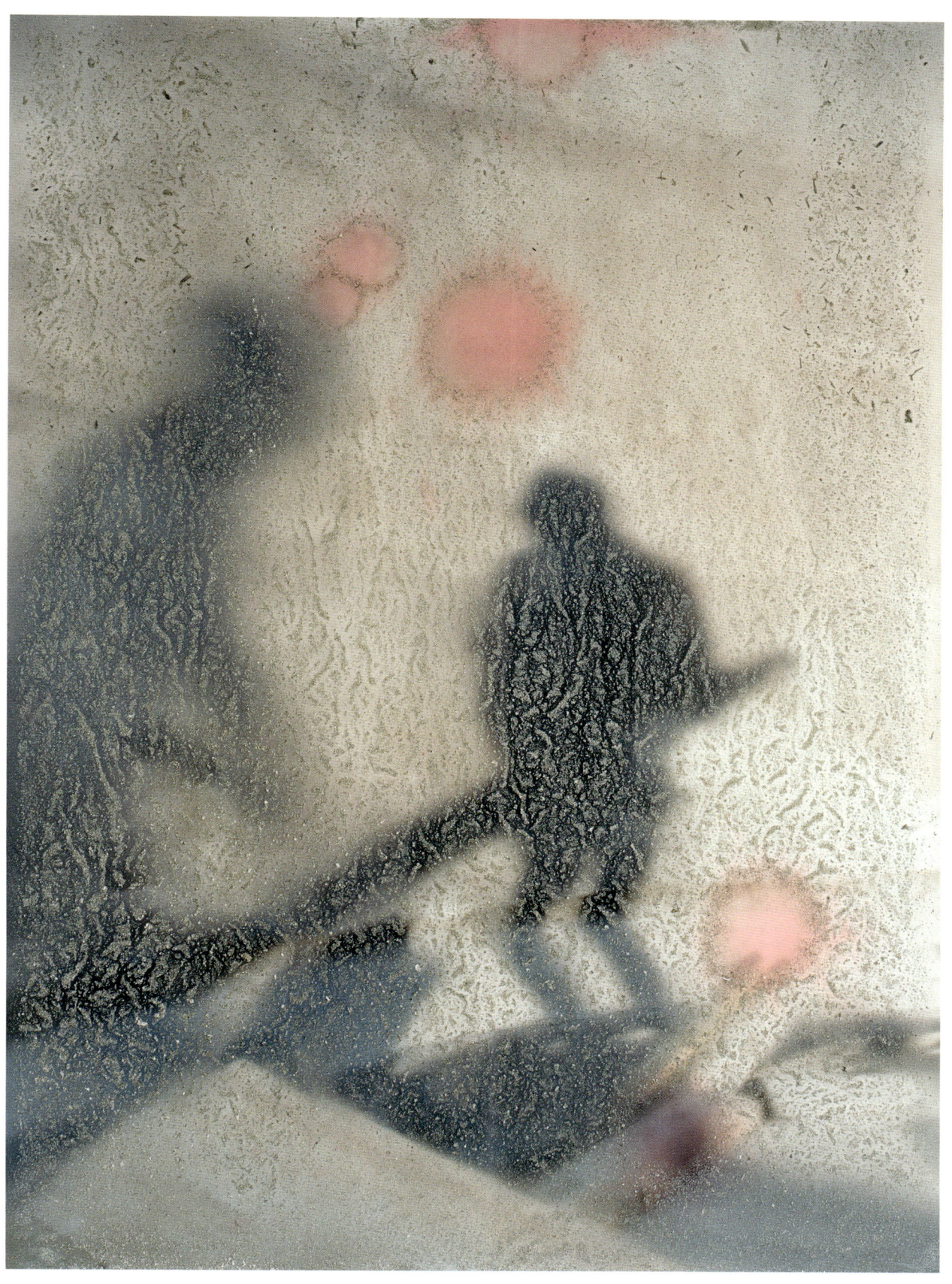

Secret Universe is the title of the exhibition series under which, in 2011, the late Horst Ademeit's work was first presented to a museum audience. It was a fitting choice for an exceptional corpus of Polaroid (and later digital) photography that was neither conceived as an artistic project nor intended for public exposure. Compiled over some fifteen years, beginning around 1990, these images were made for strictly personal, utilitarian ends.

Trained as a textile designer, Ademeit entered Joseph Beuys's class at the Kunstakademie Düsseldorf in the late 1960s. When his work was rejected as too conservative—too academic—he left not only Beuys's class but the art world at large. Thereafter Ademeit supported himself primarily as a manual laborer in the building trade. He took up photography in order to contend with a mounting concern: his belief that he was increasingly subject to the deleterious effects of what he referred to as "cold rays" and invisible radiation, emanating from electrical sockets and fittings in his apartment. To contain and counter the harmful yet undetectable rays, Ademeit photographed their sources at home, and, by extension, in his neighborhood, notating his feelings and impressions— as well as detailed data from electricity meters, thermometers, clocks, and other devices—in the narrow margins of his Polaroid prints. While capitalizing on the ease and immediacy offered by this particular process, Ademeit may also have valued the fact that, exceptionally among photographic media, the Polaroid camera produces a unique and unrepeatable image. On the evidence of those few among his six-thousand-plus Polaroid shots made public to date, it seems, however, that the making of the image— the pointing, shooting, transfixing, and hence warding off of the feared effects— took priority over the character of what was produced. The more rudimentary his methods, and the more seemingly happenstance his compositions, the greater the charge generated by the resulting images—as if something had, indeed, been caught on the fly. In short, these works are compelling almost in inverse relation to the degree of attention lavished on their production.

Ademeit's œuvre has been likened by critics to a Conceptual art project of the kind that fueled the practices of On Kawara and Hanne Darboven. It might equally well be compared with works by certain individuals who have felt themselves subject to the wiles of what Viktor Traub (an associate of Freud) termed "influencing machines": that is, machines that appear, in the words of the psychoanalyst, "as an outer enemy, a machine used to attack the patient." Among the most haunting precursors to Ademeit's murky testimonials, the annotated drawings of Hugo Rennert, Jakob Mohr, and Robert Gie sometimes depict their authors entangled in the immaterial coils emitted by unidentifiable contraptions, and sometimes simply record the pathways traversed by sinister impulses. Had Ademeit picked up pencil and paper, in place of a camera, while grappling with his infested environment, he too would likely be identified as an Outsider artist. Fortunately, photography has not been subject to the same disciplinary distinctions as the other visual arts: it largely eschews hierarchies between what is produced by the marginal and/ or self-taught for leisure and utilitarian ends and the panoply of artifacts produced by mainstream professionals of various ilks. In photography's short history, conventions based on notions of center and periphery, of accredited and amateur, are less determinant than they are in the discourses attending painting, sculpture, and the graphic arts. Indeed, one measure of the strength of Ademeit's singular endeavor is that it can be viewed through multiple lenses.

Horst Ademeit Secret Universe

Lynne Cooke

Curator and art historian Lynne Cooke is currently Andrew W. Mellon Professor at the Center for Advanced Study in the Visual Arts, National Gallery of Art, Washington D.C. She recently curated Rosemarie Trockel: A Cosmos, at the New Museum, New York.

This page:
Untitled (11.09.1991), 1991
All photographs by
Horst Ademeit
Courtesy Galerie Susanne
Zander/Delmes & Zander,
Cologne

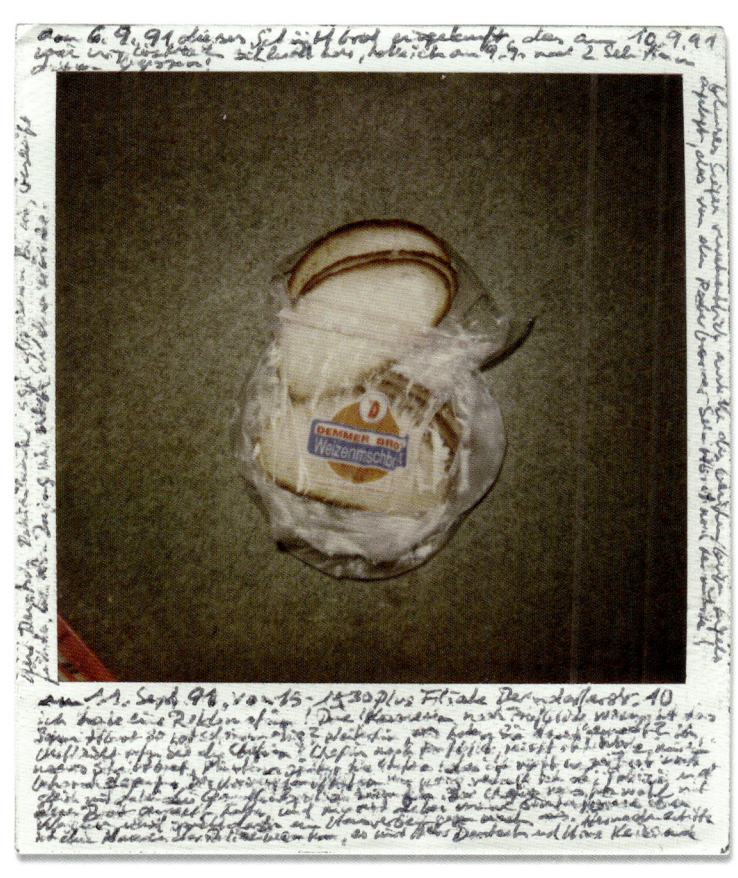

This page:
Untitled, (03.06.1992),
1992

Opposite,
top left: *Untitled
(11.03.1994)*, 1994;
top right: *Untitled
(27.09.1990)*, 1990;
bottom left: *Untitled
(27.05.1992)*, 1992;
bottom right: *Untitled
(19.02.1994)*, 1994

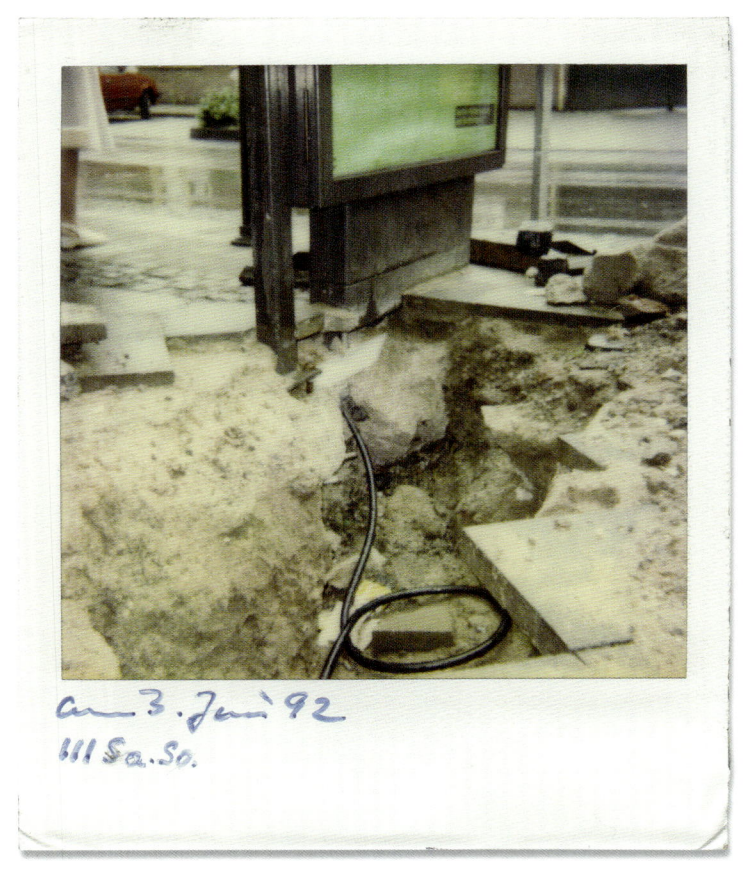

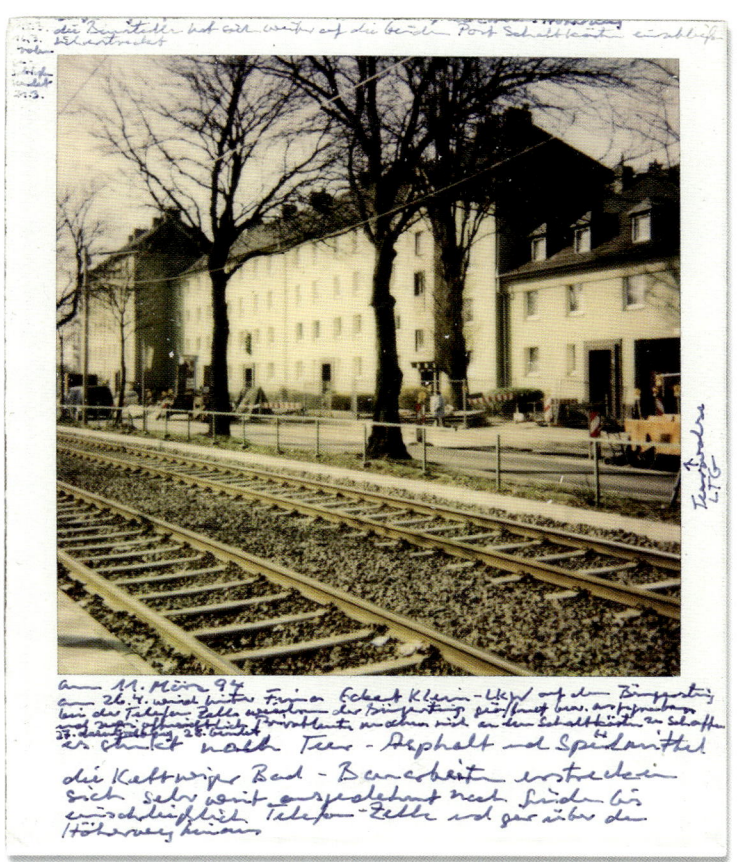

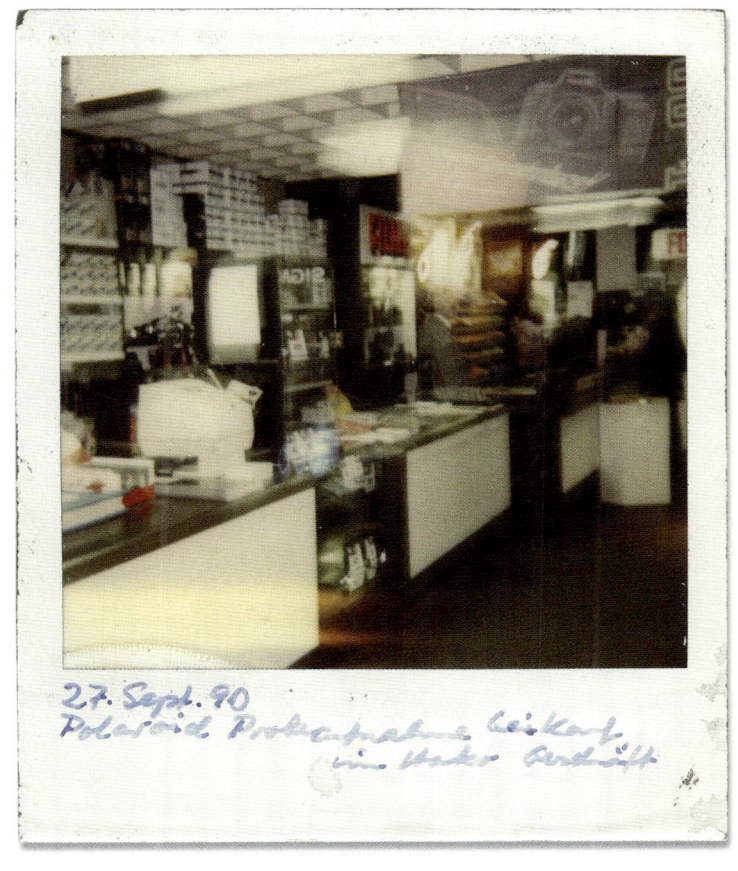

27. Sept. 90

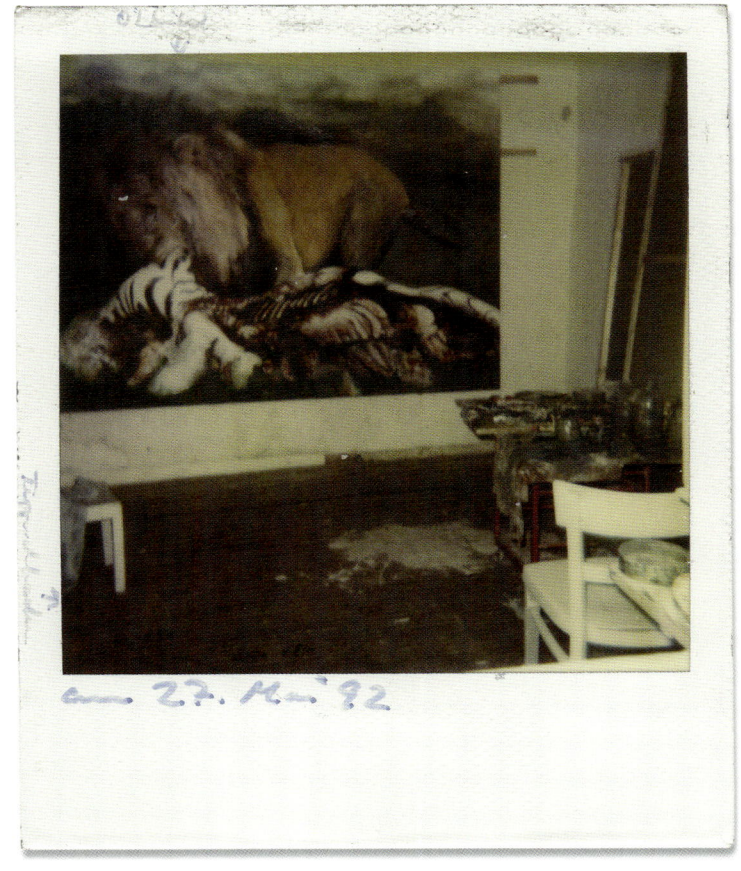

am 27. Mai '92

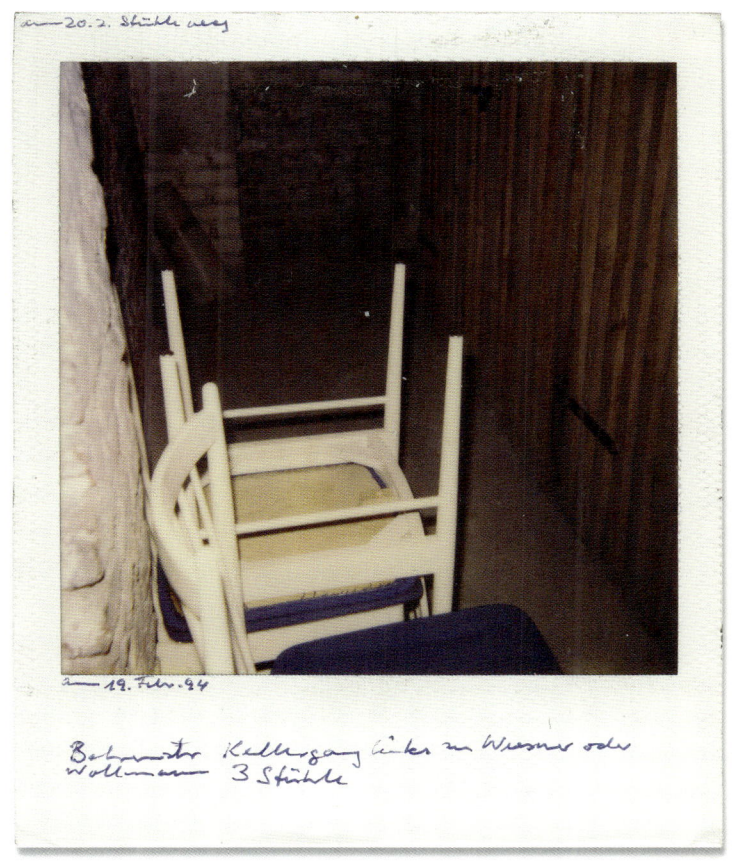

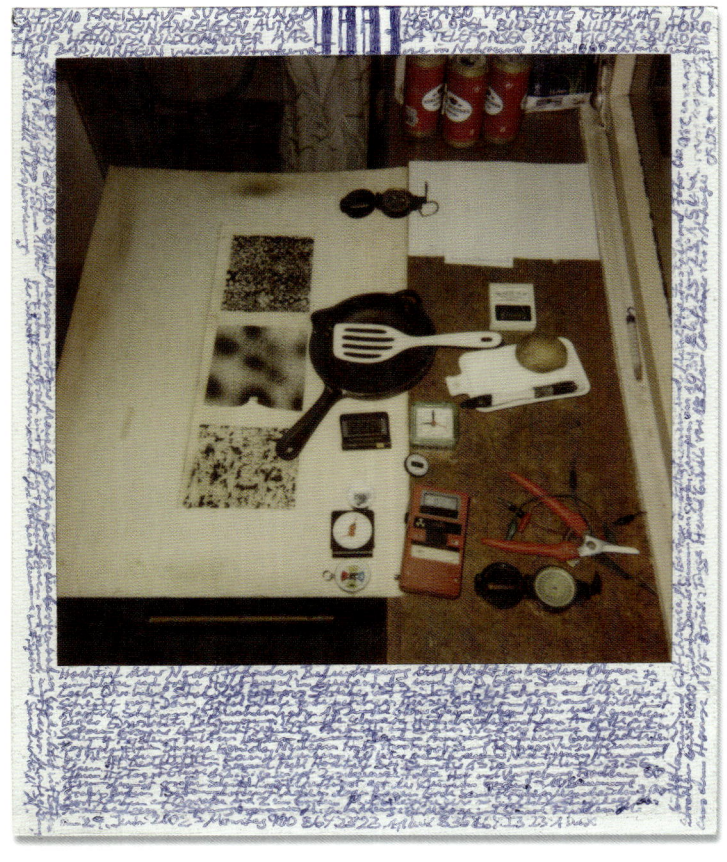

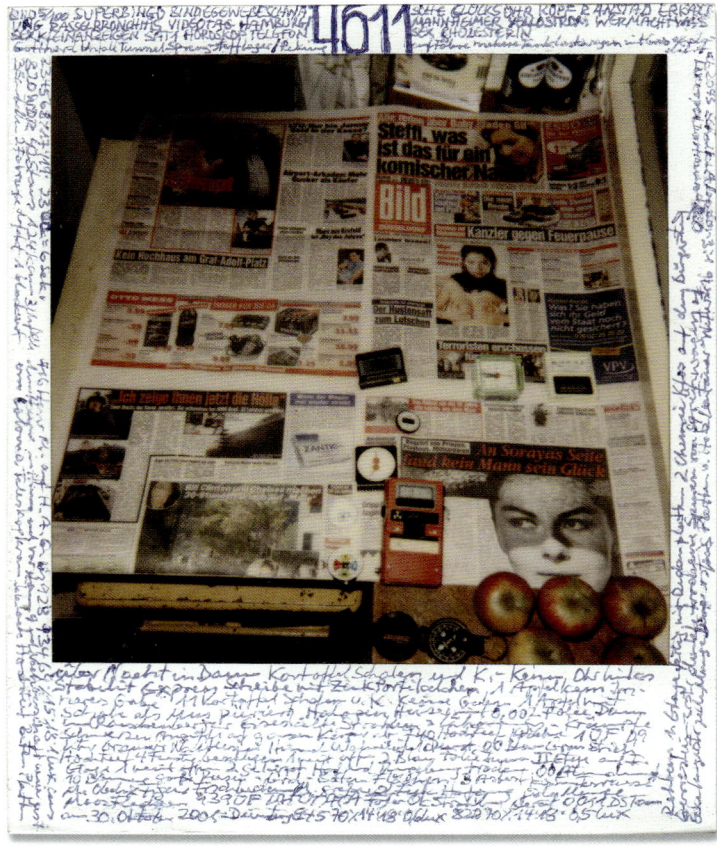

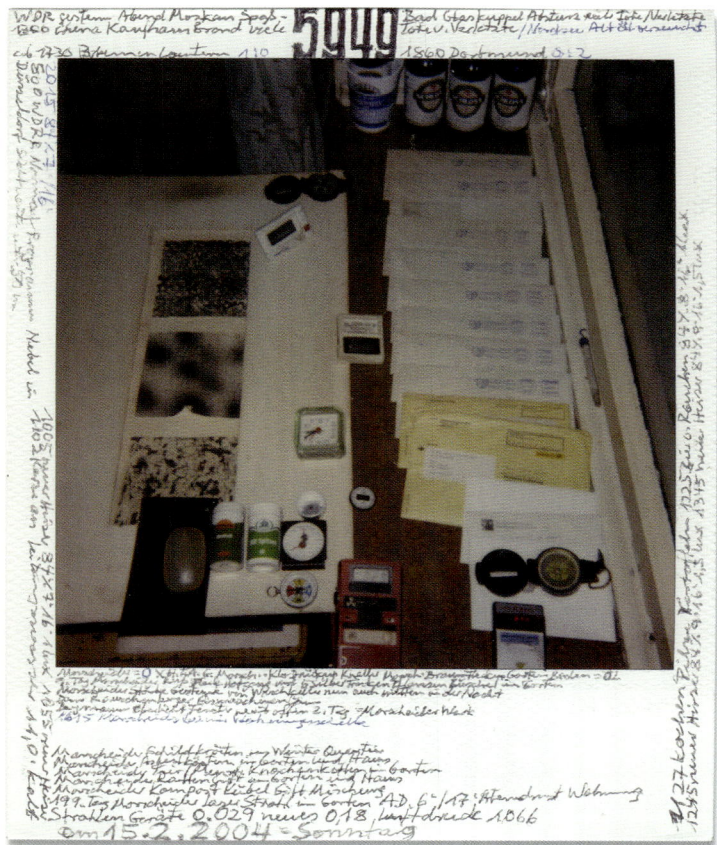

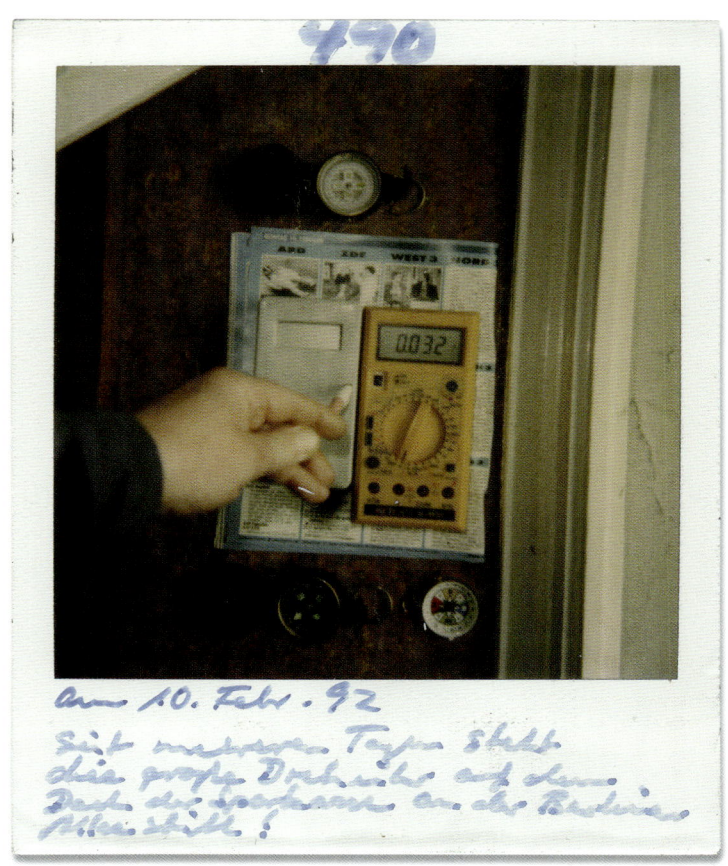

Opposite,
top left: *4883
(29.07.2002)*, 2002;
top right: *4611
(30.10.2001)*, 2001;
bottom left: *5949
(15.02.2004)*, 2004;
bottom right: *490
(10.02.1992)*, 1992

This page:
3570 (14.12.1998),
1998

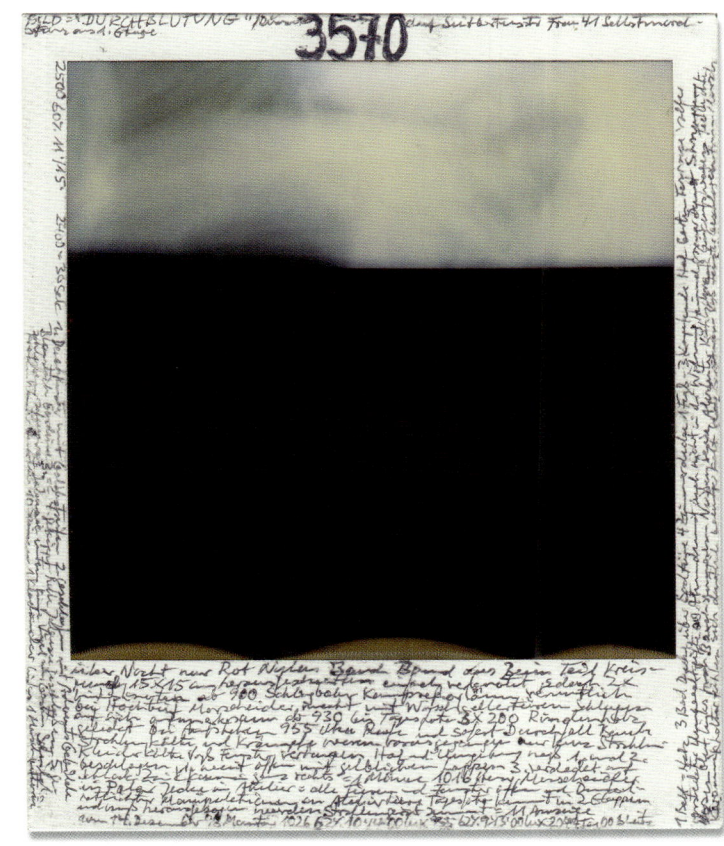

"Let a cannon-bullet pass through a room, and in its way take with it any limb or fleshy part of man." This dramatic scenario was envisaged by the great Enlightenment thinker John Locke in 1689. The bullet, he reasoned, "must touch one part of the flesh first, and another after, and so in succession." But the action would happen so instantaneously that no one would be able to "perceive any succession, either in the pain or sound of so swift a stroke." Our rational minds tell us that rapid events occur in a certain order, even though this order cannot be perceived. Since Locke's early speculations, generations of researchers have worked hard to understand an increasingly fast-paced world. With the help of electronic flash, photographers were able to arrest Locke's imagined projectile in midair: in the 1930s, Harold E. "Doc" Edgerton, working at the Massachusetts Institute of Technology, captured a rifle's bullet flying at the vertiginous speed of 2,700 feet per second.

Harold E. Edgerton

"Doc" and His Laboratory Notebooks
Jimena Canales

The first use of flash is usually attributed to one of the inventors of photography, William Henry Fox Talbot. In 1851 Talbot used a simple electric spark to illuminate a moving target—a page of the London *Times* that was pinned on a rapidly rotating wheel. To his amazement, the resulting photograph was legible. At the turn of the century, the British physicist A. M. Worthington used sparks to illuminate splashing drops, and in France during the 1920s the Seguin brothers developed the "stroborama"— a machine made first with mercury and then with neon arc lamps. As scientists extended the field of flash illumination beyond the spark, they increased the range of their visual studies.

Edgerton's first announcement of strobe technologies appeared in a 1931 issue of the journal *Electrical Engineering*. James R. Killian, a young science writer (later president of MIT and one of Dwight Eisenhower's most trusted scientific advisors), was immediately fascinated by strobe lights. For more than forty years, Edgerton and Killian worked as a team: one taking the photographs and the other writing about the "meaning of the pictures."

In 1932 Edgerton's images were published in *Technology Review*, a student-run MIT journal edited by Killian, who also wrote the preface to Edgerton's first book about strobe technology, the handsomely illustrated *Flash! Seeing the Unseen by Ultra High-Speed Photography* (1939). When the United States joined World War II, Edgerton went on active duty; his night-reconnaissance work (using a 40,000-watt-per-second xenon flash) won him the Medal of Freedom. Upon returning home, he cofounded a highly lucrative defense-contract business from which he and his partners made a munificent living. Among their many endeavors, they developed a shutterless "rapatronic" ("rapid" and "electronic") camera that was able to photograph the first stages of superfast nuclear explosions.

In 1954 Killian and Edgerton republished *Flash!*. The original 1939 edition had included a photograph of a golf club hitting a ball; in the later volume this image was replaced with one of an atomic bomb explosion. While much had changed during a decade and a half of war and Cold War, Killian's preface to the book was unaltered. Edgerton was, Killian noted there, "first of all a scientist and an electrical engineer, investigating, measuring, seeking new facts about natural phenomena." Nonetheless, Killian also insisted that "these pictures are not only facts, but new aesthetic experiences," which he compared to Edward Weston's cypress trees and rocks, Edward Steichen's sunflowers, and Alfred Stieglitz's clouds and hands. He described Edgerton's images as "literal transcriptions" of nature, broadly fitting within a realist theory of representation. They were, Killian asserted, "scientific records" written in a "universal language for all to appreciate."

For Edgerton himself, strobe photographs were something else: records of the unforeseen and the unexpected. As he would put it decades later: "A good experiment is simply one that reveals something previously unknown to the student." Many aspiring young engineers arrived at his MIT Strobe Lab believing otherwise: "Some students expect the results to prove the initial assumption, but I have always empathized with the student who sees new discoveries and knowledge that were not anticipated flowing from the laboratory." According to Edgerton, there was "no such thing as a 'perfect' result or a complete study of the phenomenon." His laboratory notebooks, filled with notes, hand-scrawled diagrams, and snapshots documenting his work, reveal the flowing stage of production—often referred to as "science in action"—which belies the static, "ready-made" outcome presented at the end. In contrast to the published photographs, those in his lab notebooks show a different behind-the-scenes spectacle: most interestingly, scientists (including Edgerton himself) working their machines.

Killian was not concerned with the production process of science or with unexpected results that could suddenly surface in real time. For a number of like-minded thinkers—including Aristotle and Albert Einstein—time was as predictable as space. Edgerton's machines "manipulate time as the microscope or telescope manipulates space," Killian wrote. Modern science "enabled us to see and understand by contracting and expanding not only space but time."

Edgerton was not as optimistic as Killian. "Although I've tried for years to photograph a drop of milk splashing on a plate with all the coronet's points spaced equally apart, I have never succeeded." But he was hardly disappointed: "In many ways, unexpected results are what have most inspired my photography."

Edgerton expected the unexpected. In 1952 came an ultimate case in point: in approximately ten nanoseconds, one of the handheld cameras he and his associates had developed captured the initial stages of the first hydrogen bomb explosion, which obliterated Elugelab Island, part of the Enewetak Atoll in the Marshall Islands of the Pacific. Even those who had witnessed atomic tests were stunned by the bomb's capacity for destruction: the explosion was more than twenty times the size of the Hiroshima fireball. Not only was Elugelab vaporized, but life on the surrounding islands was destroyed. Radiation blanketed most of the atoll, and hundreds of natives expelled from the island were left with nowhere to return to. As in Locke's seventeenth-century description, the pain on the ground did not match with the knowledge of the succession of events—this time on a scale never before imagined.

Jimena Canales is
associate professor of
the history of science
at Harvard University.
She is the author of
*A Tenth of A Second:
A History* (University
of Chicago Press, 2010)
and numerous articles
on the history of science,
film, photography, art,
and architecture.

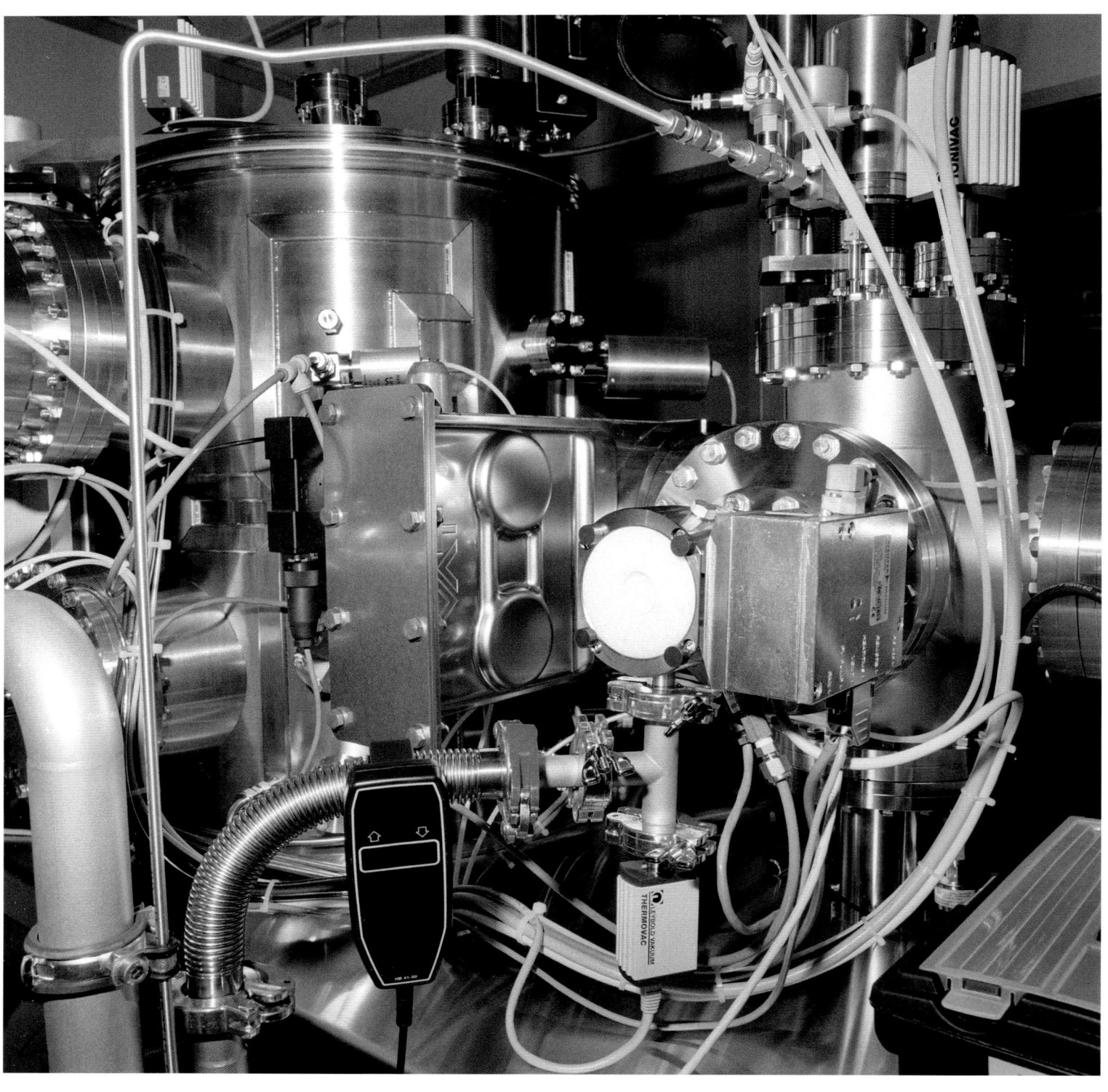

Mårten Lange has made a career of
disorienting spectators with off-kilter
points of view and high-contrast
photographs in which ordinary objects
and scenes are transformed into riddles
of perception. His book *Another Language*
(MACK, 2012) presents tightly composed
images of the natural world transmuted
into uncanny scenes. Before embarking
on these projects, though, Lange made
a curious body of rigorously composed,
square-format images of the surprisingly
expressive, even beautiful, machinery that
facilitates the study of nanotechnology,
microscopy, and nuclear physics in
high-tech laboratories at Sweden's
University of Gothenburg, in Lange's
hometown. The workplace is a mainstay
of photography (think of Lee Friedlander
at the Kray Corporation, or Chris Killip
in the Pirelli factory). Lange, though,
takes a singular approach, cropping
out the laboratory environments
to focus entirely on these machines,
which are complex to the point of chaos.

—The Editors

Mårten Lange
Machina

All photographs by
Mårten Lange, from the
series *Machina*, 2007
© Mårten Lange

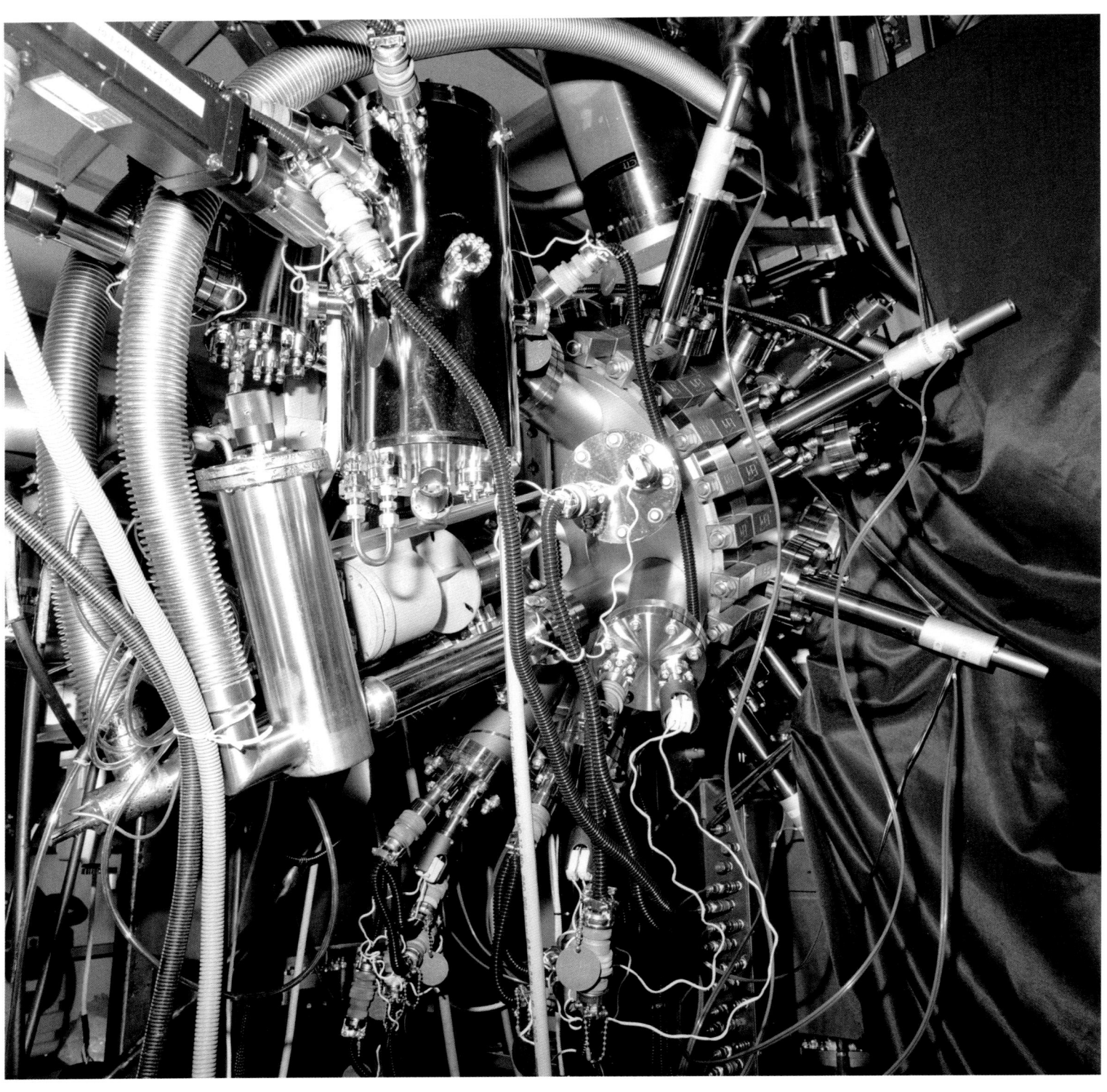

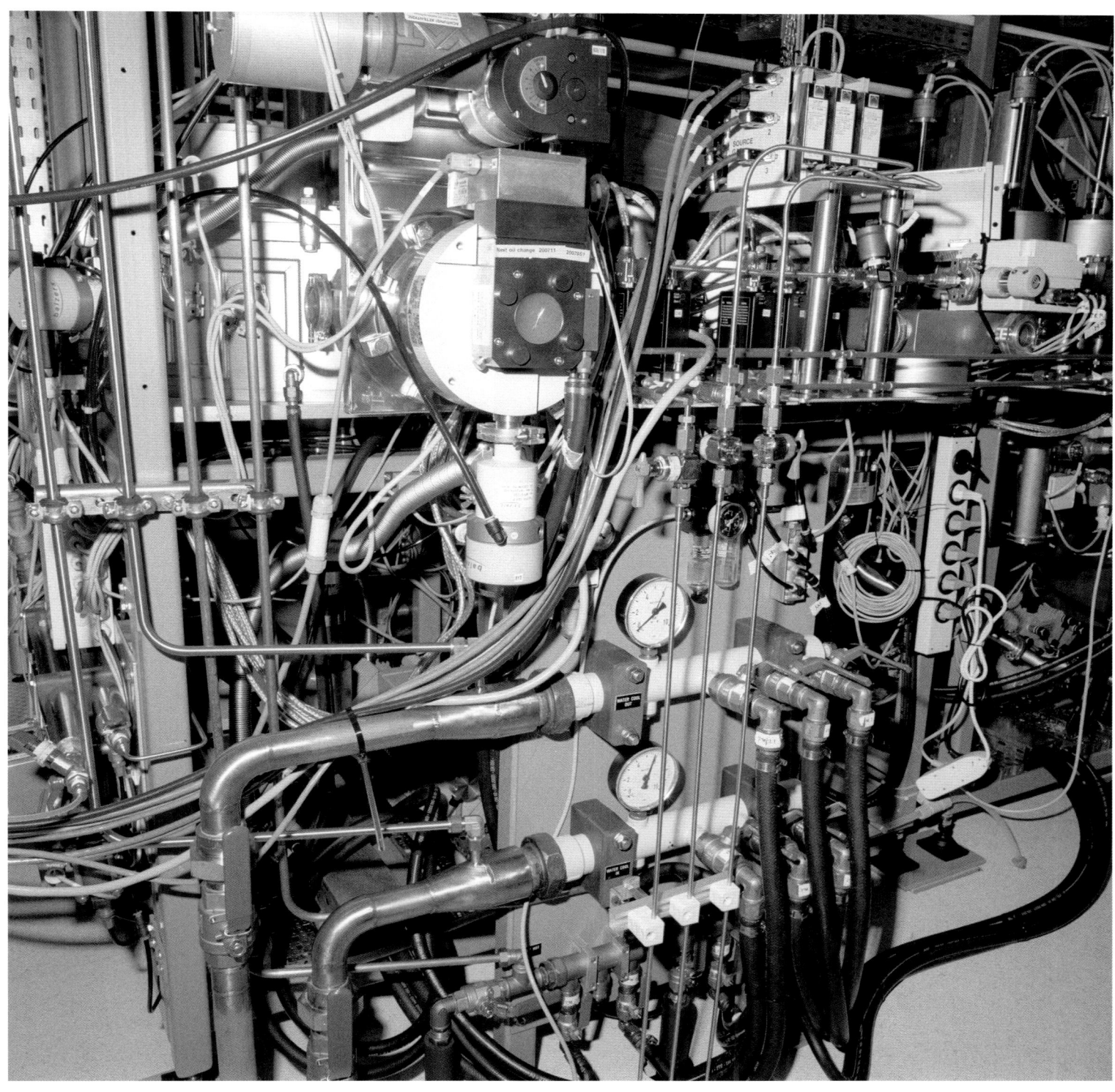

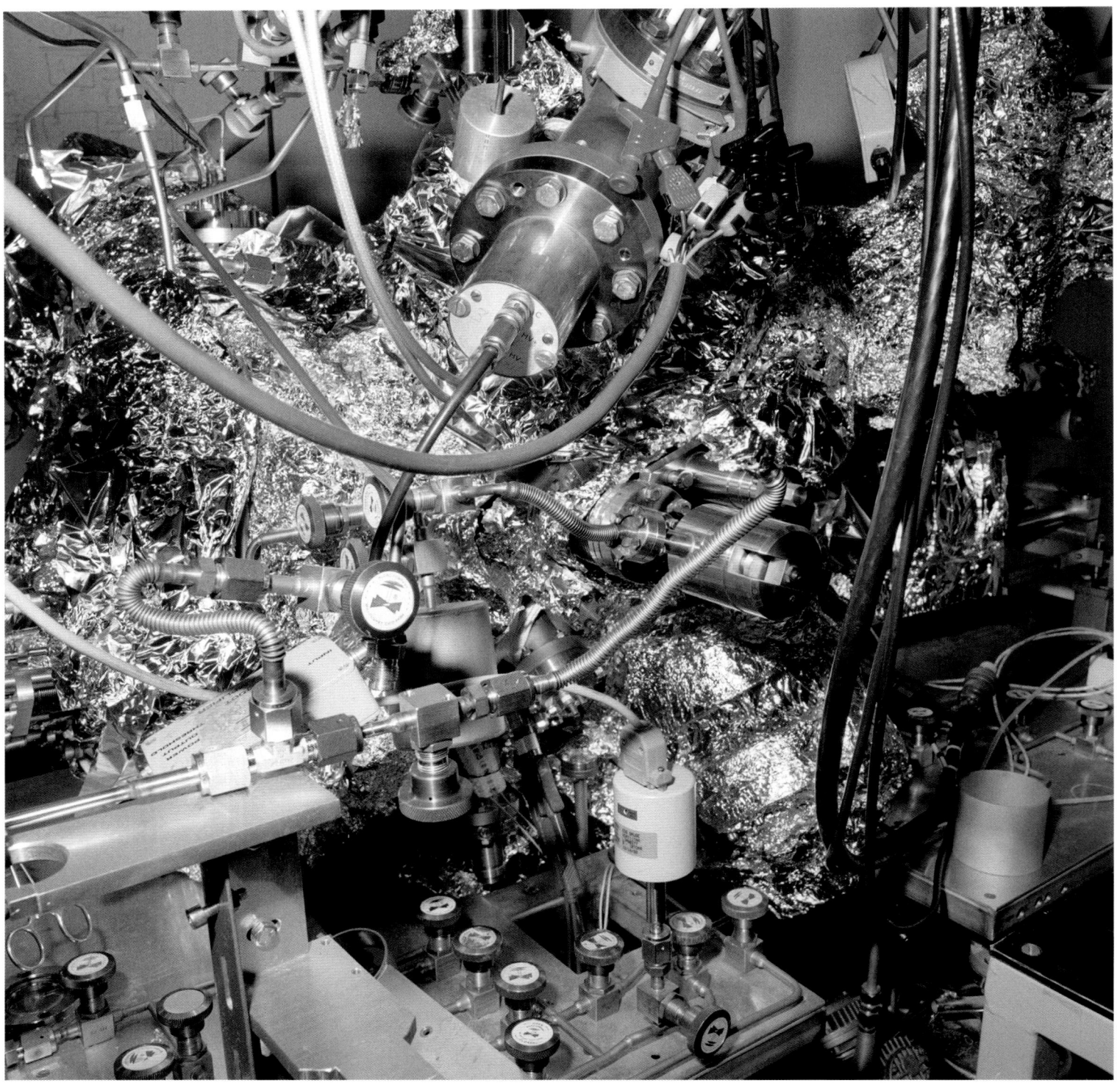

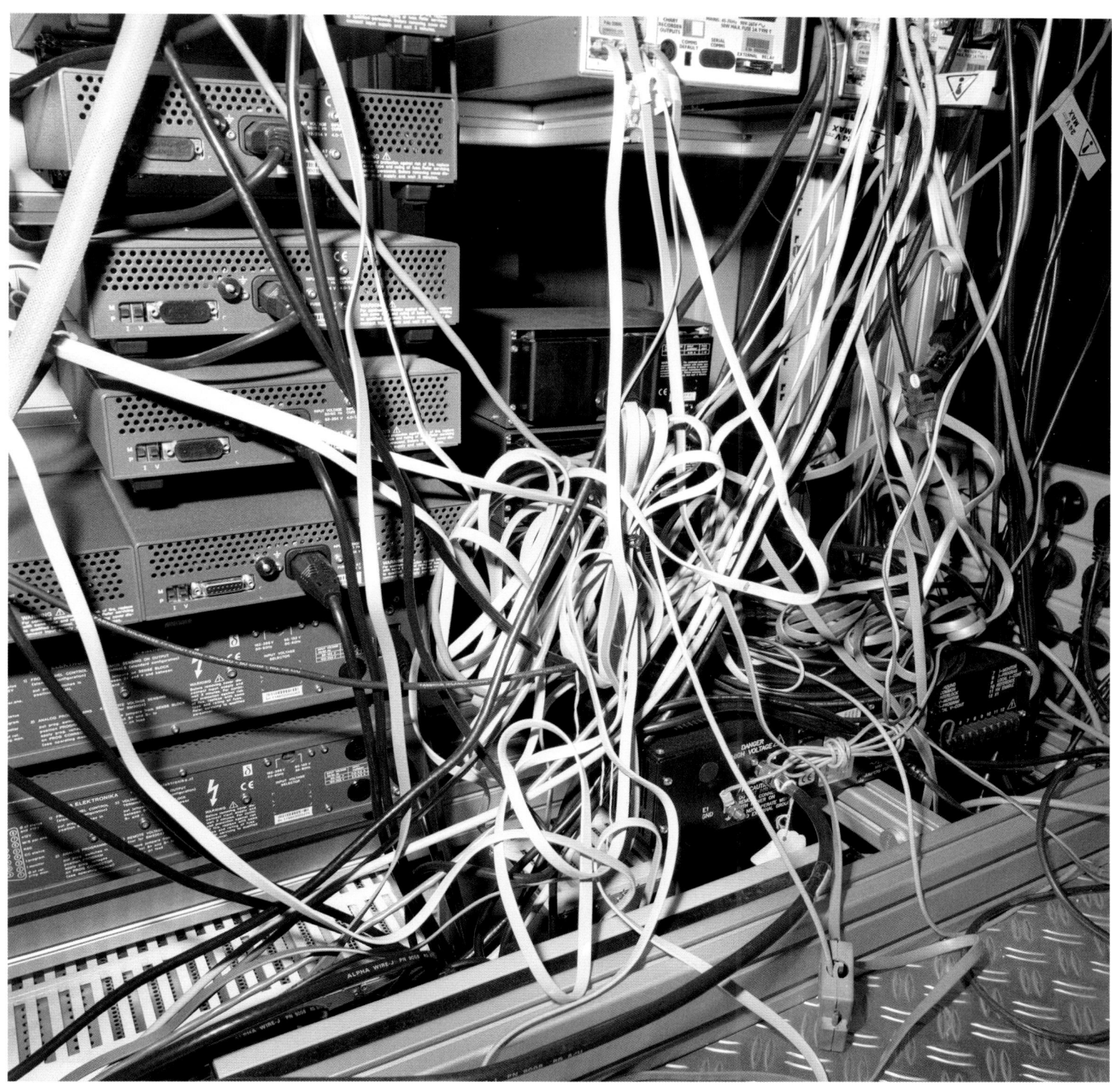

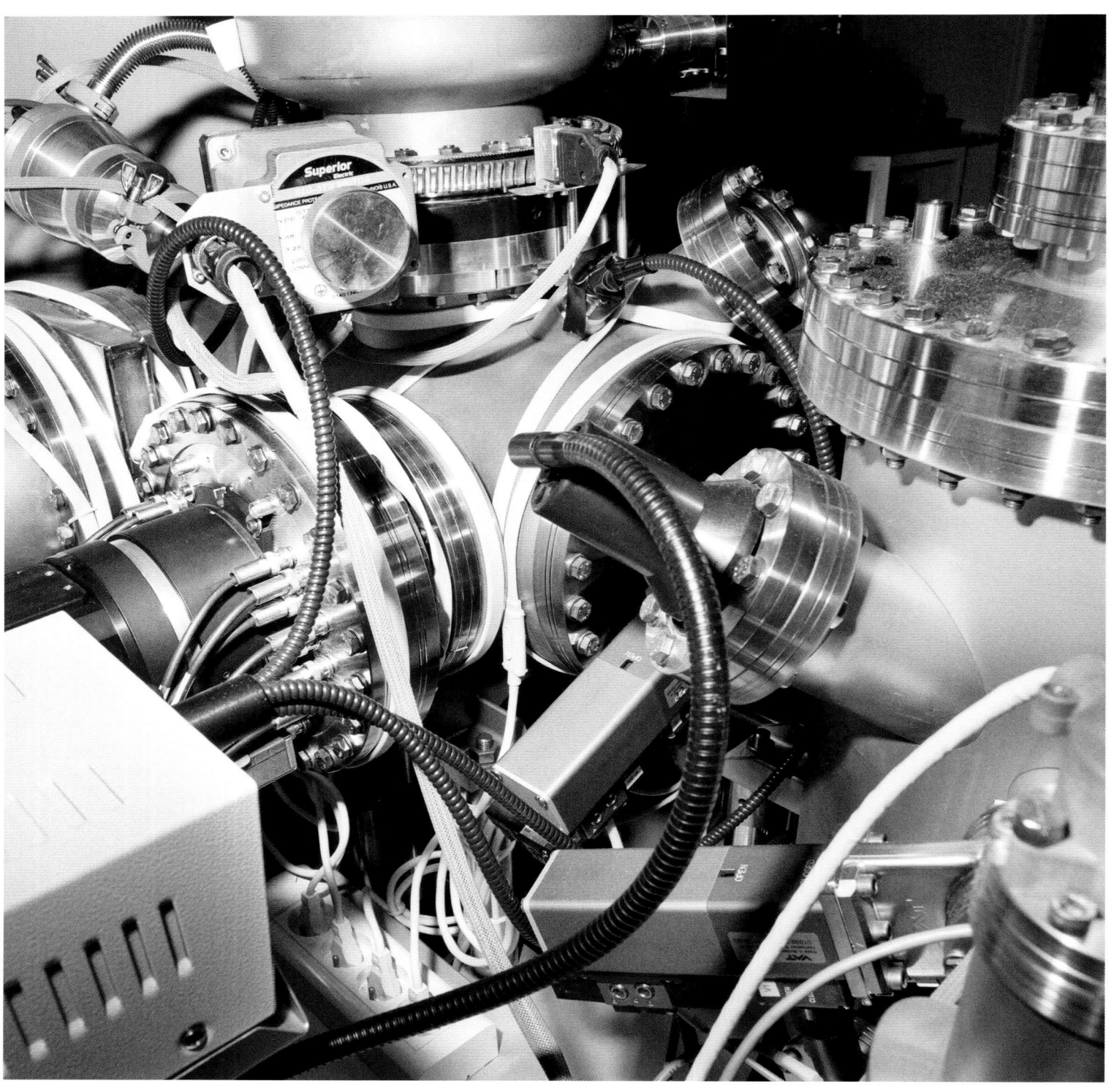

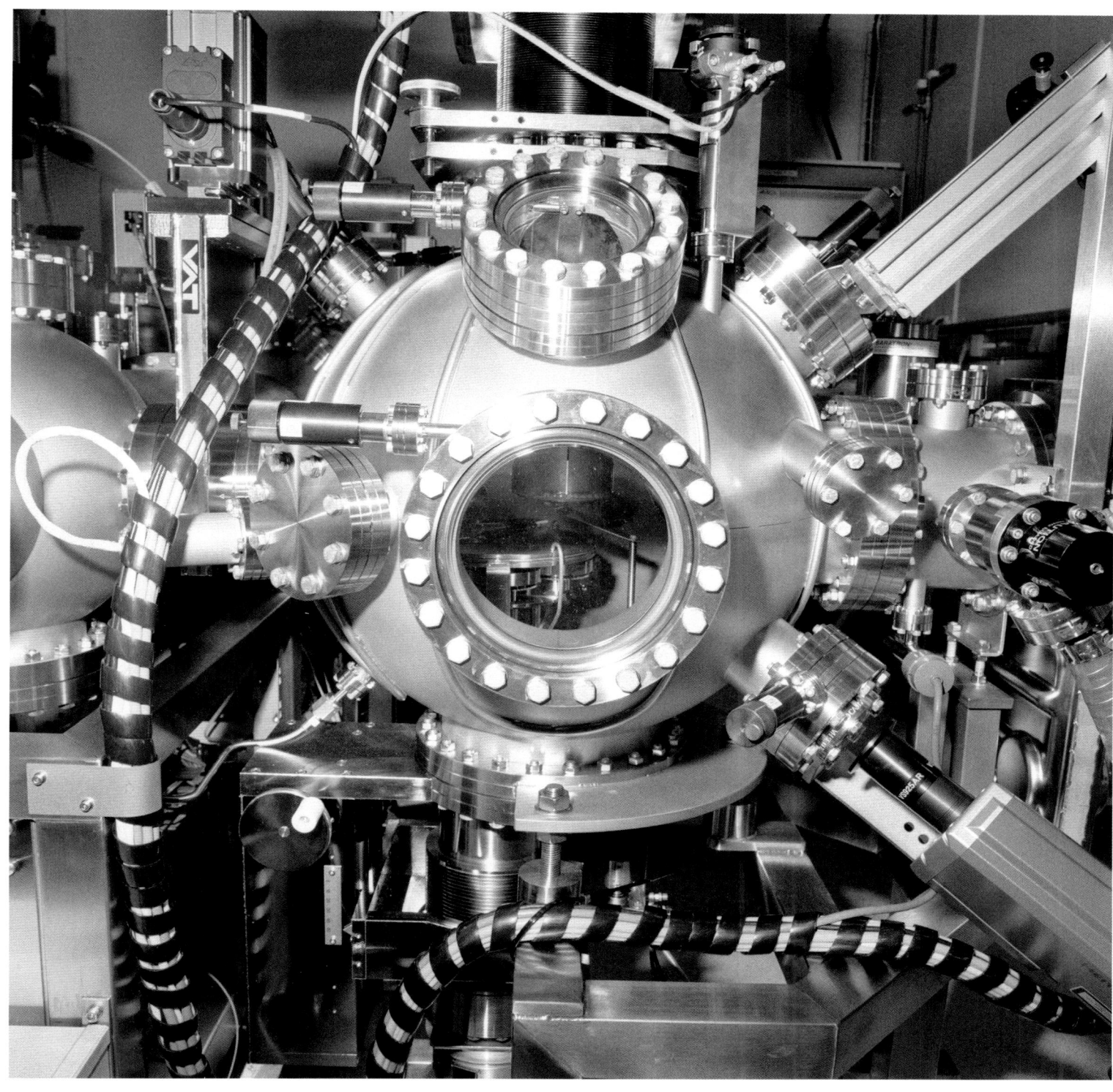

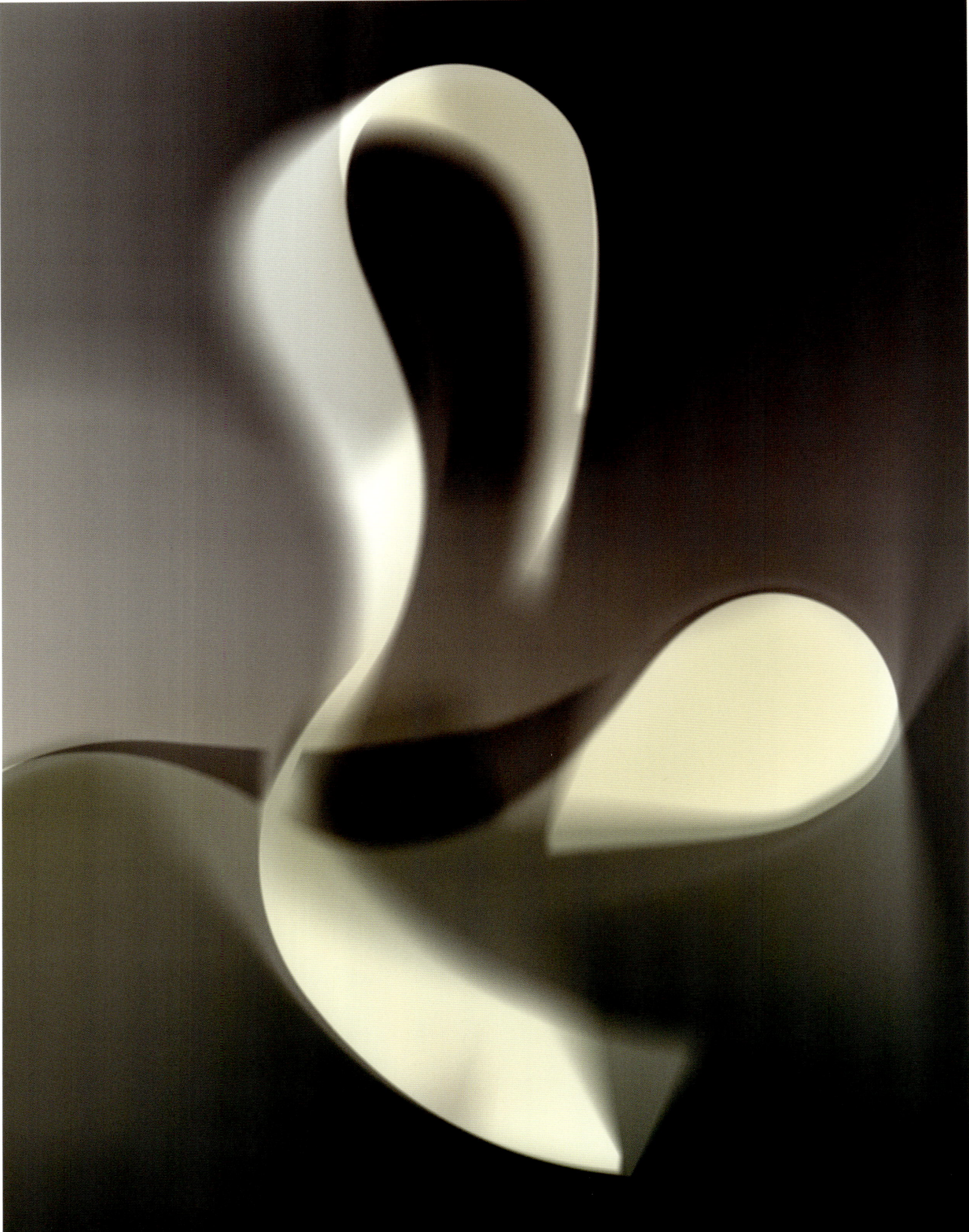

Thomas Ruff

Photograms for the New Age

Conversation with
Michael Famighetti

Michael Famighetti
is Editor of *Aperture*
Magazine.

For more than thirty years, German photographer Thomas Ruff has investigated the grammar and structures of photography, through his many celebrated series, *Sterne/Stars* (1989), *maschinen/machines* (2003), and *cassini* (2008)—to name just a few. After turning away from straight photography in the mid-1990s, Ruff has worked mainly with found imagery culled from a variety of sources—from print catalogs and scientific negatives to the Internet, from which he purloined pornographic images for his *nudes* series, which he began in the 1990s. More recently, he has turned his attention to 3-D imaging software to continue his investigations of the medium. For his newest project, Ruff has taken up a study of the photogram, updating the form for the digital era by creating his works in a 3-D digital studio environment and outputting the resulting images in the large scale he tends to favor. Michael Famighetti spoke with Ruff, who is based in Düsseldorf, by phone in February as he finished work on this new series in preparation for its debut at New York's David Zwirner Gallery this spring.

Michael Famighetti: **Can you tell us about the process behind this new body of work? What were you after when you decided to produce photograms in a digital studio?**

Thomas Ruff: The decision was quite simple. I have two photograms by Art Siegel in my collection and I passed by them again and again. Two years ago, I had the idea to begin making some of my own photograms. When I started analyzing how these photograms were made, I realized that it would be quite complicated; photograms are limited to the size of the paper and to the limitations of the black-and-white darkroom. You don't have much color—only a brownish or bluish tone. And the other thing was if you put objects on the photographic paper and remove them, and then realize that these objects would have been better shifted to the left or the right, you have to start over again. You need a lot of luck to get a good photogram, so I considered how could I do it in a different way. I had already been working with 3-D software on my series *zycles*, so I thought, maybe this is the right tool to try with the photograms. I developed a virtual setup: the paper on the bottom, and the objects—lenses, chopsticks, spirals, paper strips, all kind of objects—I put on the paper. There is a camera above, recording the paper, and then I set the lights with different colors.

MF: **You have continuously investigated a range of mostly representational photographic types: the jpeg, the nude, the scientific image. What attracted you to the photogram as a form?**

TR: The photogram is a kind of "pencil of nature." It's cameraless photography —you don't see the objects but only shadows, which reminds me of Plato's cave. It's a very vague photography; you can't recognize things very clearly but you recognize *something*. Soon I realized that if I use too much color, it doesn't look like a photogram, it just looks strange and abstract.

MF: **The images here are reminiscent of László Moholy-Nagy's experiments with color photograms from the 1930s. How active did you want such historical references to be?**

TR: The goal was really to make a kind of "new generation" of the photogram. So it still should look like a photogram, but not old-fashioned. I tried different types of photograms: some with lenses, some with spirals. I want to experiment more with the possibilities of this kind of software

to create different kinds of images. I can imagine that Moholy-Nagy would have been absolutely glad if he could have used my technology! You can do so much more than with the limitations of the analog darkroom. I am sure he would have loved the software.

MF: **The "types" of photograms here are entirely determined by the objects?**

TR: Yes, mainly by the objects. If you look at Moholy-Nagy's photograms they show different typologies within the photograms. I wanted to make variations of these different types.

MF: **Photograms are usually quite small— they are limited to the size of the paper available, as you mentioned. Will these images be on par with the usual large scale of your work?**

TR: Yes, they will be really big.

MF: **Why is large scale important?**

TR: First of all, I wanted to break the world record of the size for the photogram! *[laughs]* The early photograms, from the 1920s and '30s, are quite small, more post-card size. Photograms from the New Bauhaus school—by Art Siegel and his colleagues, for example—are approximately fifty by sixty centimeters. I work with the large format; I like the physical presence of the big size.

MF: **You mentioned the connection between this new body of work and your *zycles* series, computer-generated abstract line drawings based on algorithms. Throughout your career you have worked in strictly delineated series. Is it common for one series to bleed into the next?**

TR: Yes and no. I am using the same software, the same techniques—but one series doesn't emerge from the other. It's more like you have a Leica, and then you have a Linhof: a 4-by-5 camera, and then an 8-by-10 camera. They are just different tools, or cameras, or techniques. The output looks completely different.

MF: **Much of your work investigates "systems" and the role of genre in photography. You've worked with many forms of found photography, from catalog to online imagery. Considering how much photography has transitioned in recent years—this explosion of imaging —do you see new systems and genres emerging?**

TR: I see photography as a very classical medium, with of course all kind of genres— portrait, abstract, science photography, and so on. What I am also interested in right now is the negative, since it seems that it is going to disappear soon. When I ask my nine-year-old daughter: "What's a negative?" she can't say, as she knows only digital photography. "Polaroid? What's that?" she asked me some time ago. What interests me is the outcome of all these different kinds of photography and how they change our lives and our perception of the world. I just turned some photographs that I own into negatives, and they look strange. My interest in this process comes from working on the photograms— I make reverse photograms. And you still have these strange, old-fashioned darkroom techniques, like solarization, which I now also practice in the photograms series.

MF: **How do you see photograms, or abstract images, shaping our perception of the world?**

TR: The photograms are not so much about the perception and influence of photography in our daily lives. Maybe I just want to recall that artists used techniques in photography that enabled them to make completely artificial and abstract photographs and that these techniques are, unfortunately, nearly forgotten.

MF: **You've taught at the Kunstakademie Düsseldorf, where you also studied. How does your interest in the history and evolution of photographic technologies come into play in the classroom?**

TR: I've used a lot of different photographic techniques in the past thirty years. I realize there isn't just one way to take a photograph, there are a thousand different ways—and that's what I've taught the students. They should not insist on their beautiful Leica, or their Hasselblad, or whatever they use. The technique must result from the *idea* that you have—and you may have to develop your own technology to bring out the images. I'm not much interested in "straight" photography anymore. It has been practiced for more than 150 years, and most of it is too conventional. I've always wanted to go beyond the limits.

MF: **But you are interested in photographic conventions. Why?**

TR: I think photography is still the most influential medium in the world, and I have to deconstruct these conventions.

MF: **Do you ever take pictures, in the traditional sense?**

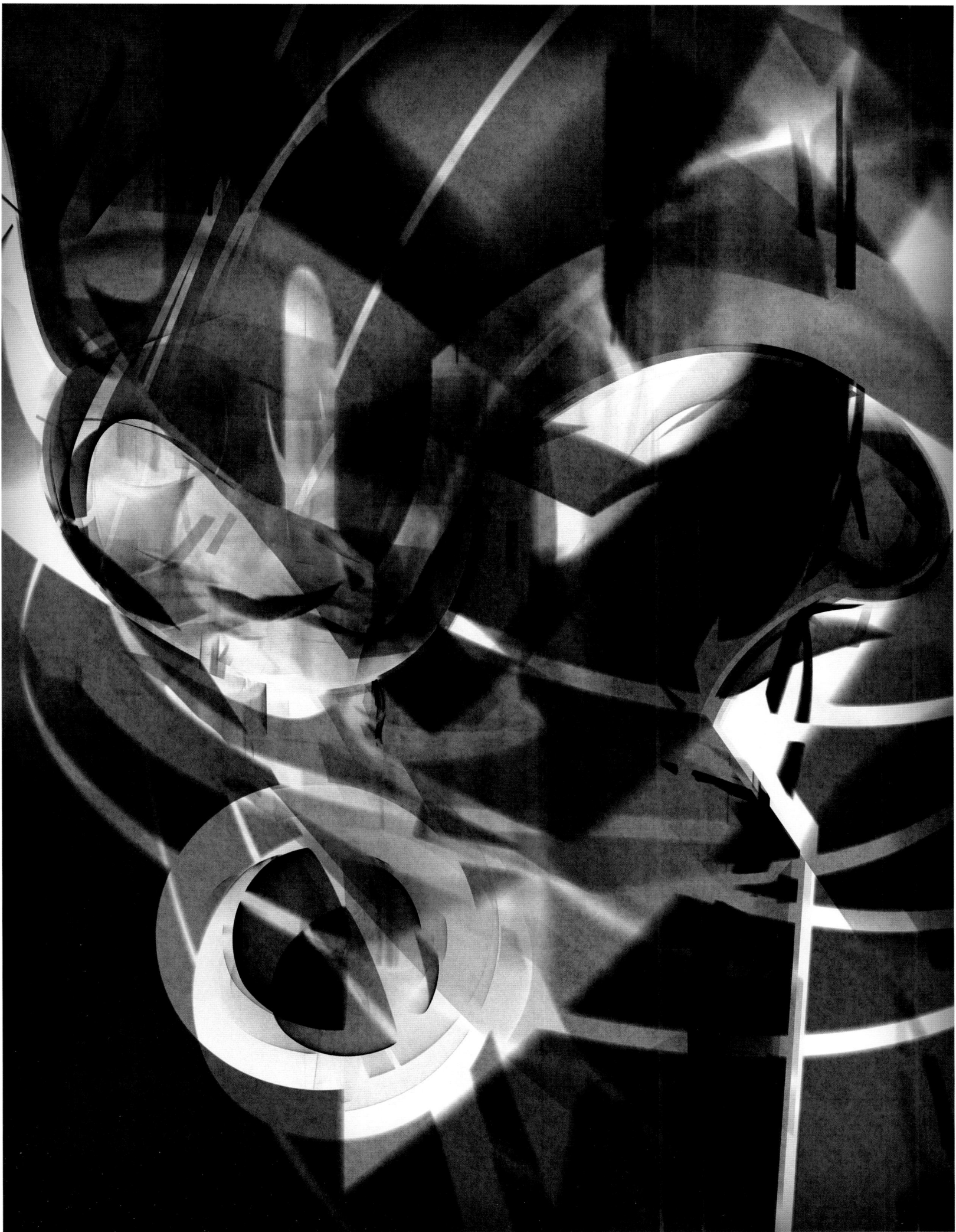

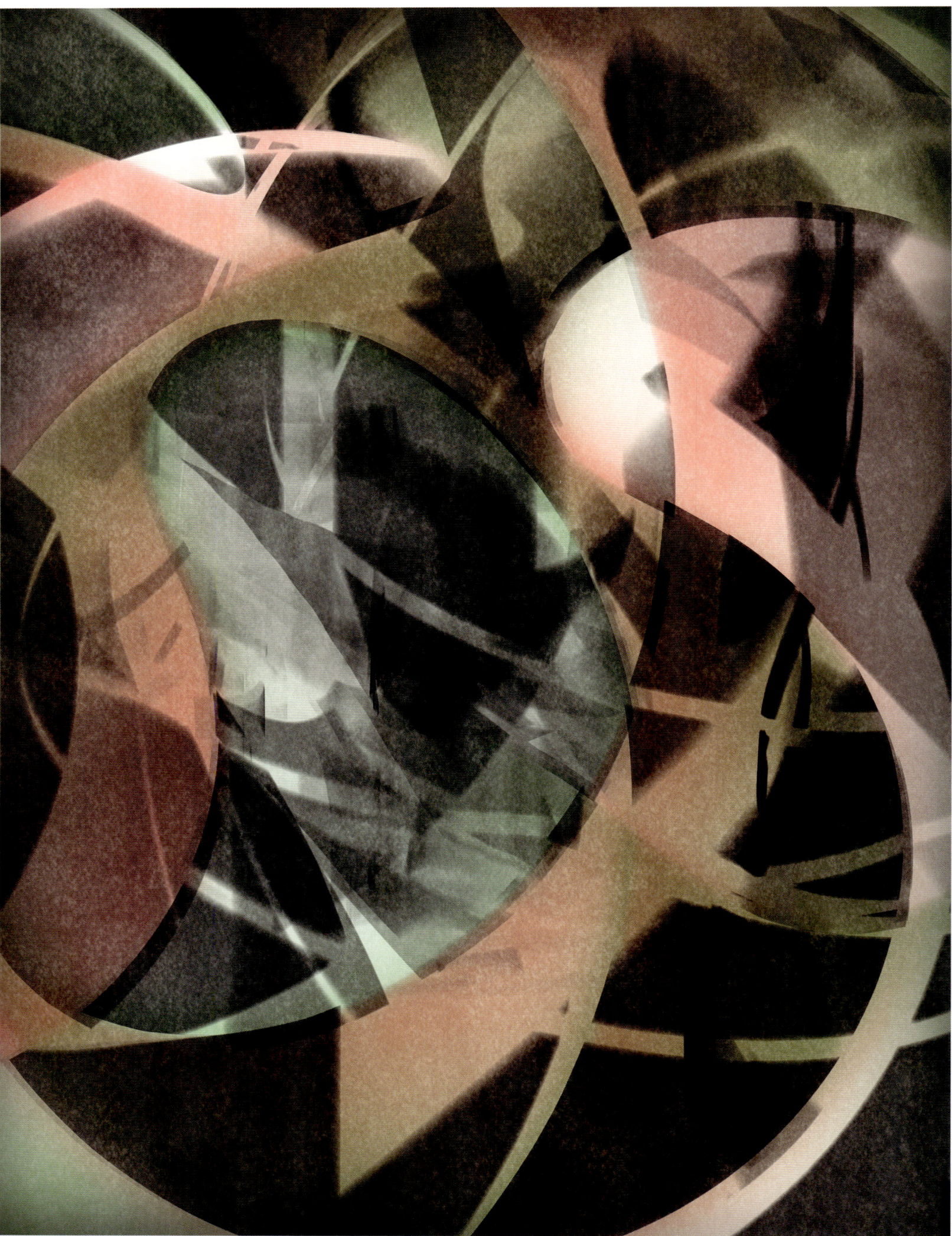

TR: The last photographs that I took in the traditional way, with an 8-by-10 camera and negative film, were architectural photographs of my studio some months ago. And, of course, if an idea for a new series requires a traditional analog photograph, I will use the camera again.

MF: **Could you talk about the role of research in your work? Where does a project begin?**

TR: If I see an image that attracts, upsets, or astonishes me—one that stays in my mind for a long time—I begin working. This is the starting point of the research: I try to find out how the image was created and in what context—historical, political, or social—the image belongs. After clarifying these questions I begin to create "my own" image, the image I have in my mind, the image that was triggered by the image I saw. Sometimes it can be done in a straightforward way, with a camera, but sometimes you need to reflect on how you can manage to make this technically. For example, when I had the idea of photographing the night sky, I realized that with my small telescope, I had no chance of getting high-quality images of stars, so I looked for an observatory with a big telescope where I could take the photographs myself. But they wouldn't let me in. So I had to give up the idea of being the author of the photograph, and worked with large-format negatives from the observatory's archive.

MF: **It's been written that when you were in high school you wanted to be either an astronomer or a photographer. Your *cassini* series connects the two occupations.**

TR: I have an affinity for astronomy, so from time to time astronomical issues show up in my work. The *cassini* series consists of images of Saturn, its moons and rings, taken by a machine camera within the *Cassini* spacecraft. They are black-and-white photographs with an abstract quality that I really like. To highlight the abstraction, I colored these photographs so that they resemble a kind of "post-Suprematist" image.

MF: **You've spoken of your interest in the writings of Vilém Flusser, whose ideas about imaging, written in the 1970s and '80s, feel prescient today.**

TR: [Flusser's 1983 *Towards a Philosophy of Photography*] is a book I read twenty years ago. He was writing about the shifting of photography. There are a lot of different photographs, and different photographs have different intentions. Fine art, medical, propaganda, and of course the most influential image-production machine is advertisement. This transformation, let's say, of the scientific photography into the art world, or advertising photography into politics (as seen in the last U.S. election)—this modification of images from one intention to another brings about interferences. The image, and the *meaning* of the image, changes.

MF: **This notion of shifting contexts—and thereby shifting meanings—is central to your work. This is true with your *nudes* series, your first using Internet imagery. How does your image-collecting process work?**

TR: I have a particular curiosity; I see things, I collect them, with no intention or without knowing what to do with them. I just keep them, because they trigger something within myself. A couple of years later, maybe even ten years later, these things appear in my mind again and lead to a new body of work. There's no straight line or conscious scheme of collecting. It could be any kind of image—it's just that I'm attracted to it.

MF: **Does the medium continue to surprise you?**

TR: No, not really. But of course I'm always happy when I see a new, never-before-seen example of a photograph. An image is just an image—it all depends on what you do with it.

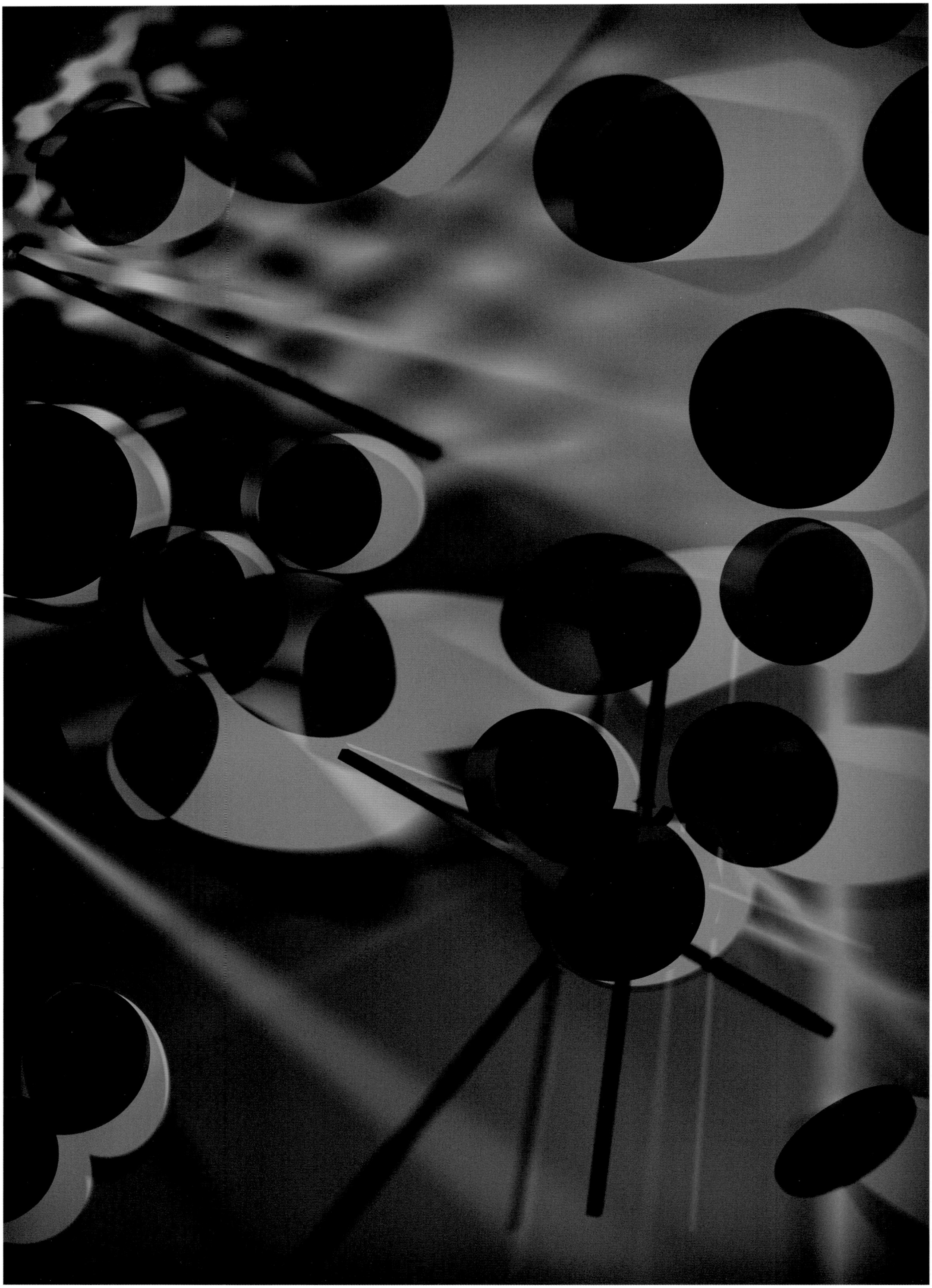

This page: *phg.s.03*, 2012; opposite: *phg.s.01*, 2012

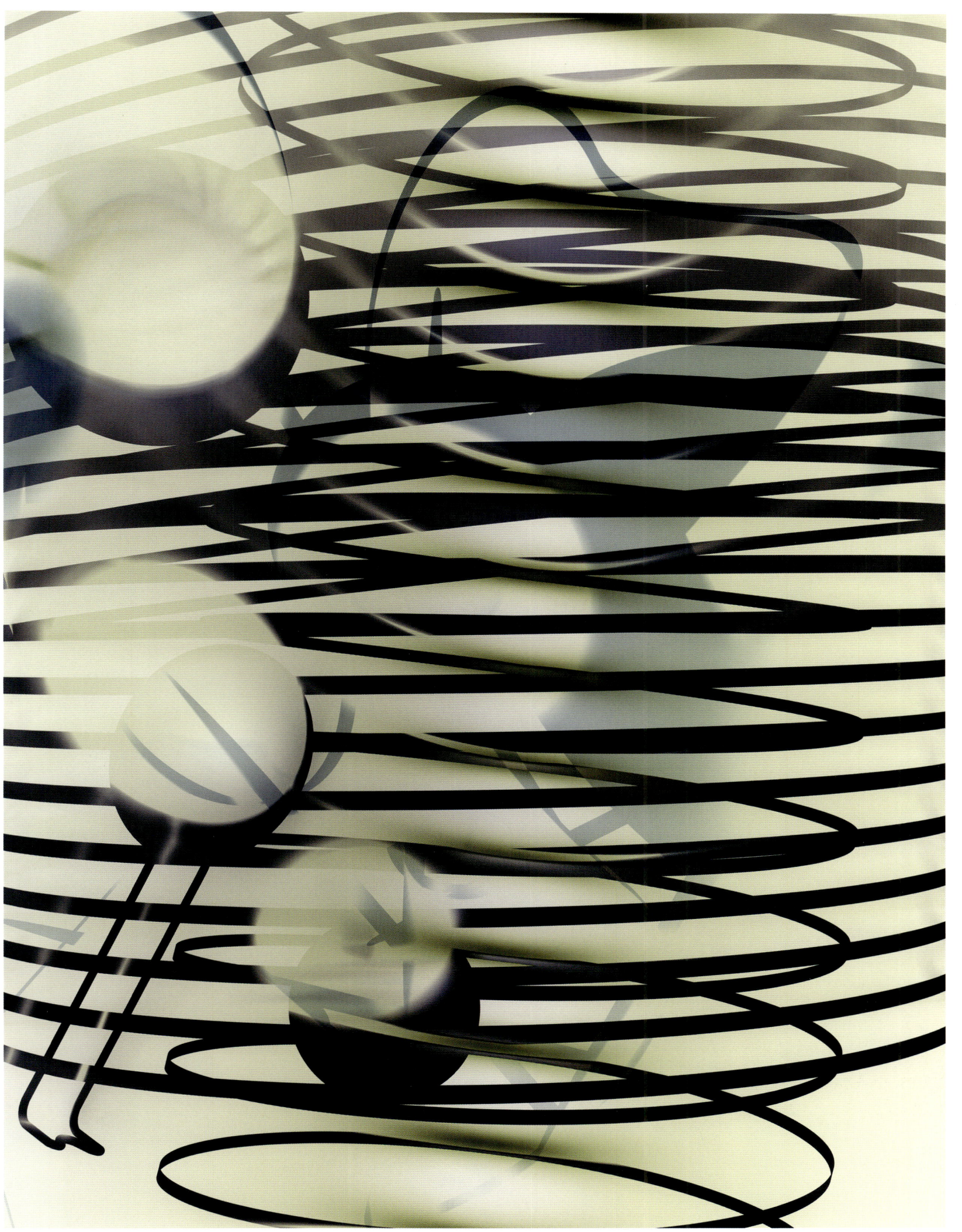

Photographs of Nothing

Joel Smith

In the 1890s, with the rise of Kodak products and the standardization of halftone reproduction in print, photographs became the wallpaper of daily life. Anyone and everyone, now, could create pictures full of detail, and the reading public's mental picture of current events was, increasingly, a camera-derived image. By 1900 art photography, by an epicurean law of contraries, began to distance itself from the banal factuality of the mass medium. Pictorialism, in its embrace of murky Whistlerian shimmer as both style and message, inaugurated the modern-era tradition of the counterphotograph.

Since then, through a series of willfully perverse gestures, artists have tested the aesthetic and epistemological boundaries of the photograph by making it do that which common sense says it cannot: doubt as well as certify, negate as well as indicate, embody absence as well as substance. The plates that follow trace this discontinuous history in five chapters. Herewith, five guidelines for making photographs of nothing.

Joel Smith is the Richard L. Menschel Curator of Photography at the Morgan Library & Museum in New York. His publications include *Edward Steichen: The Early Years* (Princeton University Press, 1999); *Saul Steinberg: Illuminations* (Yale University Press, 2006); and *The Life and Death of Buildings: On Photography and Time* (Yale University Press, 2011).

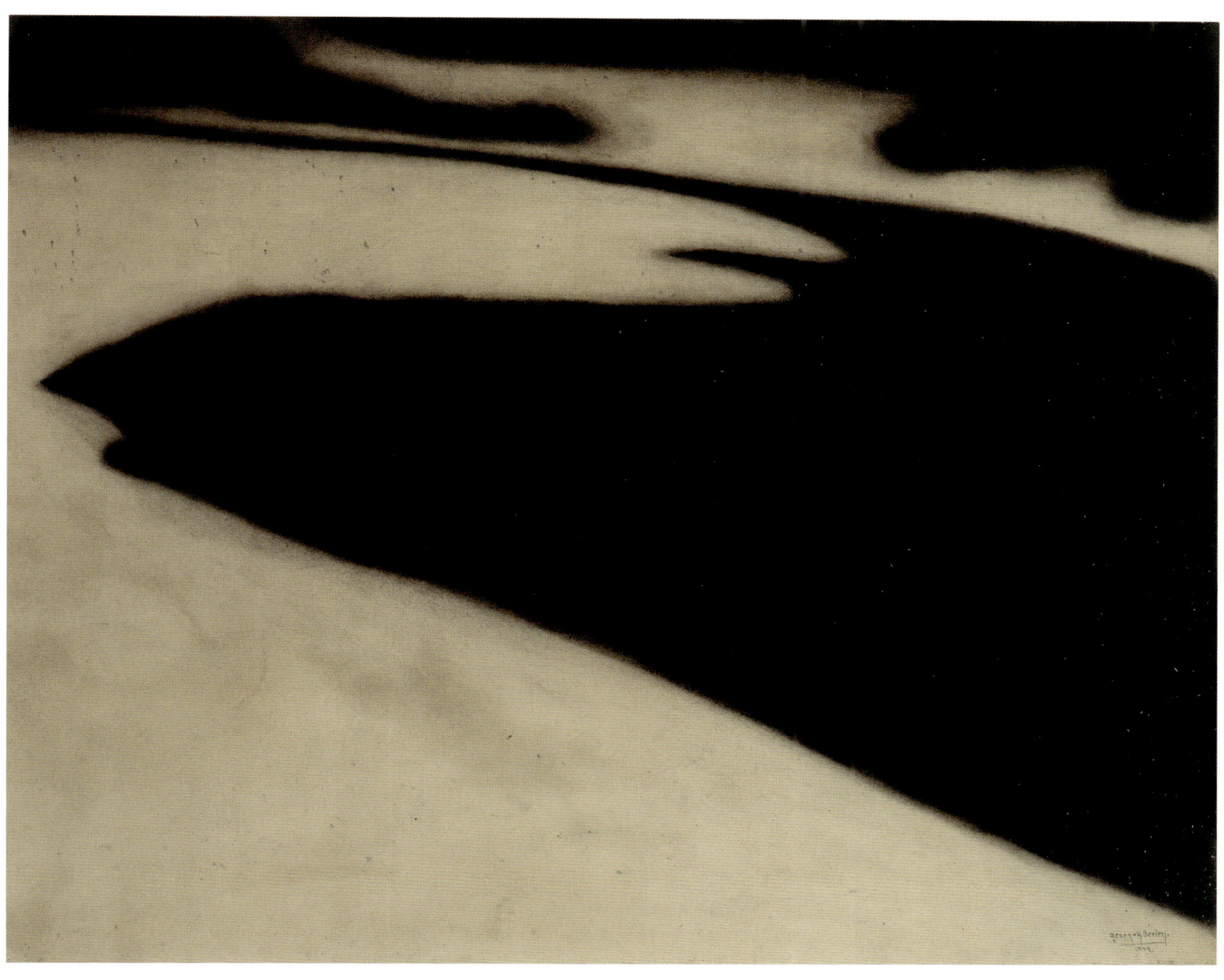

1.

Take a conventional camera exposure
and, with Japanese woodblock prints and
Stéphane Mallarmé's "nuance, only nuance"
as your aesthetic models, progressively
empty the plate of tangible detail. Risk
working the image until it loses its basis
in lens-borne projection and becomes
a design, a scrim, a sketch.

George Seeley,
***Winter Landscape,* 1909**
© Metropolitan Museum of
Art/Art Resource, New York

2.
Invent an aesthetic mode that is identifiably photographic, yet non-representational, abstract. Create a photograph that is not a photograph *of* by strategically outwitting (or, as a snapshooter, fortuitously failing) the medium. Lose track of the horizon. Exclude the subject (or the camera, or the negative, and so on). Assign light a performative instead of an interpretive function. Leave us guessing.

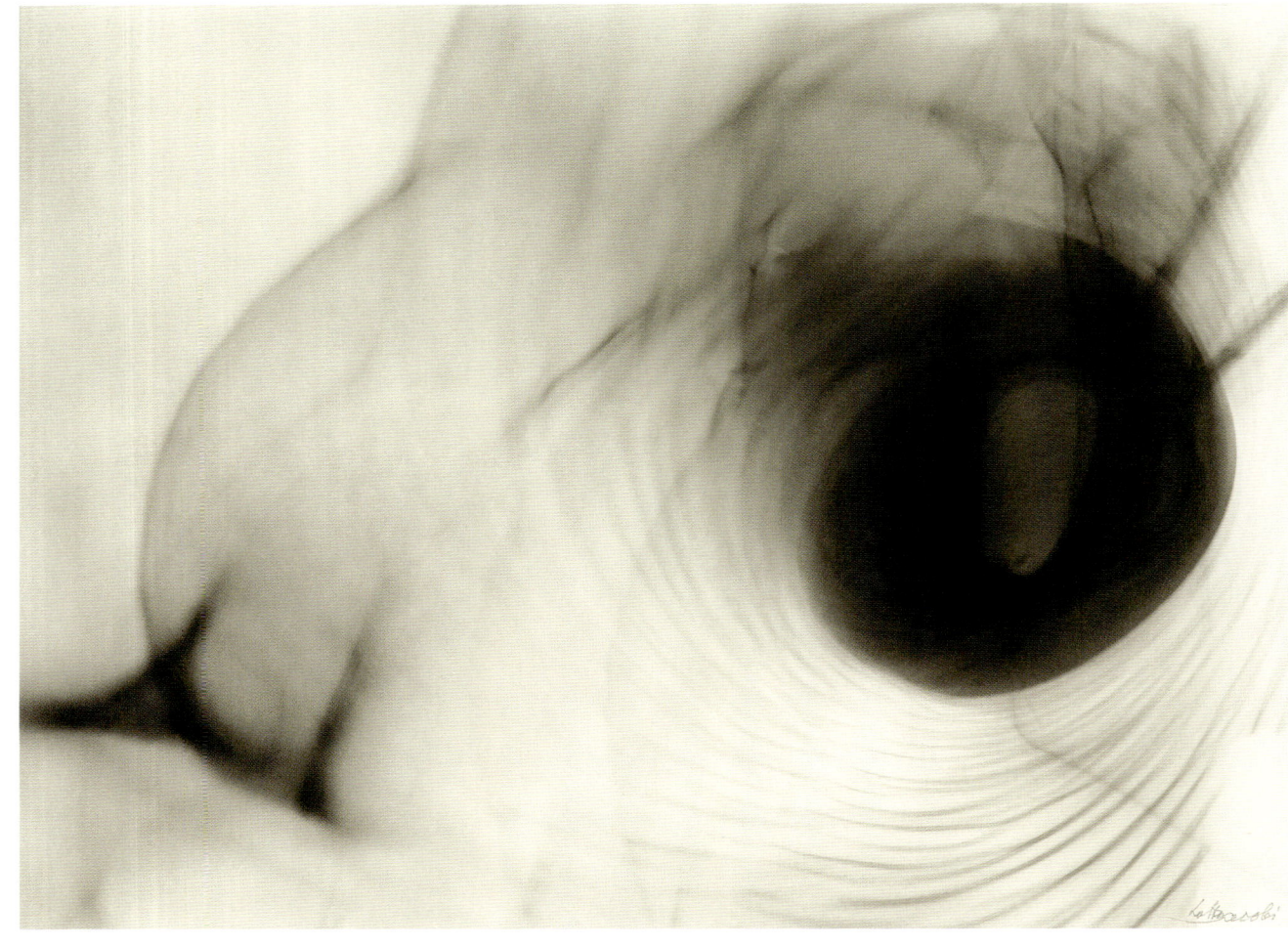

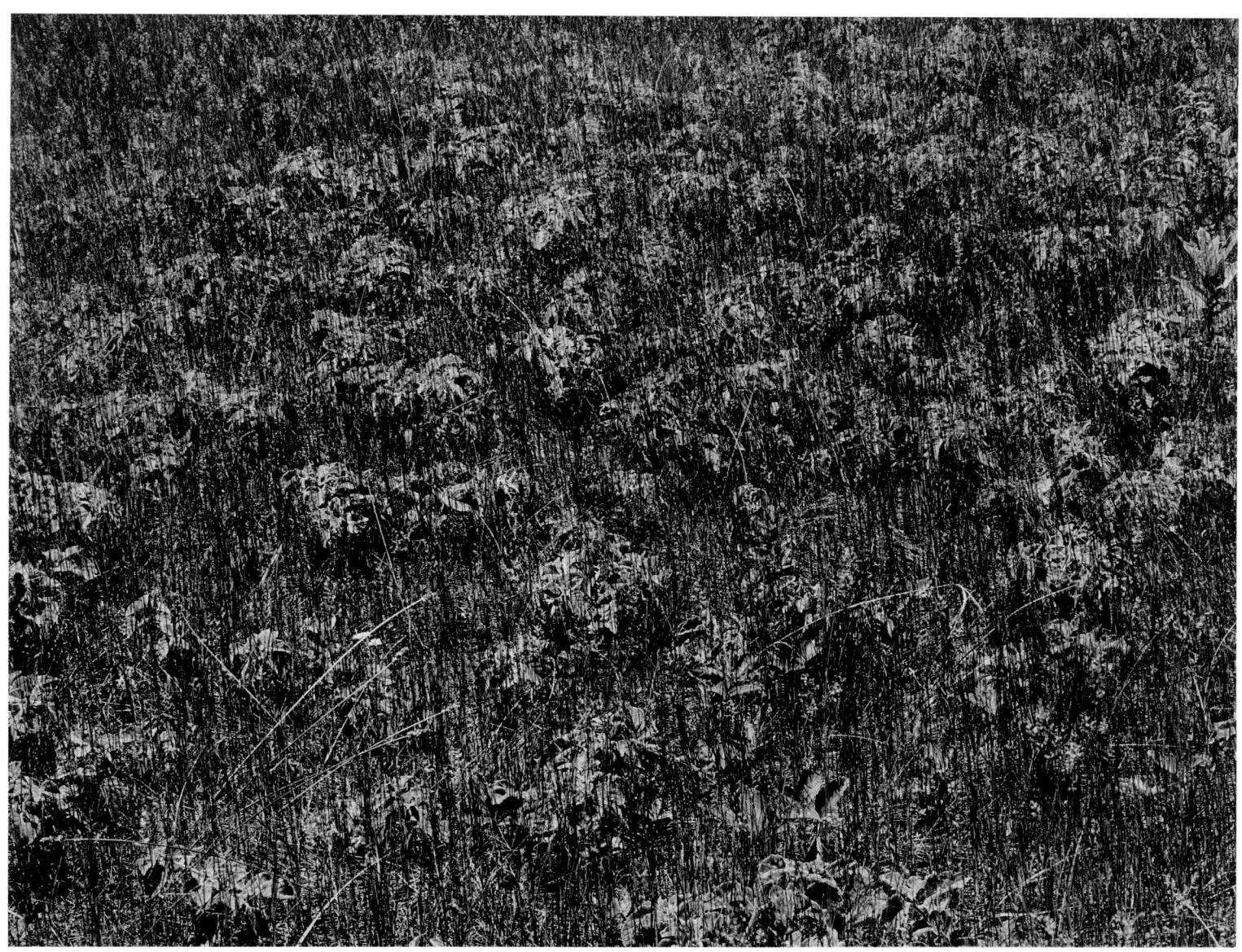

3.
Engage viewers in a Zen-like exercise,
marrying rigorous craft to perceptual
paradox. Meet the highest standards
of camera technique, but end up by
manifesting topics on a nonmaterial,
subjective level, such as vertigo or visual
error. A tip: volume, void, and plane provide
the coordinates by which a photograph
says "You are here," so invite cognitive
confusion among them. For example,
what looks like a deep vacant middle-ground
in Gohlke's highway view (seen on following
page) is the face of a frontage wall.

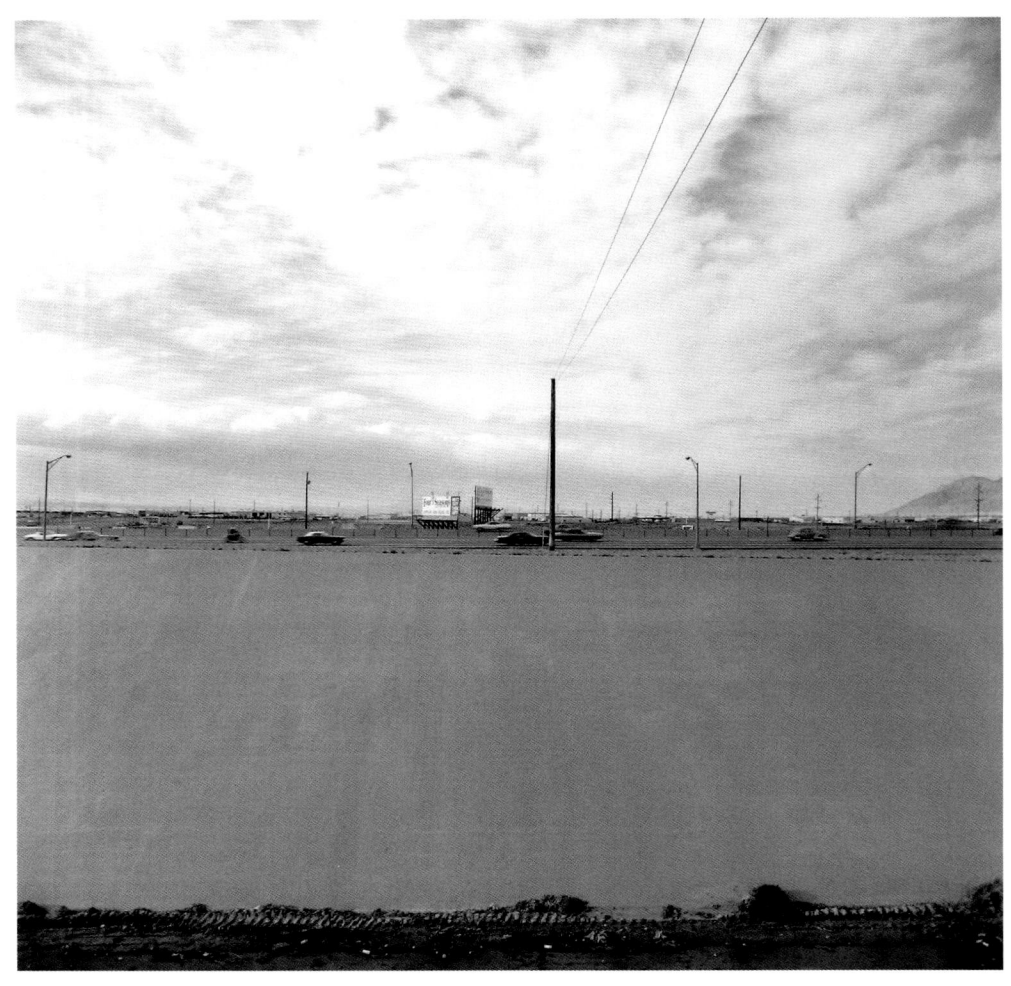

Frank Gohlke,
Landscape, Albuquerque,
New Mexico, **1974**
Courtesy Howard Greenberg
Gallery, New York

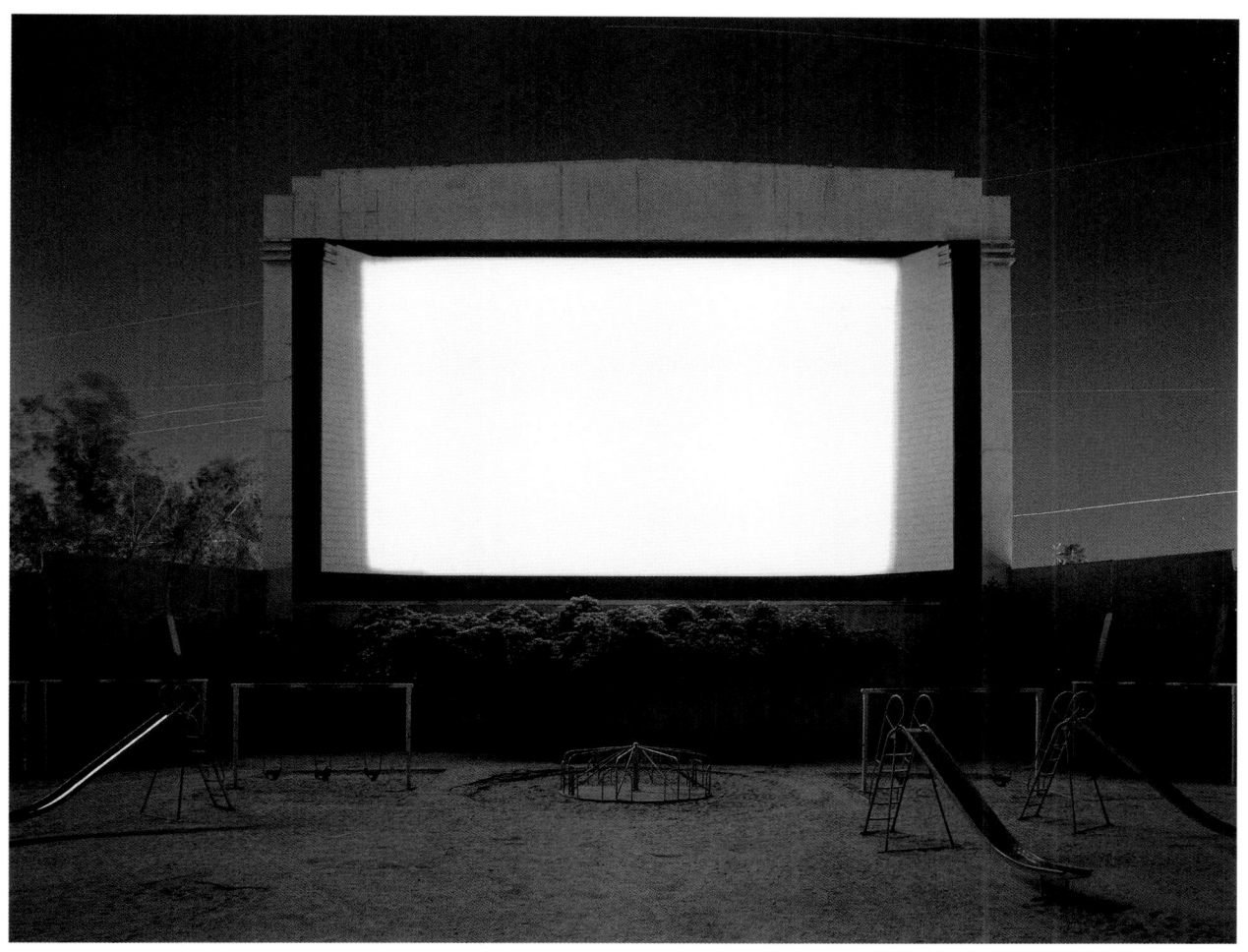

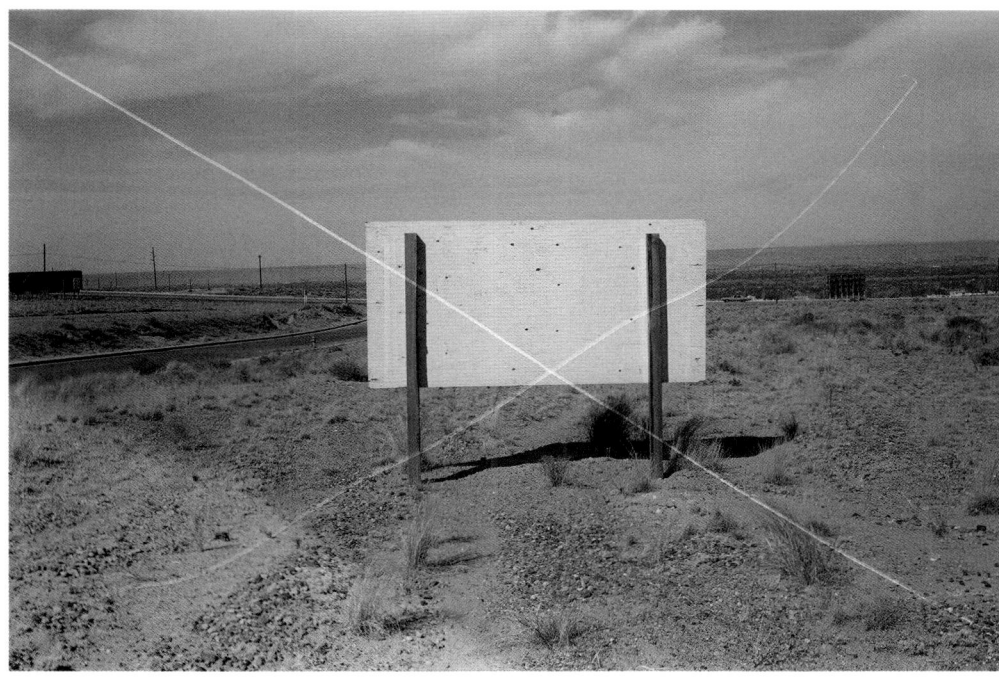

4.

For images that spur skepticism about
the crude materialism of photographic
testimony, blatantly violate camera etiquette.
Prolong an exposure until, like Sugimoto,
you make a subject of the blindness
generated by attention. Cross out a negative
as if it were an expired item on a "to do"
list. Instead of an image that says, "This!"
make an image that says: "Not! This!"

Top: **Hiroshi Sugimoto,**
Tri-City Drive-In,
San Bernardino, 1993
© Hiroshi Sugimoto, courtesy
Pace Gallery, New York

Bottom: **Thomas Barrow,**
***Sun Sign,* 1974, from**
the series *Cancellations*
© Thomas Barrow, courtesy
Joseph Bellows Gallery,
La Jolla, California

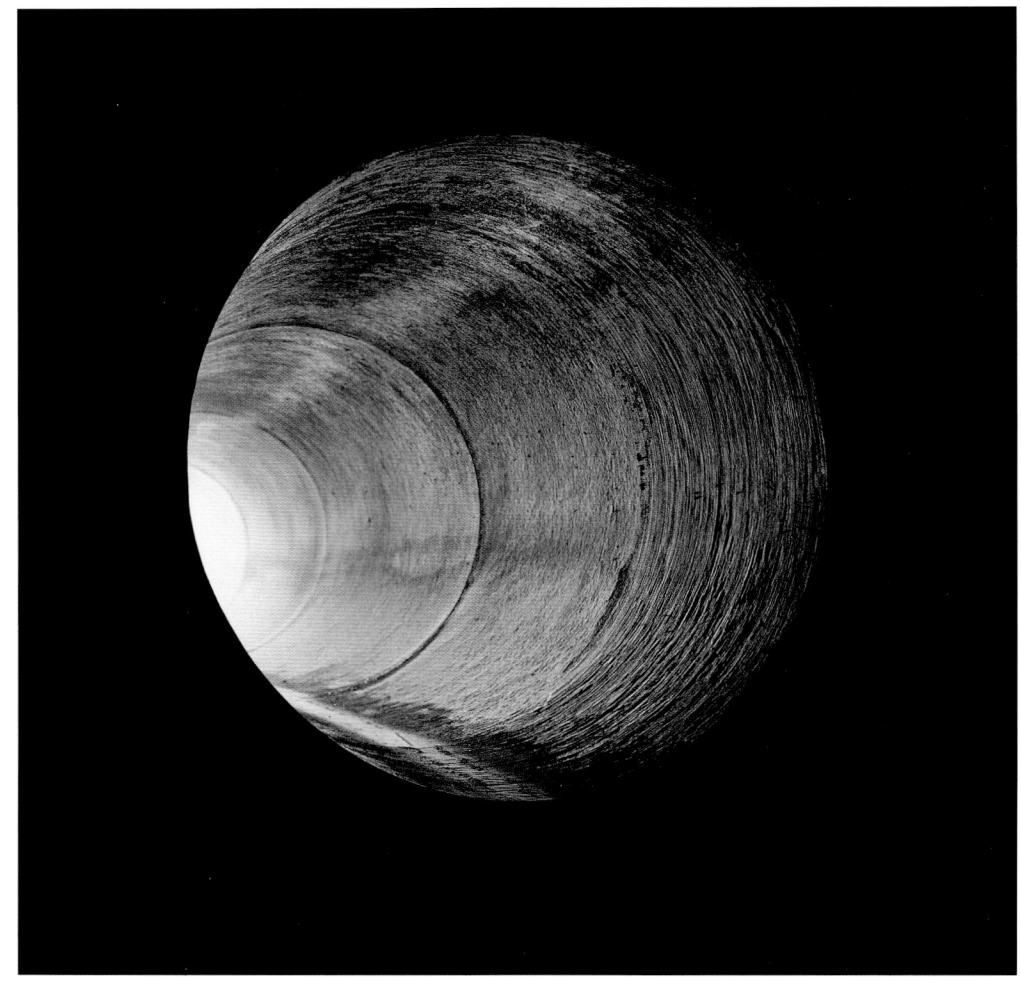

Naoya Hatakeyama,
Underground/River
(Tunnel Series) #6109, 1999
© Naoya Hatakeyama,
courtesy Taka Ishii Gallery,
Tokyo

5.

Turn photography inside-out, creatively
misusing its technical vocabulary to symbolic
effect. Within an otherwise straightforward
picture, promote a marginal, extreme feature
of photo-aesthetics (too much or too little
light) to a central role. Hatakeyama's flash
unit, glimpsed through a subterranean
culvert, becomes the moon's unromantic
antipode. Grannan portrays Washington
State's ill ex-governor, a proponent of legal
assisted suicide. Standing in full sunlight, yet
rendered as a black silhouette, he casts the
eloquent shadow of death in the midst of life.

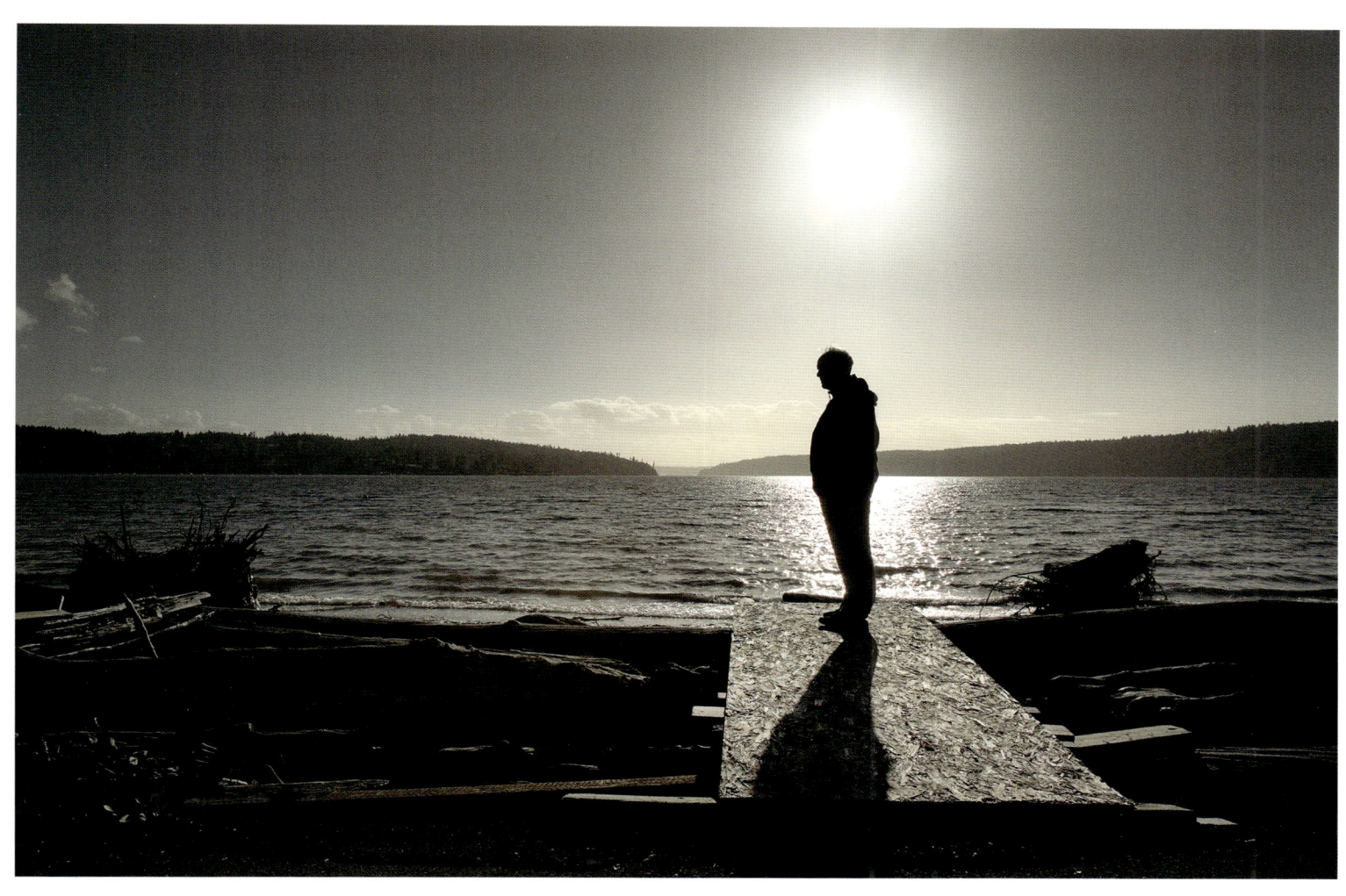

Katy Grannan,
Booth Gardner, ca. 2005
© Katy Grannan,
courtesy Fraenkel Gallery,
San Francisco, and Salon 94,
New York

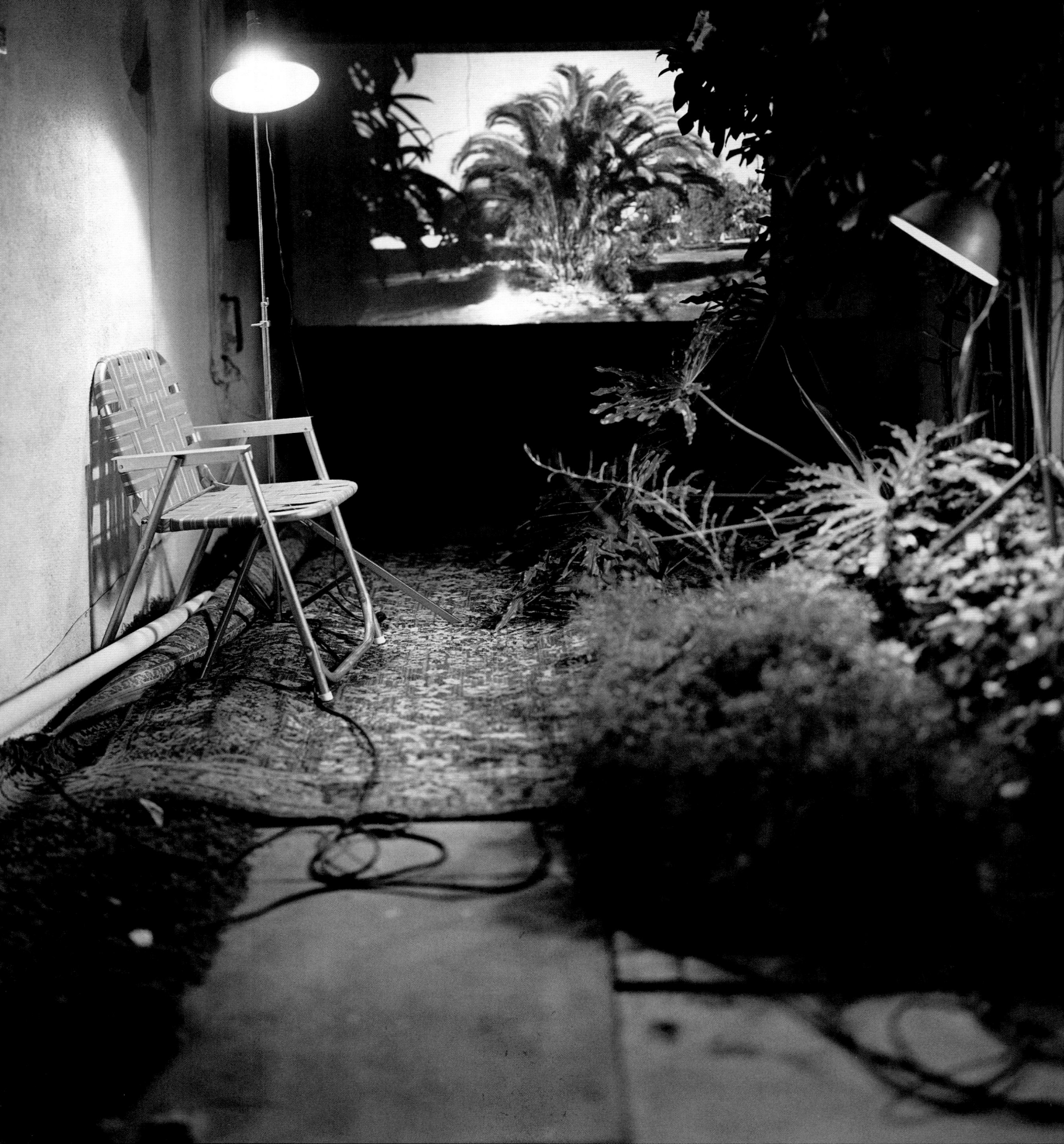

In the early 1970s Robert Cumming spent a lot of time in movie memorabilia shops in Hollywood. These shops—filled with flotsam and jetsam from the classic era of Hollywood cinema—were a curious brand of cultural repository for the young artist from Massachusetts, schooled in the Midwest. Cumming honed in on studio photographs, 8-by-10 black-and-white contact prints commissioned in the name of maintaining continuity between scenes, or for testing particular hairstyles or wallpaper samples. The slightly battered stills—bent, inked with notes, and often hole-punched—were nonetheless beautifully photographed, and they had infinitely more detail than the movie-goer ever saw onscreen, as images traveled by at twenty-four frames per second.

Cumming was discovering the curious language of film illusion. A small set light tucked into a corner of an otherwise domestically tepid living room; dolly tracks installed on a wooden platform leading up to a bucolic indoor "marsh" of ferns, grasses, and pine trees surrounding a canoe; a crewmember caught adjusting a fake pine bough on a tripod at the edge of the frame (his ghostlike arm blurred from the long exposure). Cumming wondered: *Why in the world did they have to construct that entire marsh for that canoe indoors? That's some pretty intense work when they could have just gone outside….* The photographs were certainly strange enough to pay attention to, and soon he was buying stacks of them for twenty-five cents apiece. Years later, he would say that it was stills like these that inspired him to dissect the mechanics of photographic perception.

As a painting student in the 1960s, one of Cumming's influences was Robert Rauschenberg, whose paint on canvas with collage, then photo-silk-screens and three-dimensional *Combines*, Cumming took as some of the fuel that drove him to study photography and printmaking. Later, as an MFA student at the University of Illinois, Champaign-Urbana, he took courses with photographer Art Sinsabaugh, known for his work with the massive 12-by-20-inch "banquet" camera.

Soon after receiving his master's degree in 1967, Cumming moved into three dimensions completely, and began by teaching himself a variety of sculptural practices. He made constructions that were functional-*looking*, but were intentionally useless; they often involved piping, threaded aluminum, hooks, hinges, and grommets on cotton duck, burlap, and canvas. (Few survive, but they look terrific in photographs.) He bought an 8-by-10 view camera in 1968—captivated by the precise detail of the large negative (echoes of Sinsabaugh) —and made use of that unwieldy beast to document his three-dimensional work. Soon enough, he was creating those sculptures *for* the camera, rather than to exhibit on their own.

Robert Cumming Invents the Photograph

Sarah Bay Williams

His photographs from the 1970s are a parody of the seamless illusion of film: he leaves subtle "tells" in the frame that reveal his mechanics—intentional mistakes and offscreen tools appear in the image. What unravels lets loose far more absurdity than a set light, paper fern, or plaster rock betrayed in an 8-by-10 studio still. In the diptych *Decorator Test* (1974), a visual cacophony of stripes covers a corner of wallpaper, floorboards, and steps. A swatch of more pattern is clamped to a tripod—Cumming's riff on the professional photographer's test target, used to gauge how accurately a camera depicts reality. Looking closely, however, one sees that this is not reality at all: the "wallpaper" glistens and buckles like plastic-adhesive shelf liner in the upper-left corner; the baseboard is just two flimsy pieces of wood, one wide and one thin, leaning up against the wall. Cumming wanted the viewer to get to know, personally, the process of perception—perhaps to ward off the onset of visual inertia. The pictures unfold slowly over time; the more you look, the more you see.

French philosopher Hubert Damisch mandated in his 1963 essay "Five Notes for a Phenomenology of the Photographic Image" that a true artist should never fall prey to the artificiality of photographic illusion. According to Damisch, photographs were not really "invented" in the early nineteenth century; the camera obscura had existed for centuries, and the lens even longer. It was the desire to *fix* the image that was new—a latent image was revealed, developed, and preserved; it wasn't magic: lenses and cameras complied to a spatial system dependent on distance and curvature of glass. Cumming was highly sensitive to these mechanics—for instance, the ability to transform a three-dimensional object with heft and depth into a flat representation. He celebrated this as a skill to be learned and exploited, rather than subverted as opaque—to simultaneously maintain and destroy illusion and quirks of vision with photography.

Cumming illustrates what one thinks one sees in a glance when an involuntary imagination ruptures reality: a silhouette of a cactus for a rabbit head, for example (as in *Theatre for Two—Easy Analogies*, 1978), or paper towels from a dispenser as pages on the platen of a typewriter (*Institutional Faucet*, 1971).

Cumming's images undermine the idea that a photograph, upon first glance, is as reliable as anything that reaches the unique receptors leading to our sensorium—eyes, nose, ears, mouth, skin, the liminal areas between the world around us and the world of cognition. He explores the moment of seeing, and delivers us wildly imagined permutations of the moment that follows: when perception is either uncontrollably, automatically processed or *mistakenly* processed based on remembered experience. But always with a robust and fathomless imagination.

Sarah Bay Williams is an independent curator, writer, and artist living in Venice, California. She is currently working on a monograph of Robert Cumming's photography.

Opposite: *Watermelon/Bread*, 1970

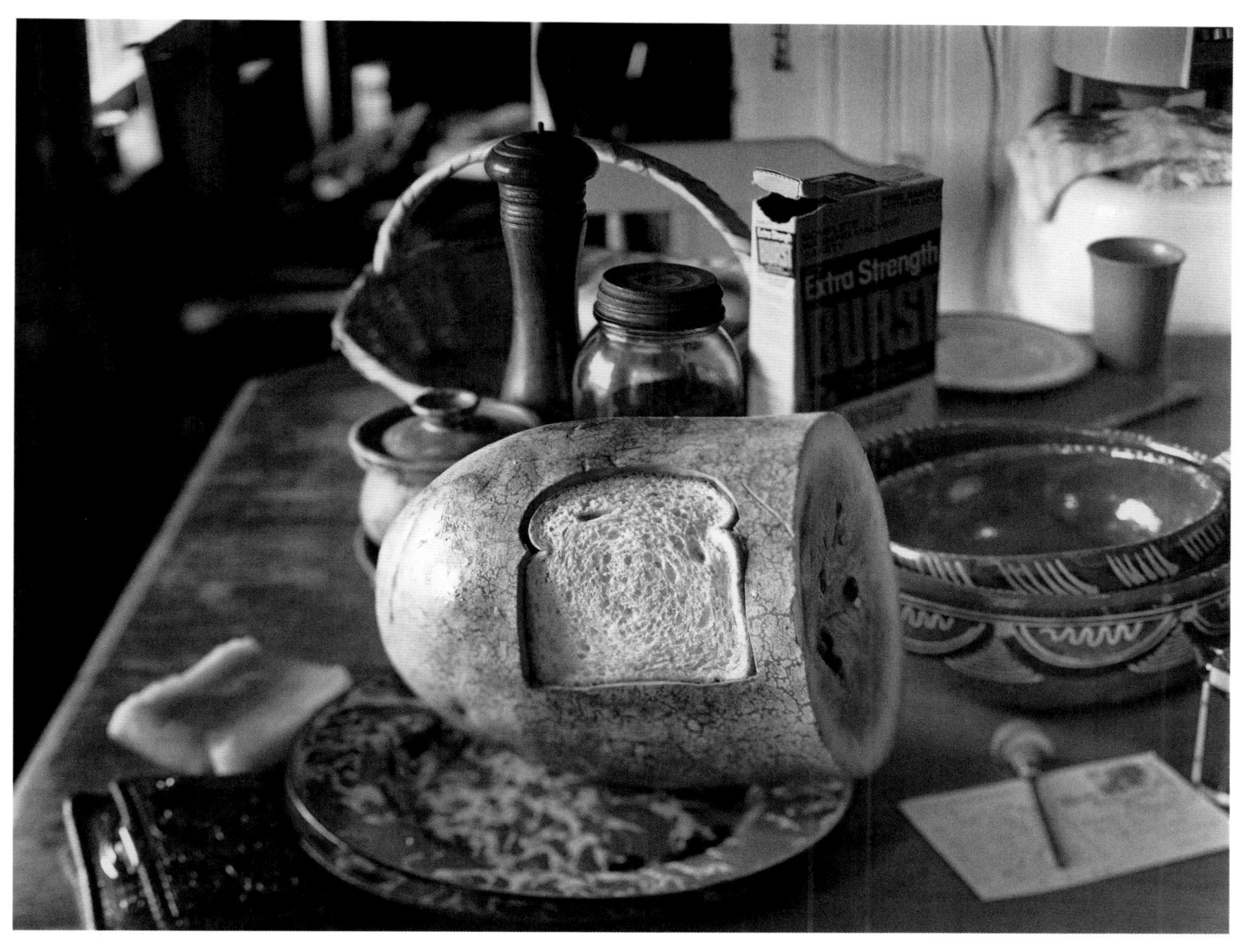

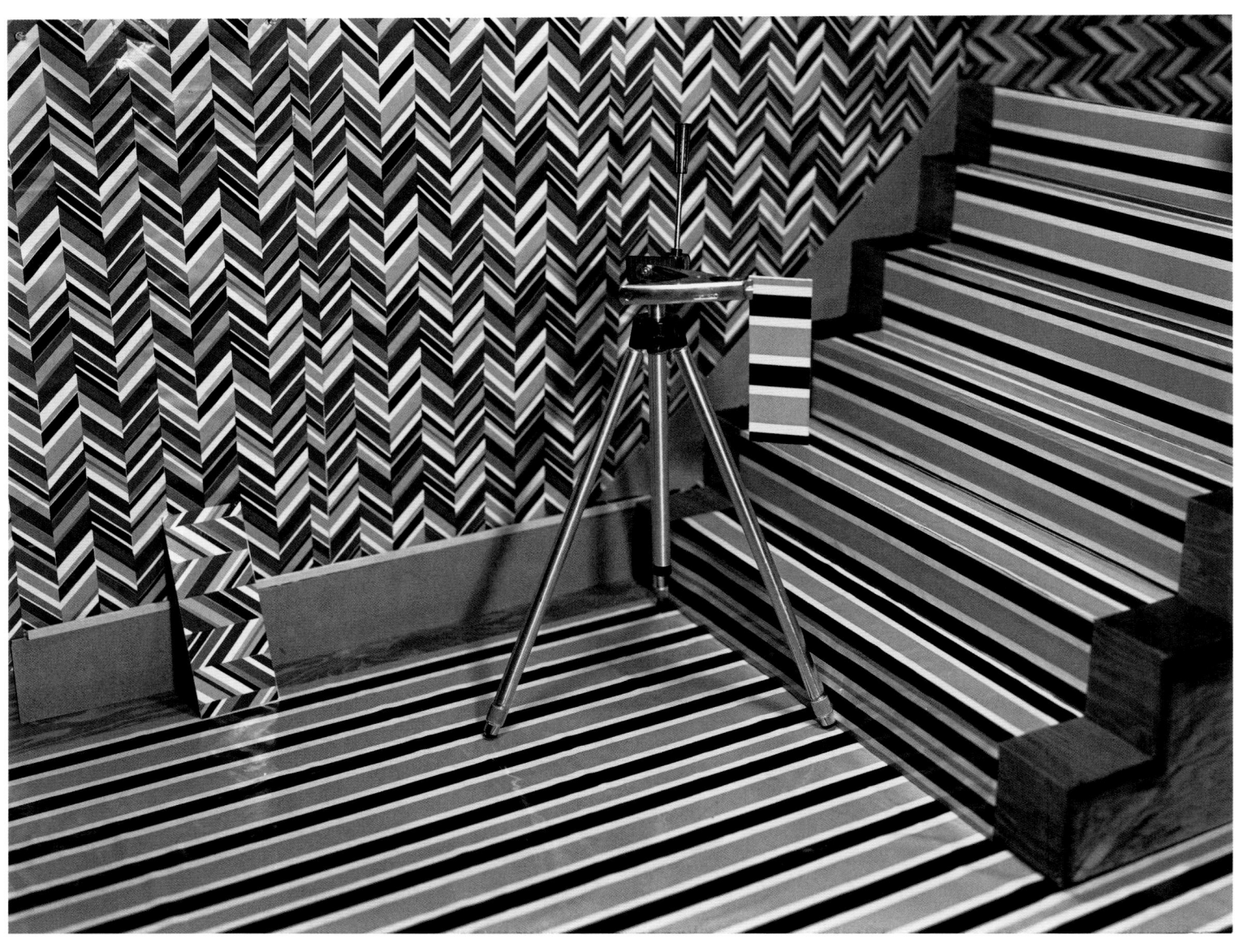

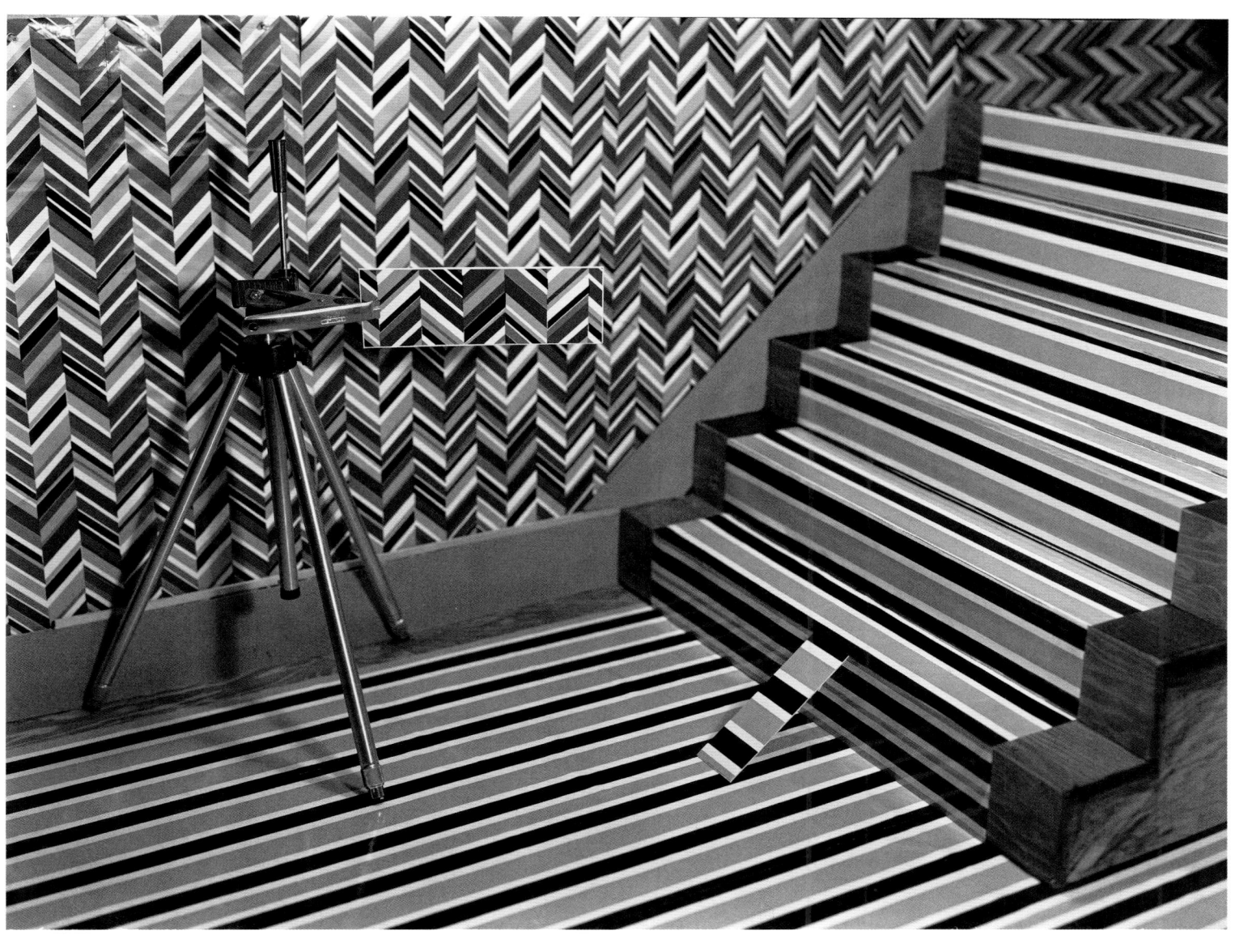

Decorator Test (diptych),
1974

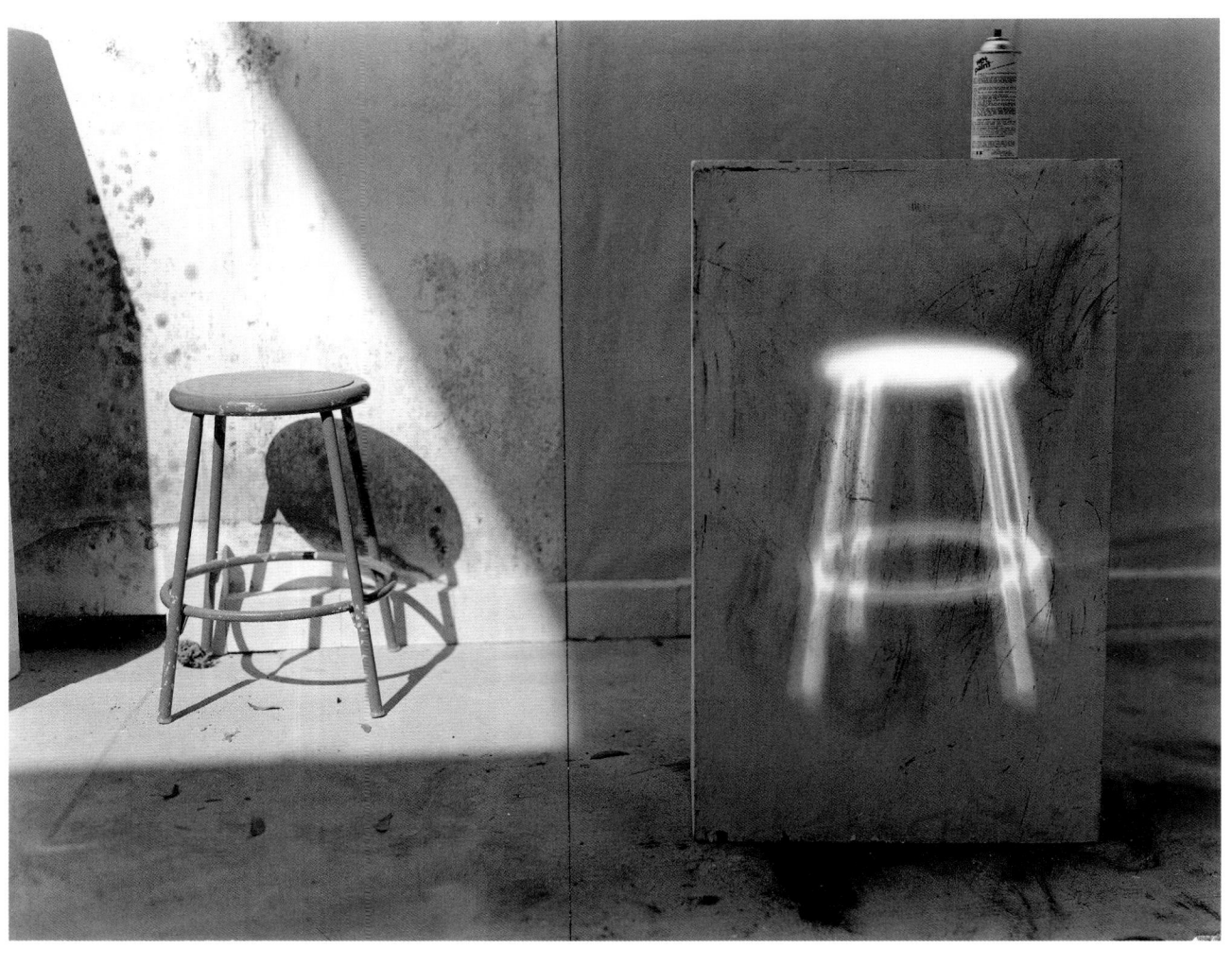

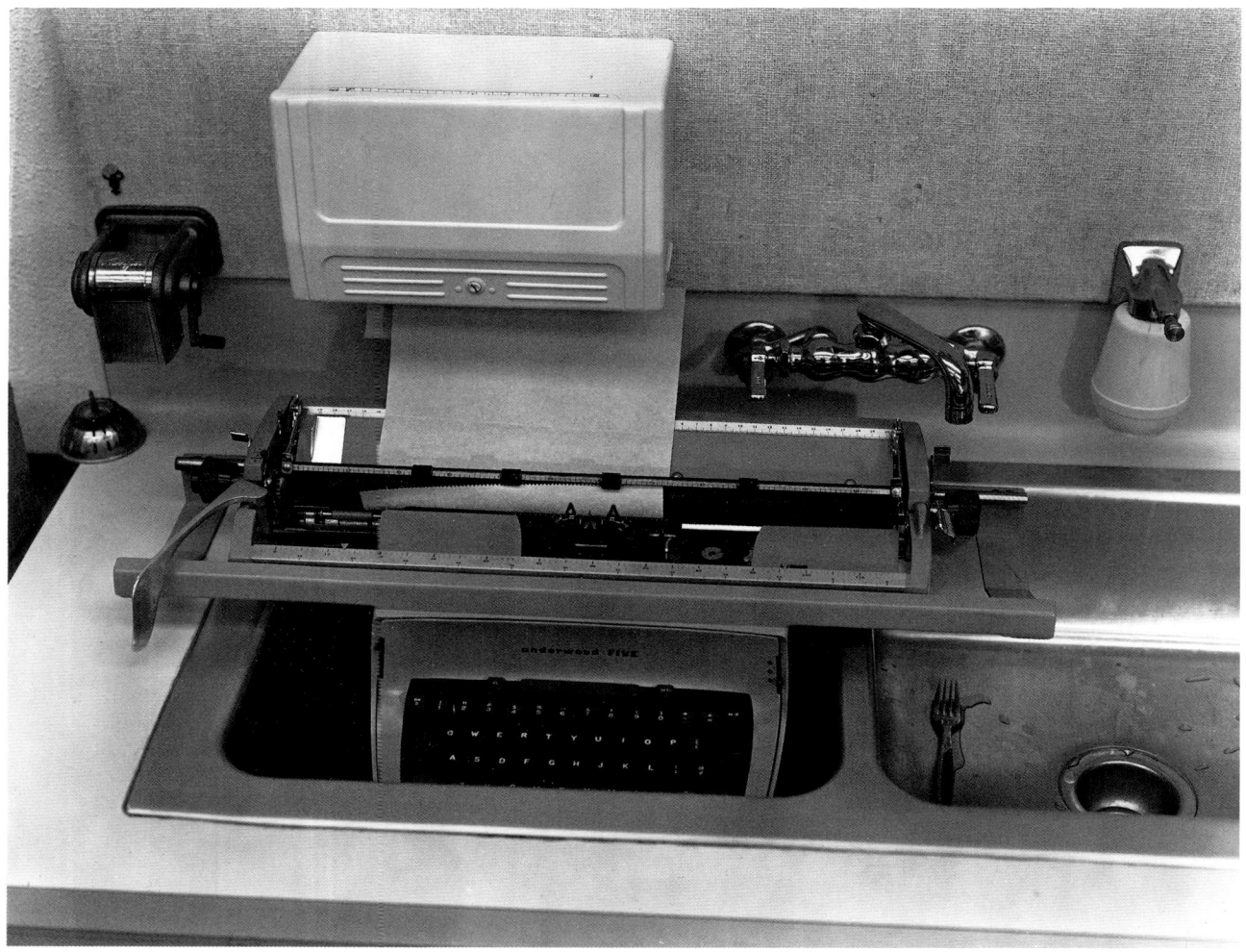

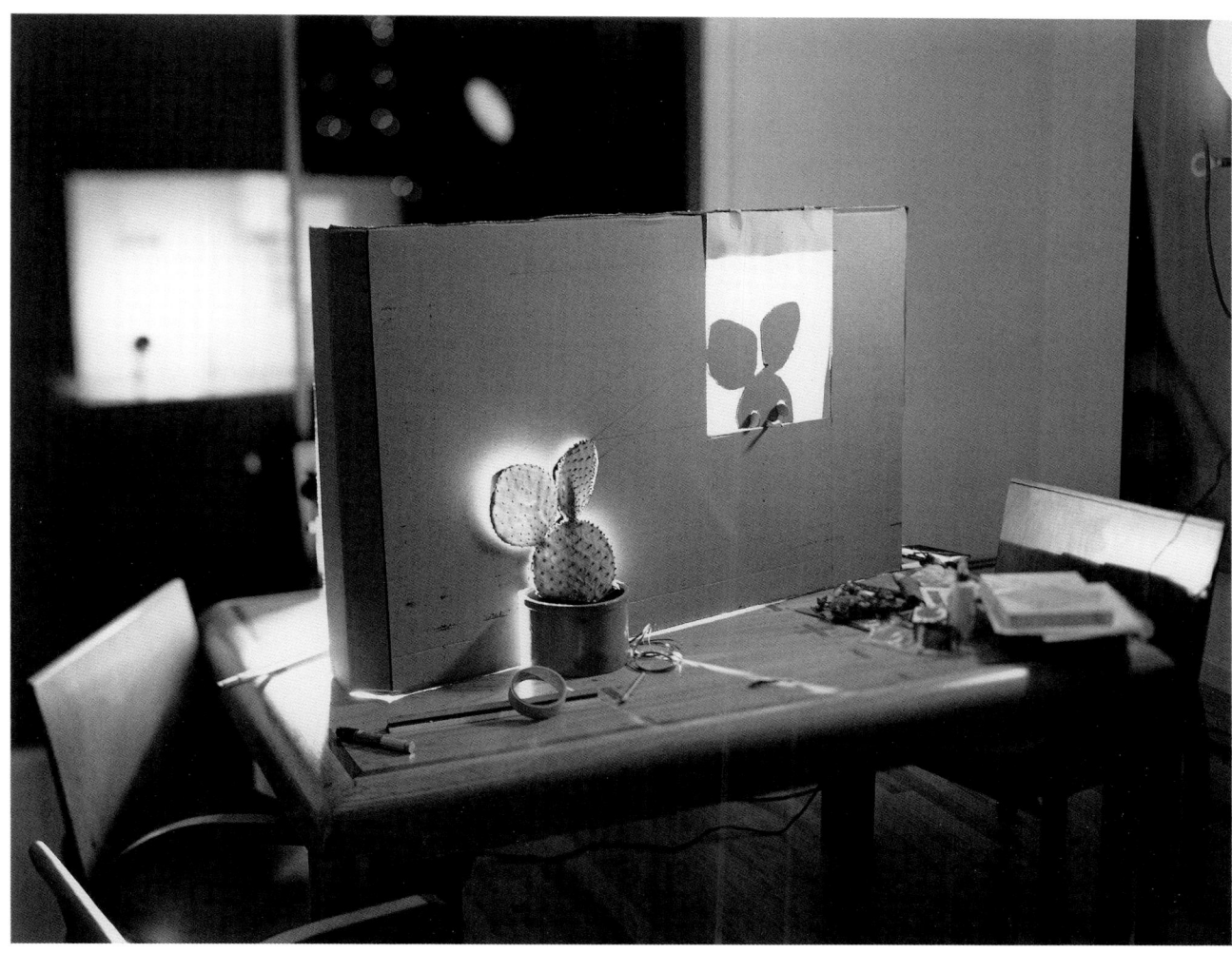

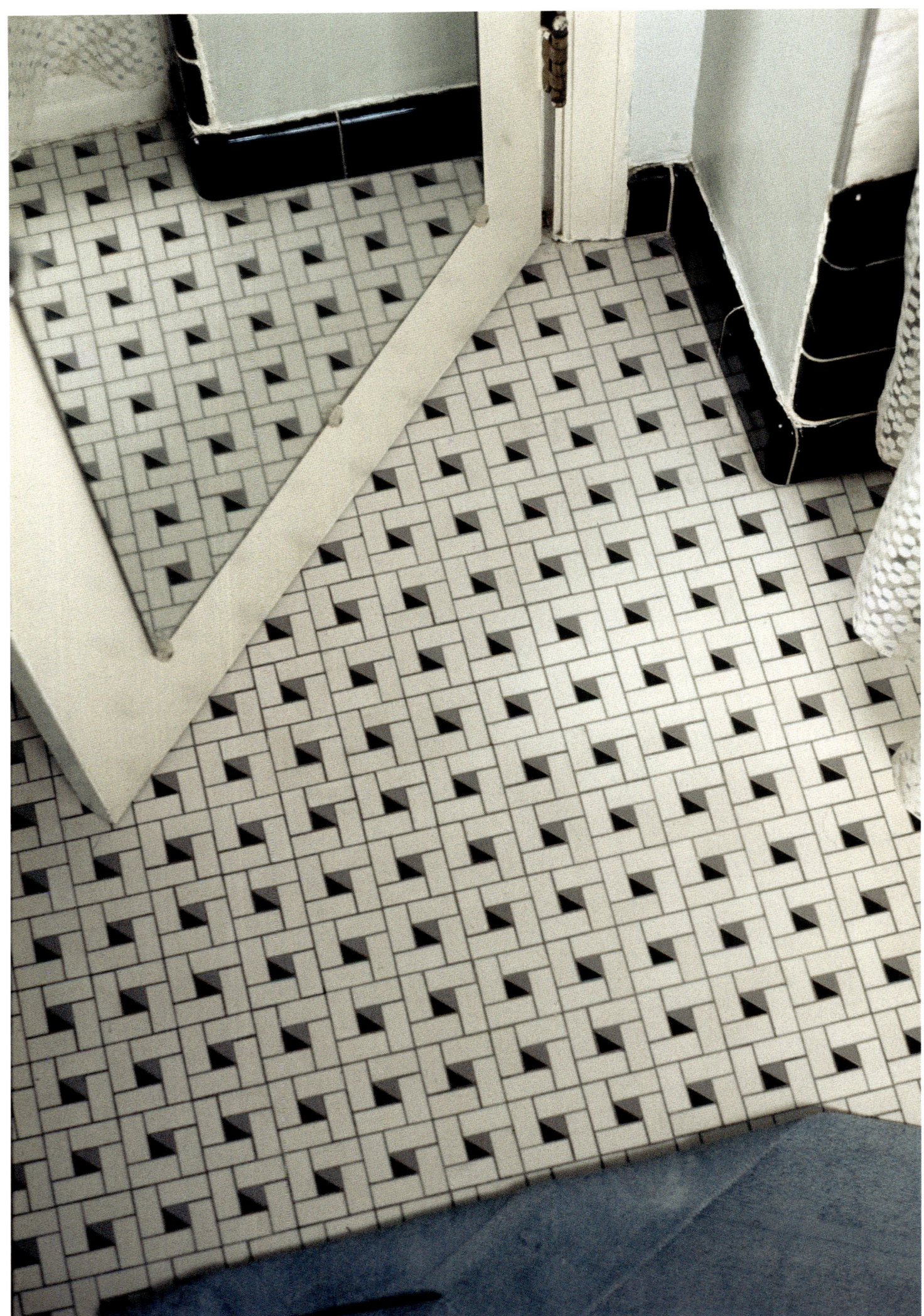

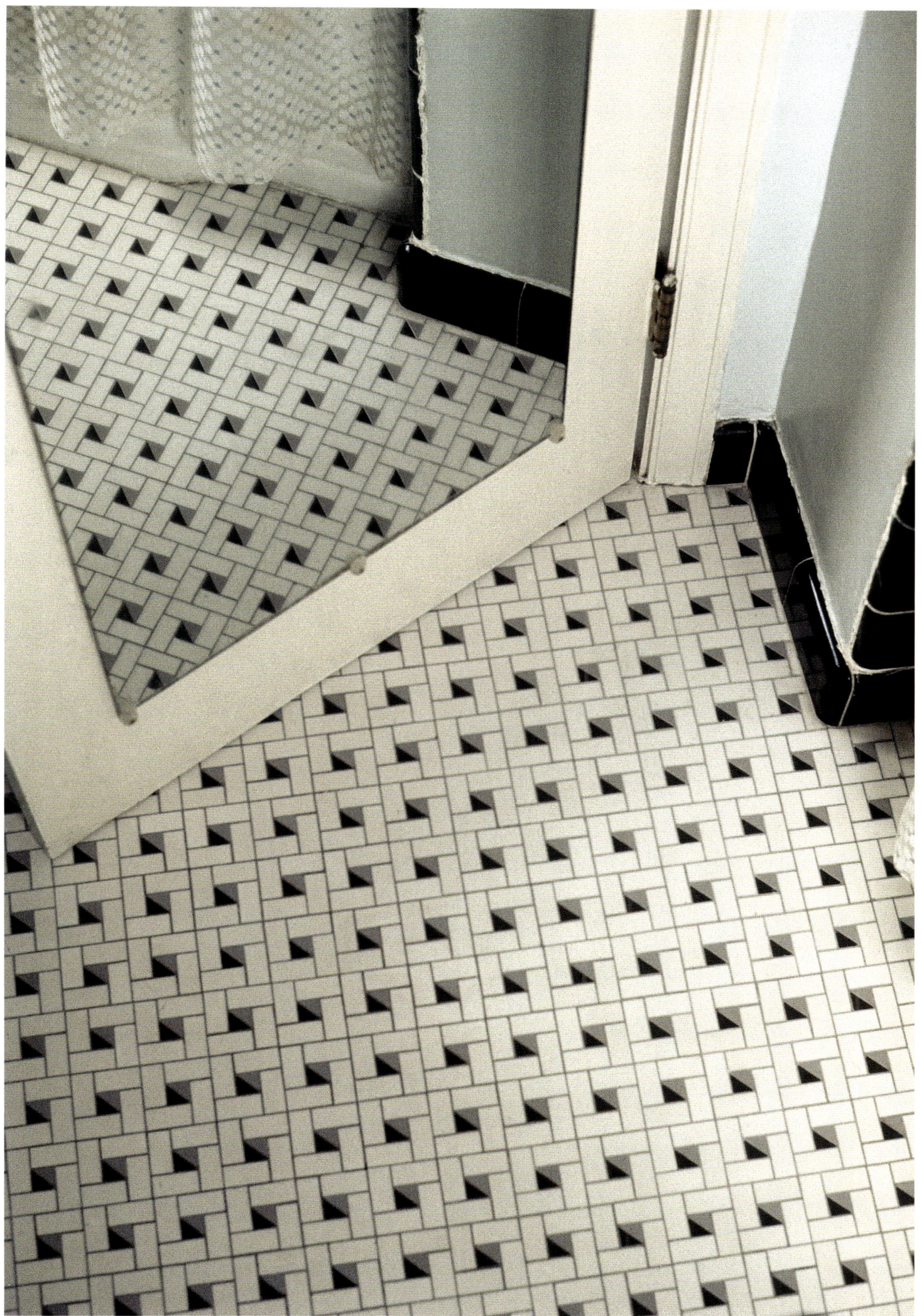

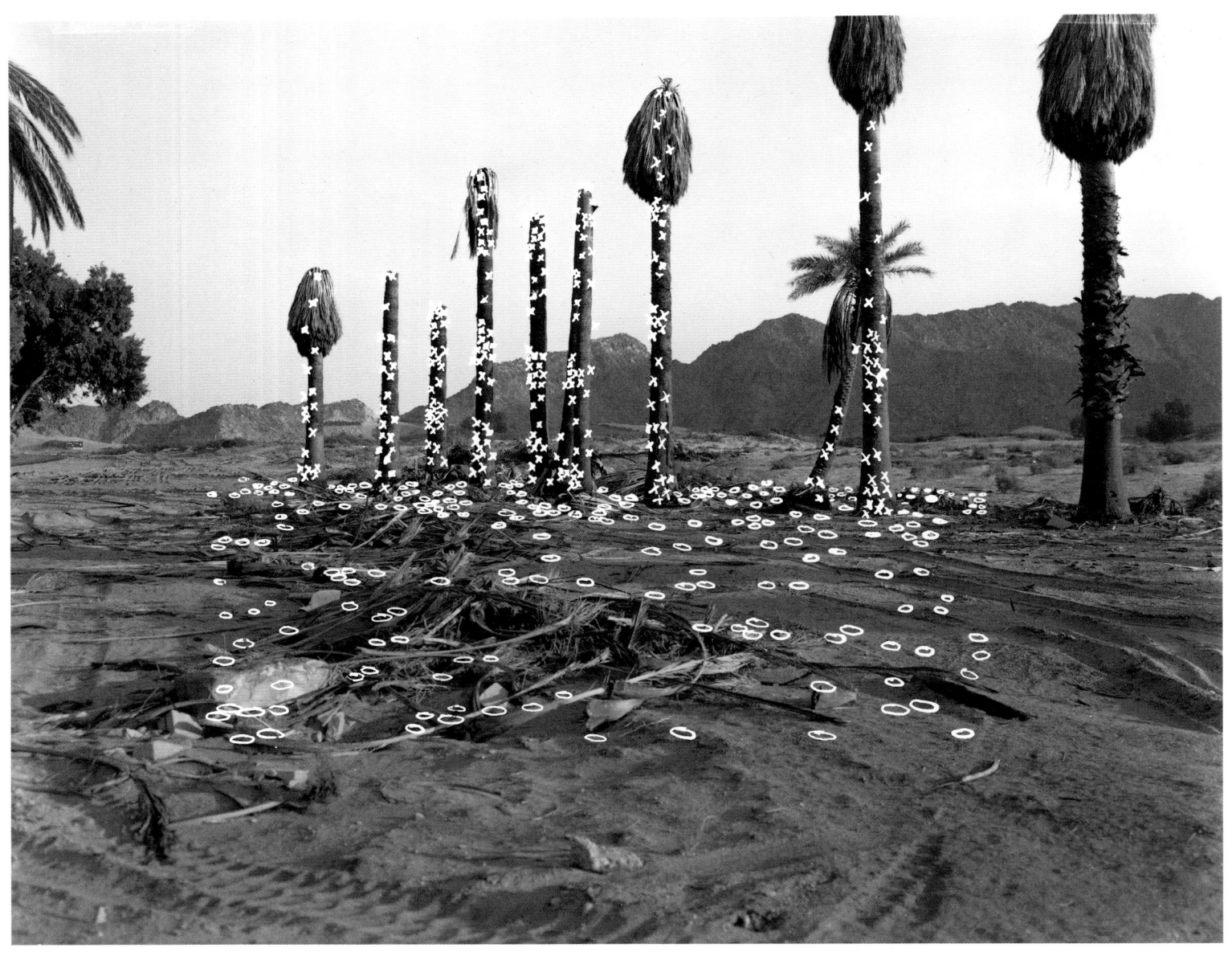

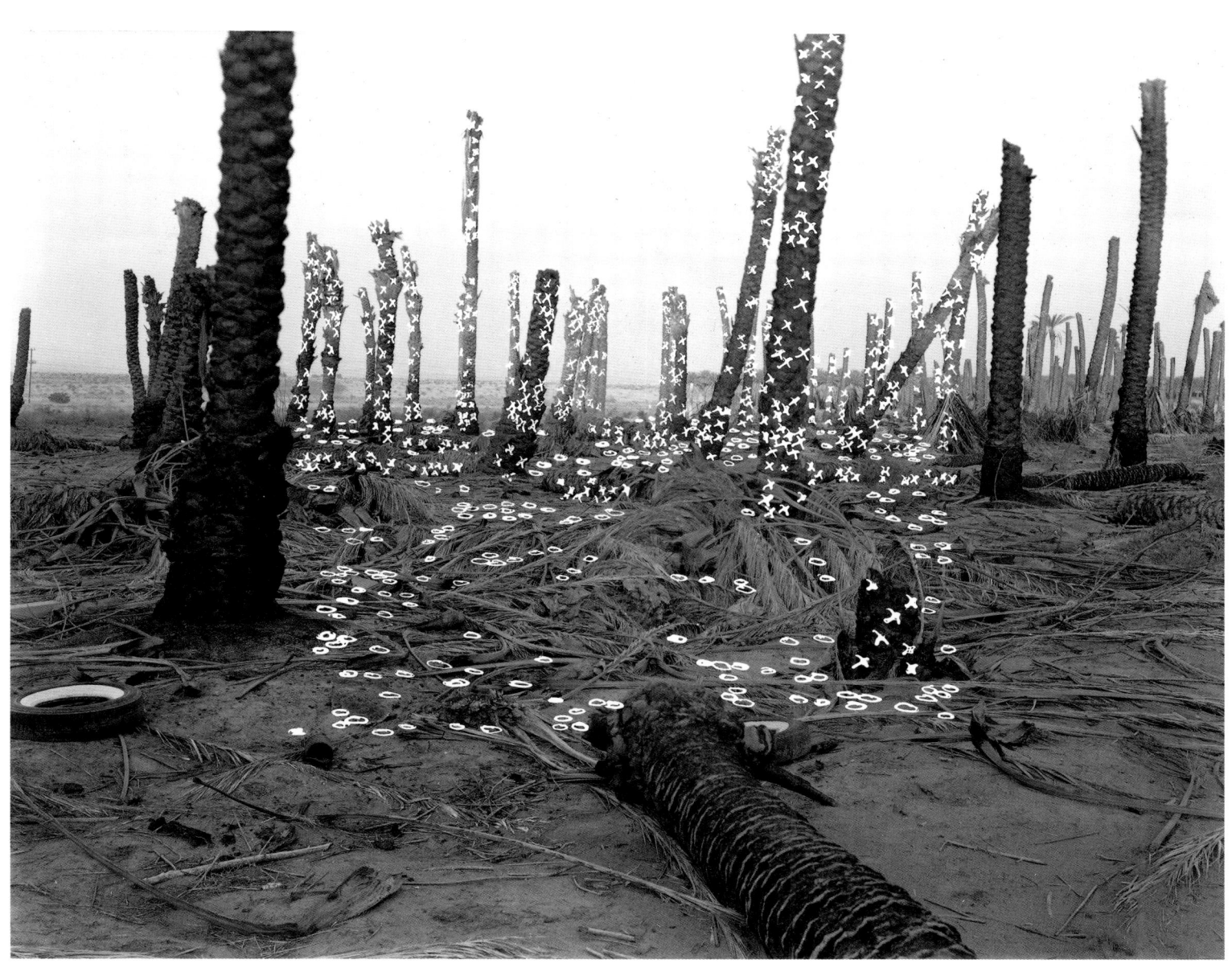

*The Effect at the Center
of the Overlay Was Most
Pleasing* (diptych), 1973

It is not surprising that Swiss photographer
Eva-Fiore Kovacovsky cites Anna
Atkins's nineteenth-century cyanotypes,
Karl Blossfeldt's 1930s studies of plants,
and Max Ernst's *Histoire naturelle*
(Natural history, 1926) as points of
inspiration. Kovacovsky's new series
of photograms continues the artist's
ongoing investigations into nature,
beginning here with perforated leaves
selected for their "found compositions"
—the result of having been chewed
by caterpillars. The leaves are then
used as "negatives," and color is added
or subtracted with the aid of filters.
The resulting images, born out of
darkroom chance and experimentation,
are abstractions reminiscent of bright
pigment on paper, camouflage, and
at times a vibrant Rorschach test.
This project follows Kovacovsky's earlier
studies of single blades of grass that
came from a period of research in the
library of the New York Botanical Gardens
on the arrangement and reproduction
of plant specimens. Here, however,
the rigor of taxonomy, or transparent
study of organic forms, is sacrificed in
favor of an elemental darkroom alchemy
that transforms the original found
compositions into disorienting, beautiful,
and at times psychedelic impressions
that have their origins in a real world
now far removed.

—The Editors

Eva-Fiore Kovacovsky
Specimens

All images by Eva-Fiore
Kovacovsky, from the
series *Photograms*,
2011 and ongoing
Courtesy the artist and
Galerie STAMPA, Basel

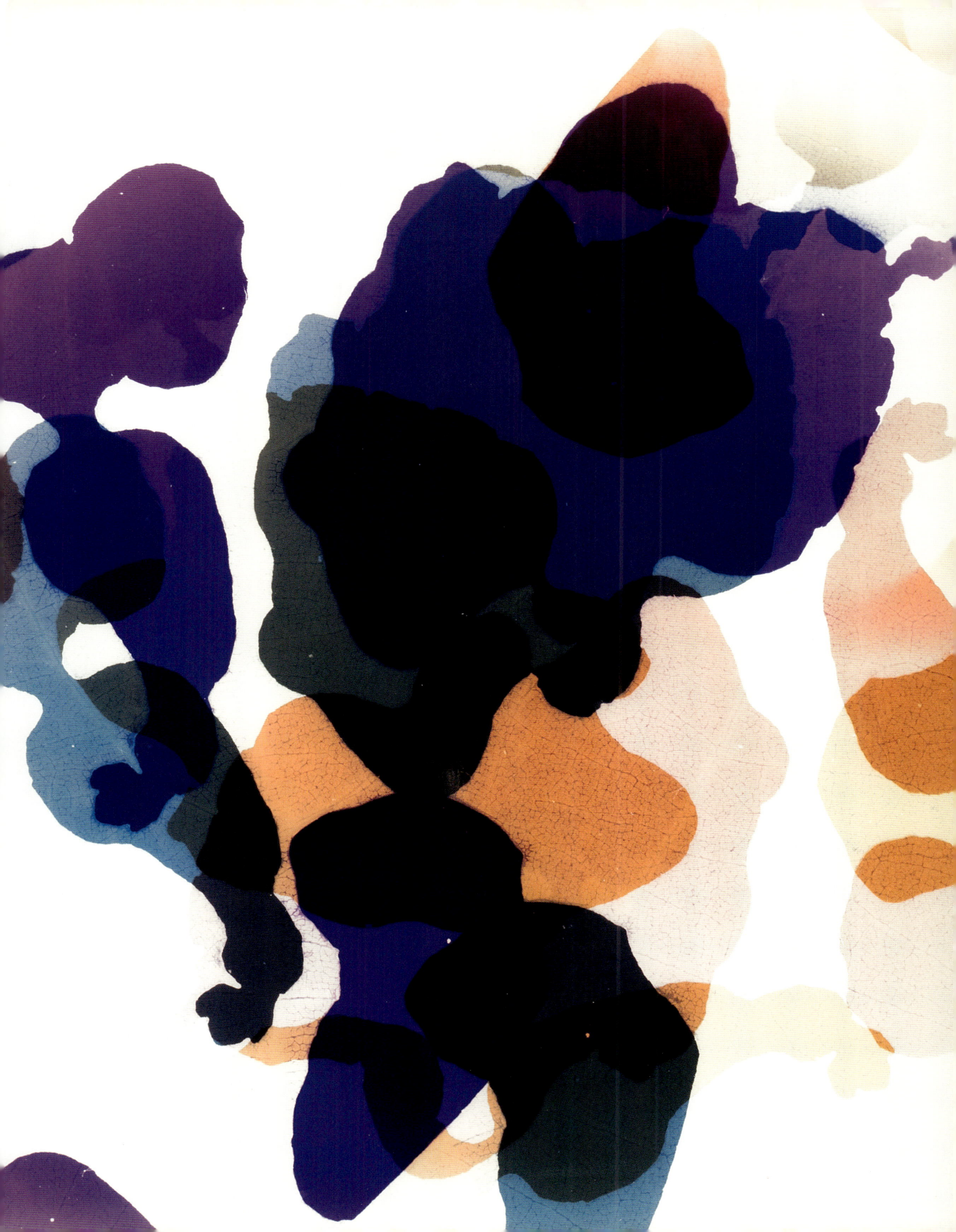

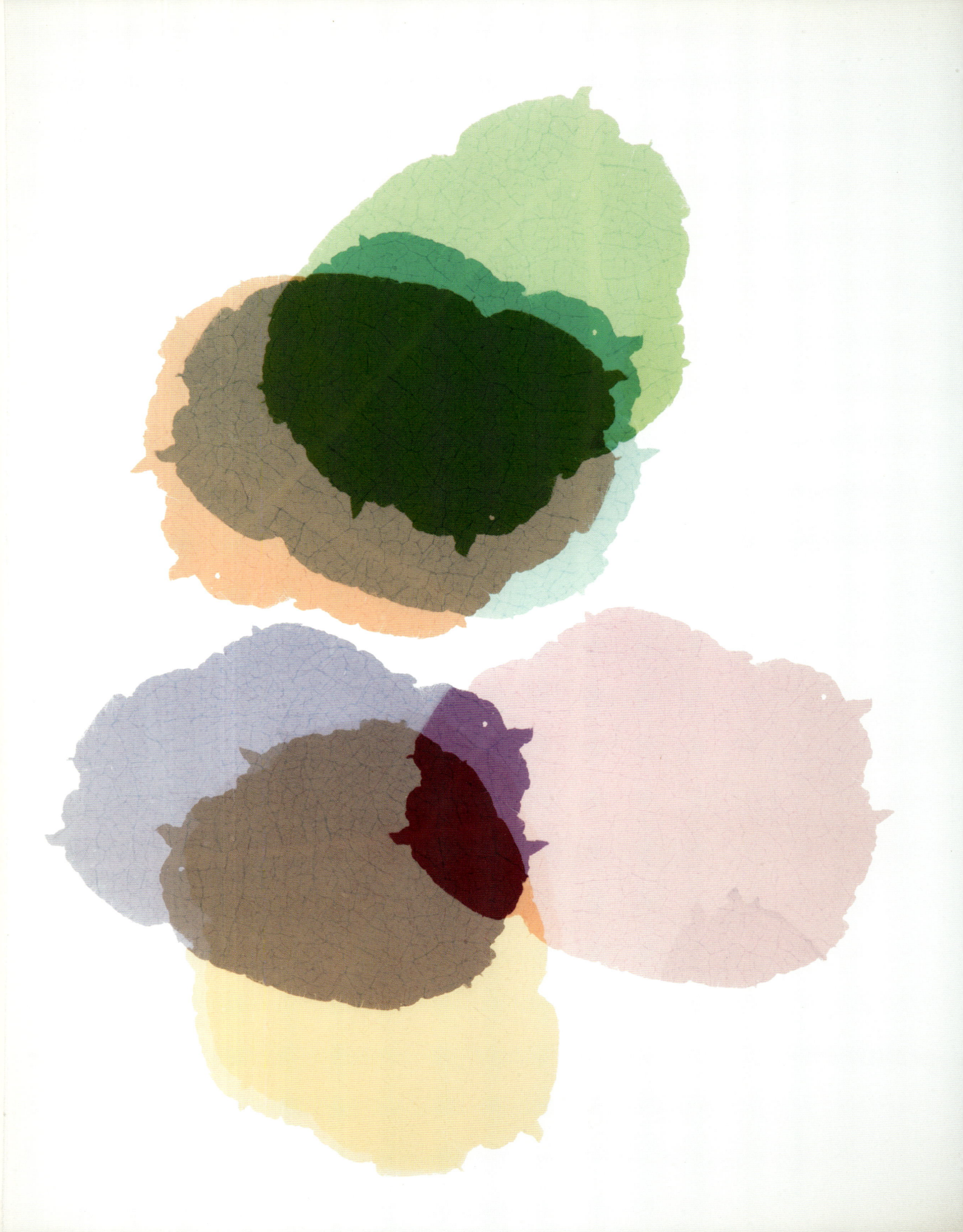

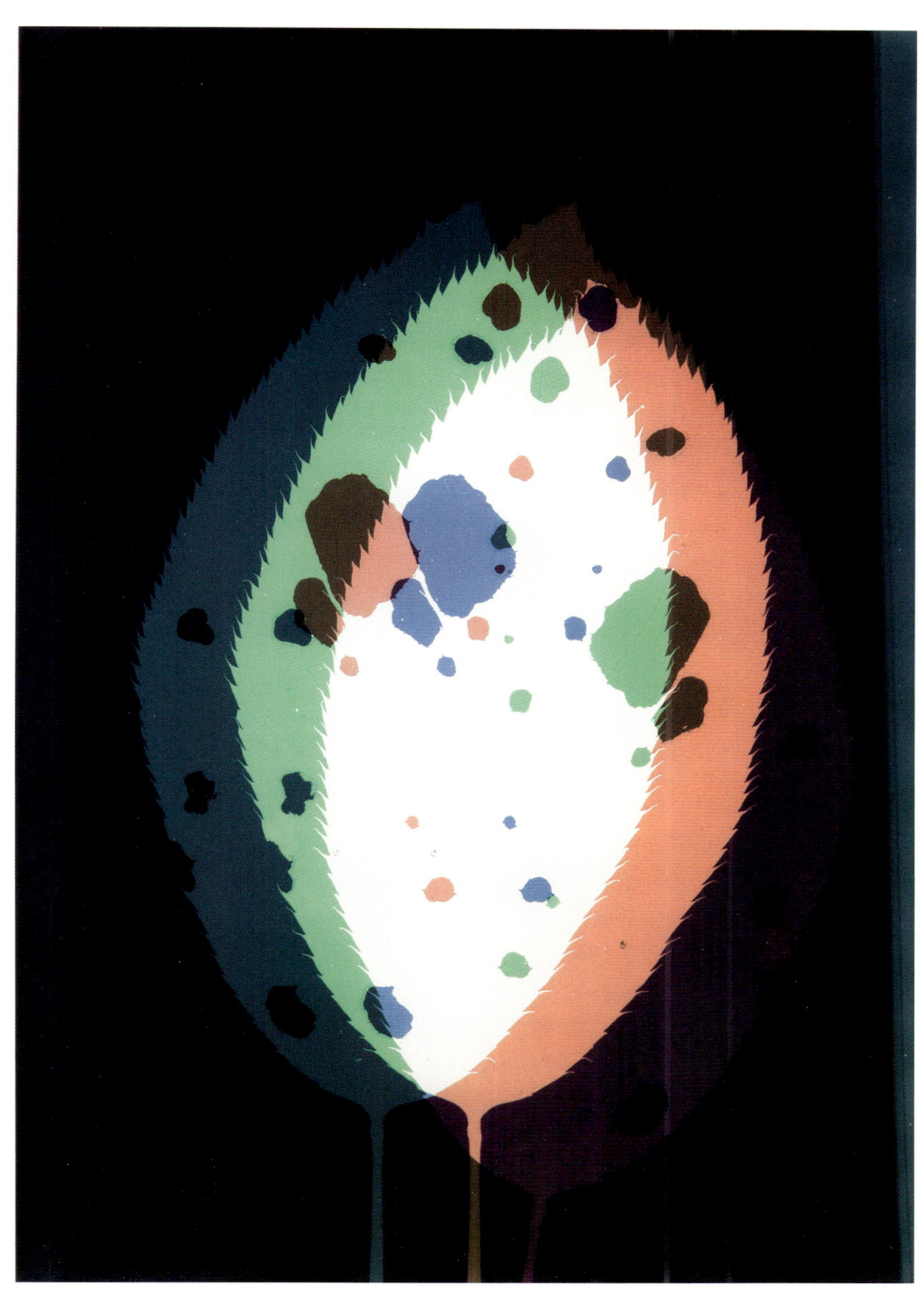

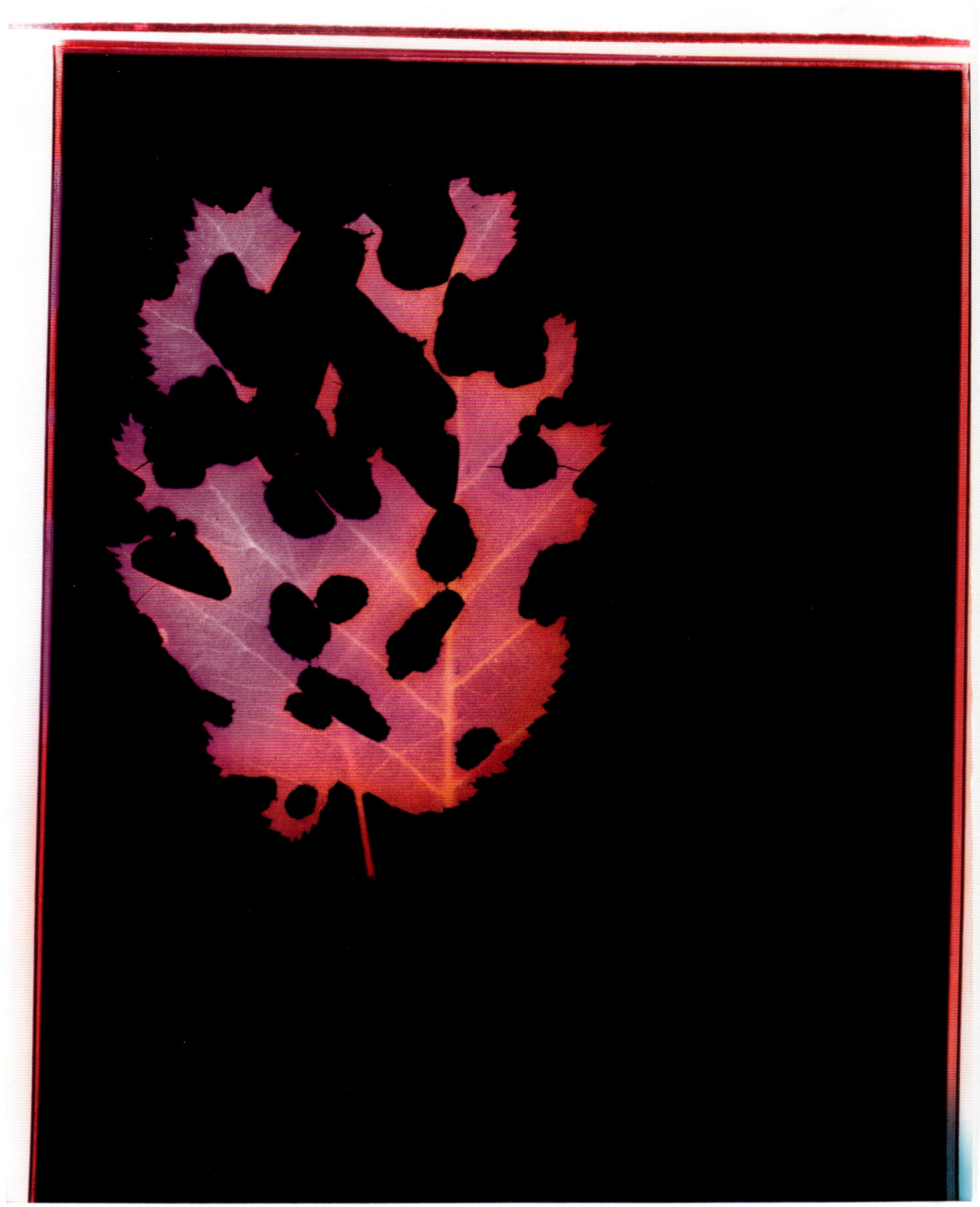

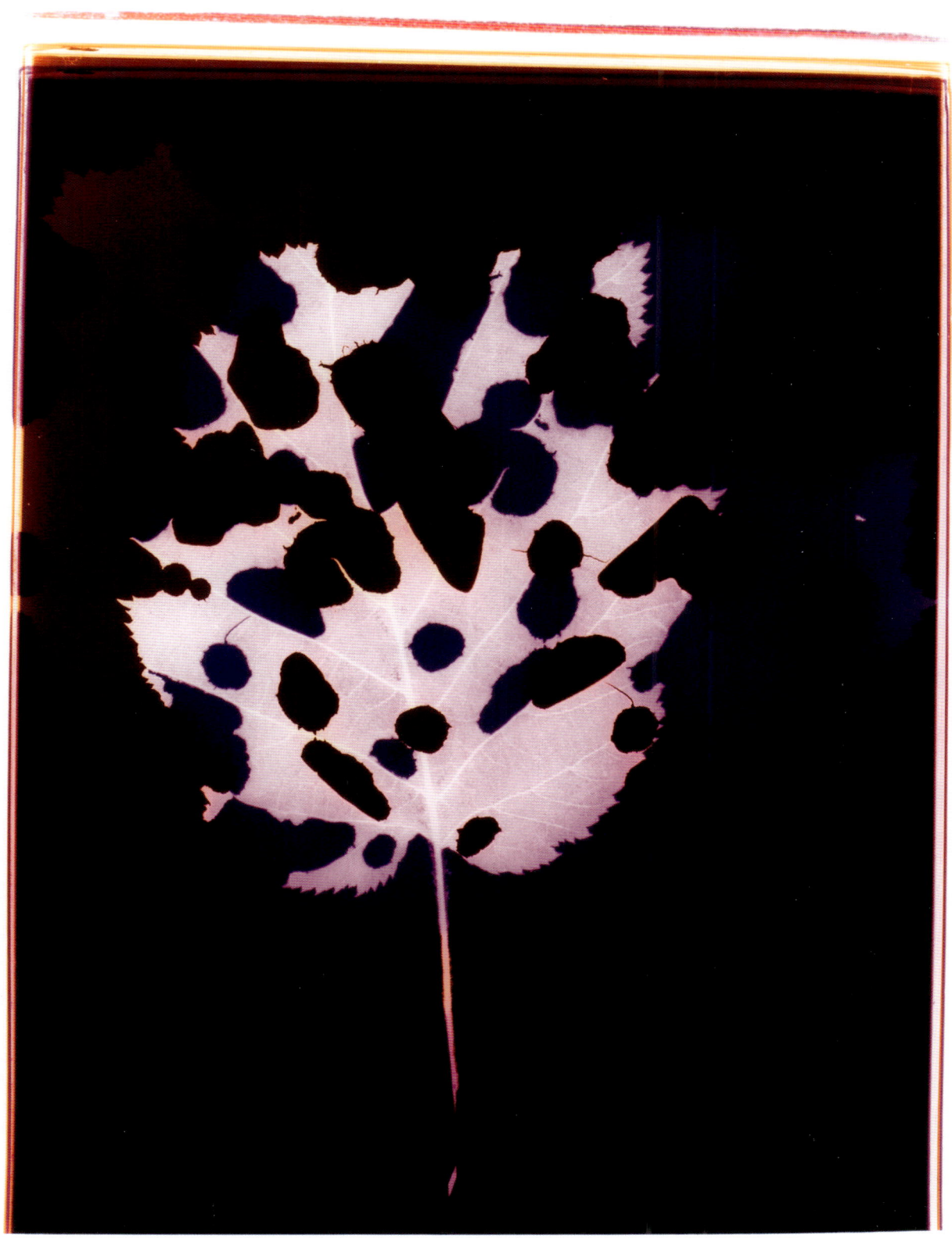

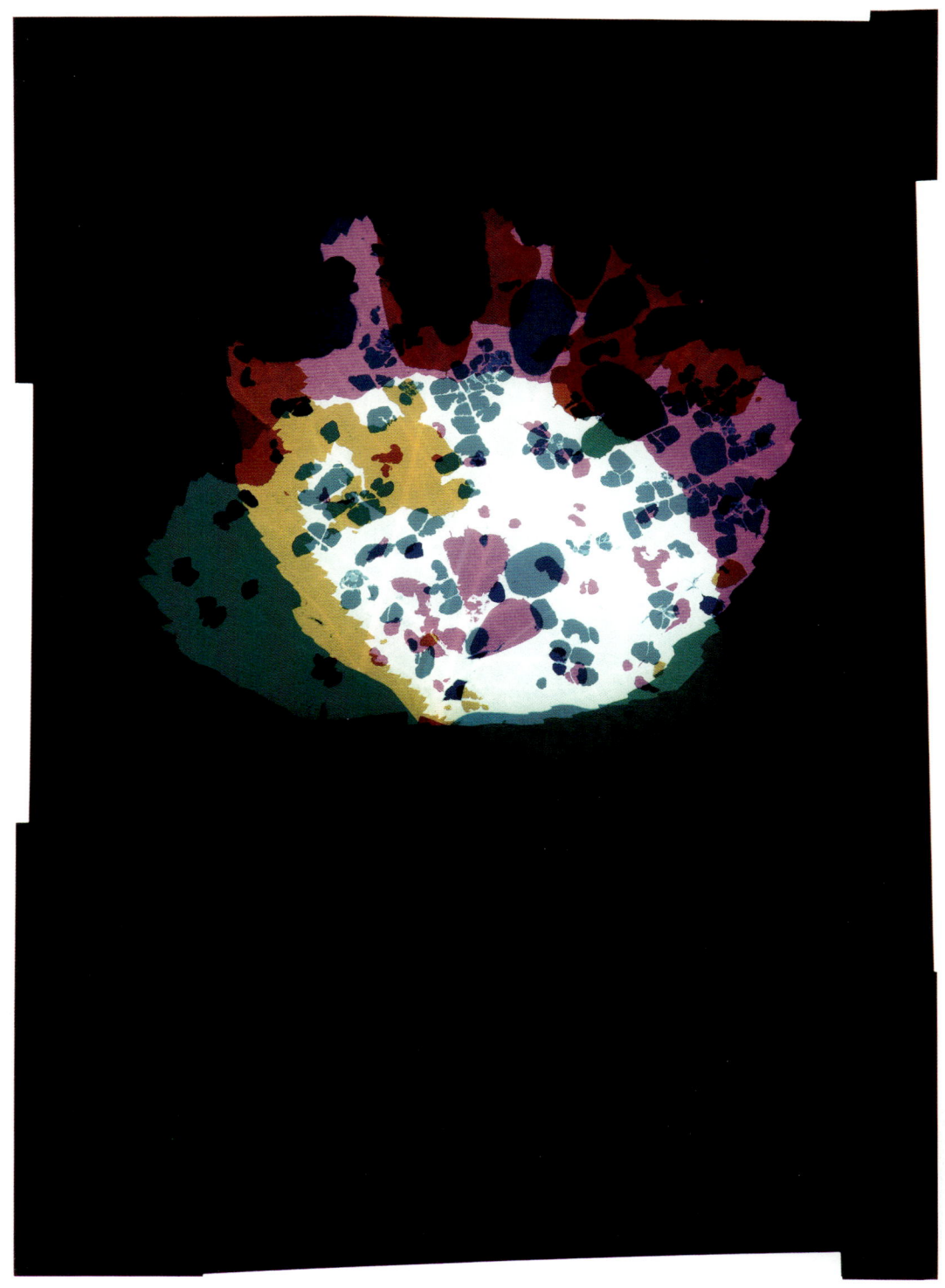

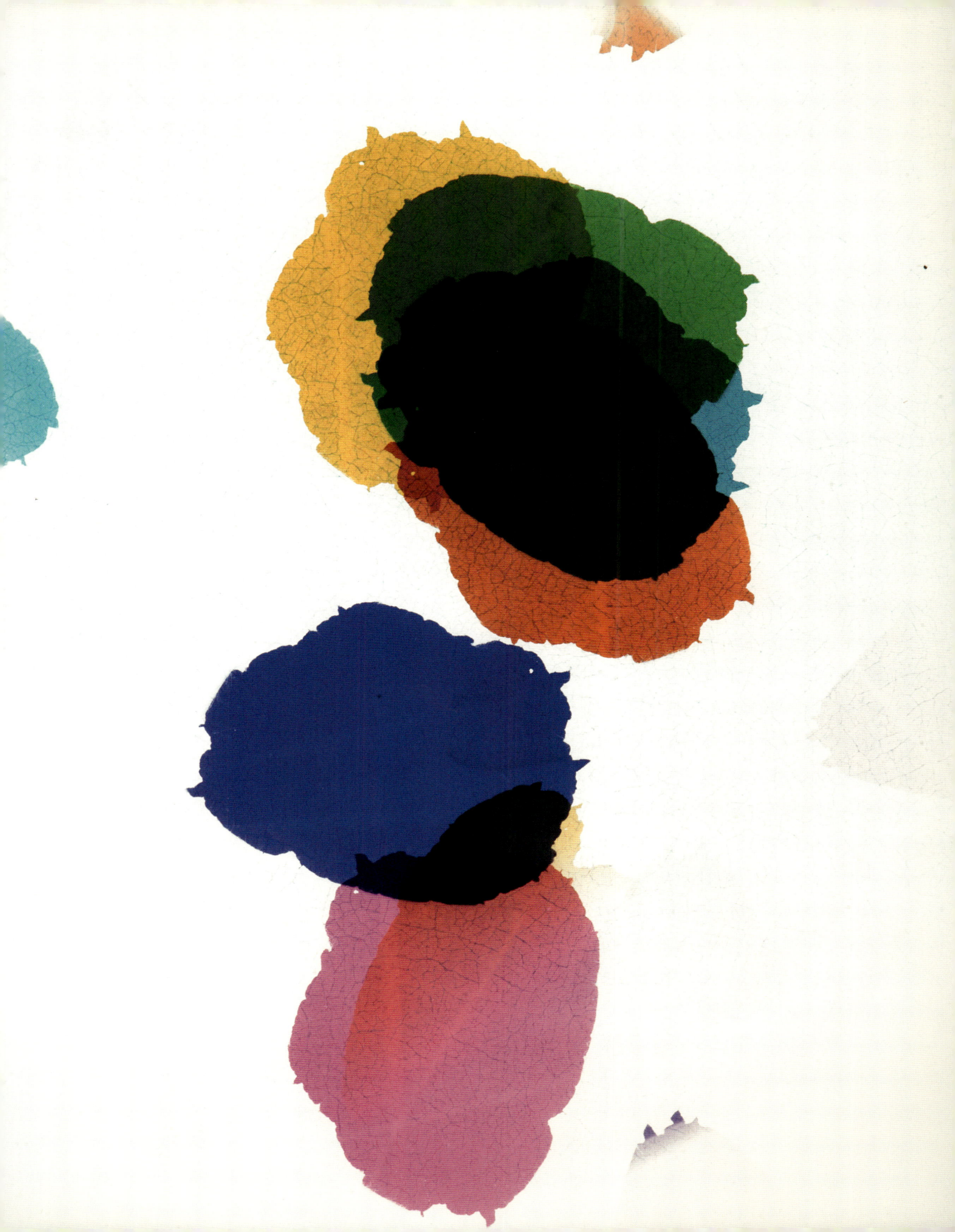

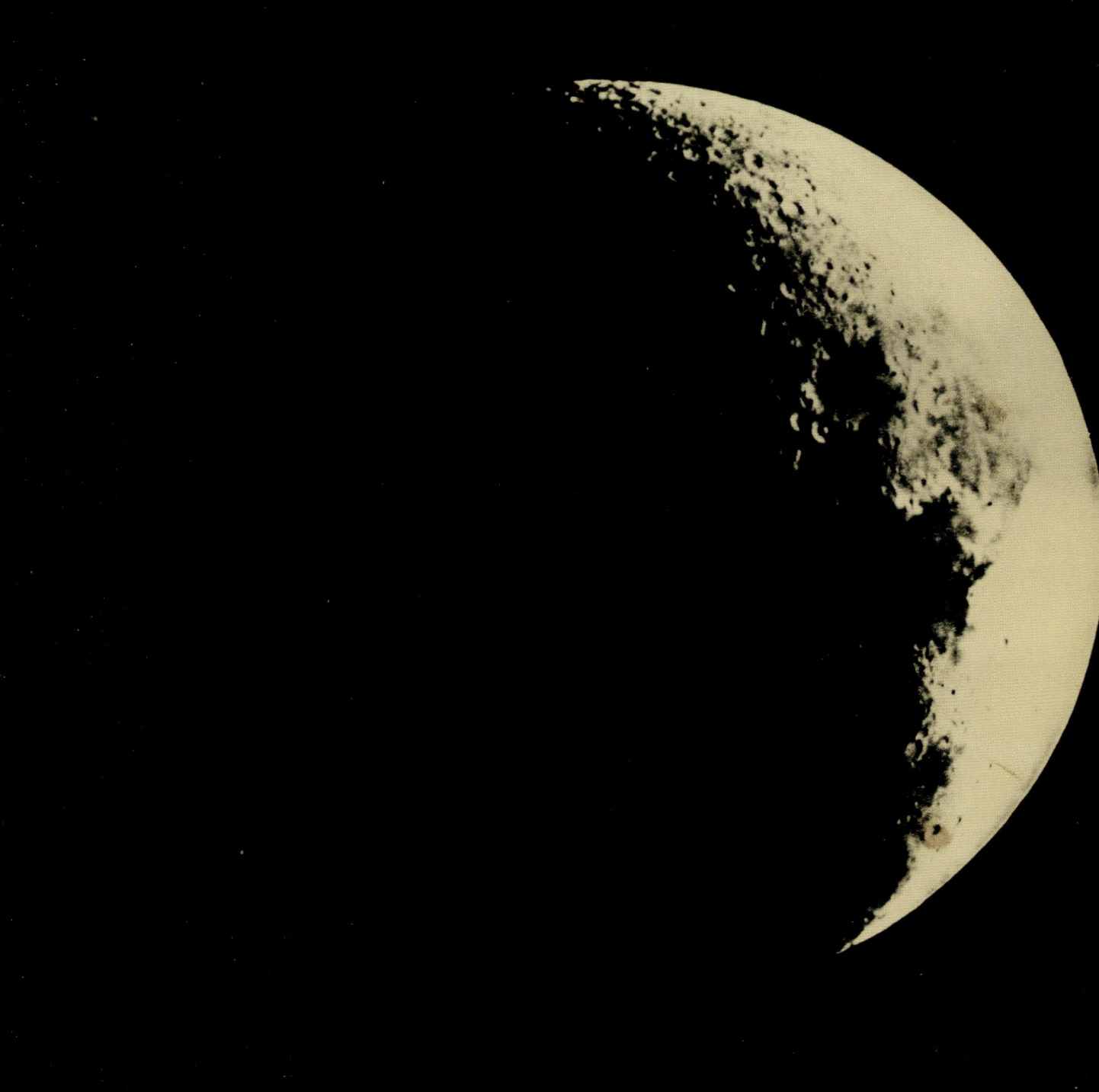

For nearly a decade, Lisa Oppenheim has teased apart the individual steps of picture-making, wringing from the medium's technical apparatus a surprisingly broad range of meanings. She is informed by the legacy of Conceptual art, but her most recent series, sampled in the following pages, reach back further in time for their inspiration. Time is itself a central focus of this work, which meditates on the various ways photography registers duration—the length of the exposure, the gap between a picture's making and its viewing—and how our sense of it dilates in a photograph's presence. This effort is in the service, the New York– and Berlin-based artist has said, of recovering the surprises offered by photography's materials, and of dwelling in "the magic of the photographic process." Through cool calculation, Oppenheim has devised an art of surprising affectiveness, equal parts romantic and rigorous.

The emotional resonance of Oppenheim's works has often rested in her use of (quite literally) universal subjects. The sun and the moon—giver of light and the ultimate light reflector—feature regularly, from a 2006 slide projection in which the artist holds postcards of sunsets in front of the real thing to a two-channel 16mm film installation, made in 2008, that is based upon images of the Earth and the moon made the night of the Apollo mission's first lunar landing. The moon recurred as the subject of a 2010 series of unique silver-toned photograms she dubbed *Lunagrams*. To make these works, Oppenheim borrowed from the archives of New York University mid-nineteenth-century glass-plate negatives by John and Henry Draper depicting the moon. She made large-format copy negatives, placed them on photographic paper, then exposed them to the moon at the time of the lunar phase depicted in the original. Decades collapse as one image, made by an enthusiast whose work was as much science as art, begets another. A related series of *Heliograms* was made in 2011: she exposed a photograph of the sun originally taken on July 8, 1876, to sunlight at different times of day during each month that year. Irregular amounts of sunlight means not every work is equally exposed, and there are gaps in the series where Oppenheim's obligations prevented her from capturing a scheduled image. The individual results once again warp our understanding of two distinct instants, but when seen in aggregate, the *Heliograms* also chart the passage of the artist's days. These silvery and golden works possess an elemental allure—the metals themselves, the primitive processes used by the medium's first exponents—but also acknowledge that copies are always already imperfect, and that life and time conspire to make them so.

Oppenheim literalizes her attempt to translate the essence of earlier images in her 2011–12 series *Smoke*. There, she isolated details of smoke from a wide range of images of fire, then turned these semiabstract compositions into digital internegatives. Rather than use the light of an enlarger to expose these negatives, Oppenheim used the flames from a match, from a culinary torch, and from other sources to expose—and solarize—these images. From a 1913 oil-field explosion to World War II–era aerial surveillance to journalists' images of the 2011 North London riots, the absent fires implied by the smoke have been made visible by altogether different flames. The resultant works, which look like polished-silver outtakes from Alfred Stieglitz's *Equivalents* series, add a canny rumination on presence and absence to Oppenheim's usual investigation of temporality. As with all her recent works, the *Smoke* series resides in interstitial spaces: between two images separated by time and place; between materialist and conceptual approaches to the medium; between intellect and emotion. In these seams Oppenheim finds a locus of mystery.

Lisa Oppenheim
Elemental Process

Brian Sholis

Opposite:
*Lunagram #1
(Version 2)*, 2010
All works by
Lisa Oppenheim
© Lisa Oppenheim
and courtesy Harris
Lieberman, New York
and The Approach,
London

Brian Sholis is Associate
Editor of *Aperture*
magazine.

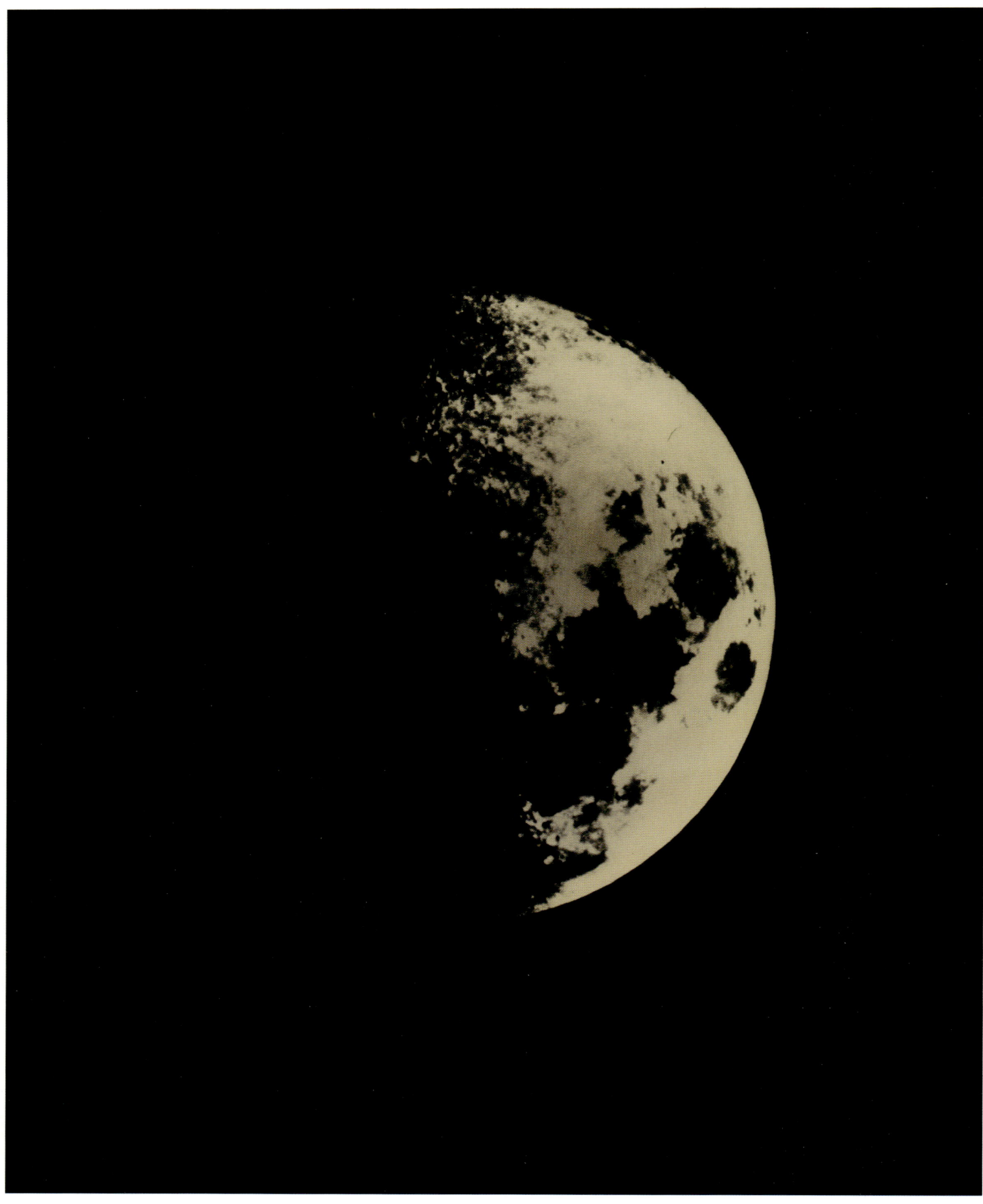

Lunagram #3 (Version 2),
2010

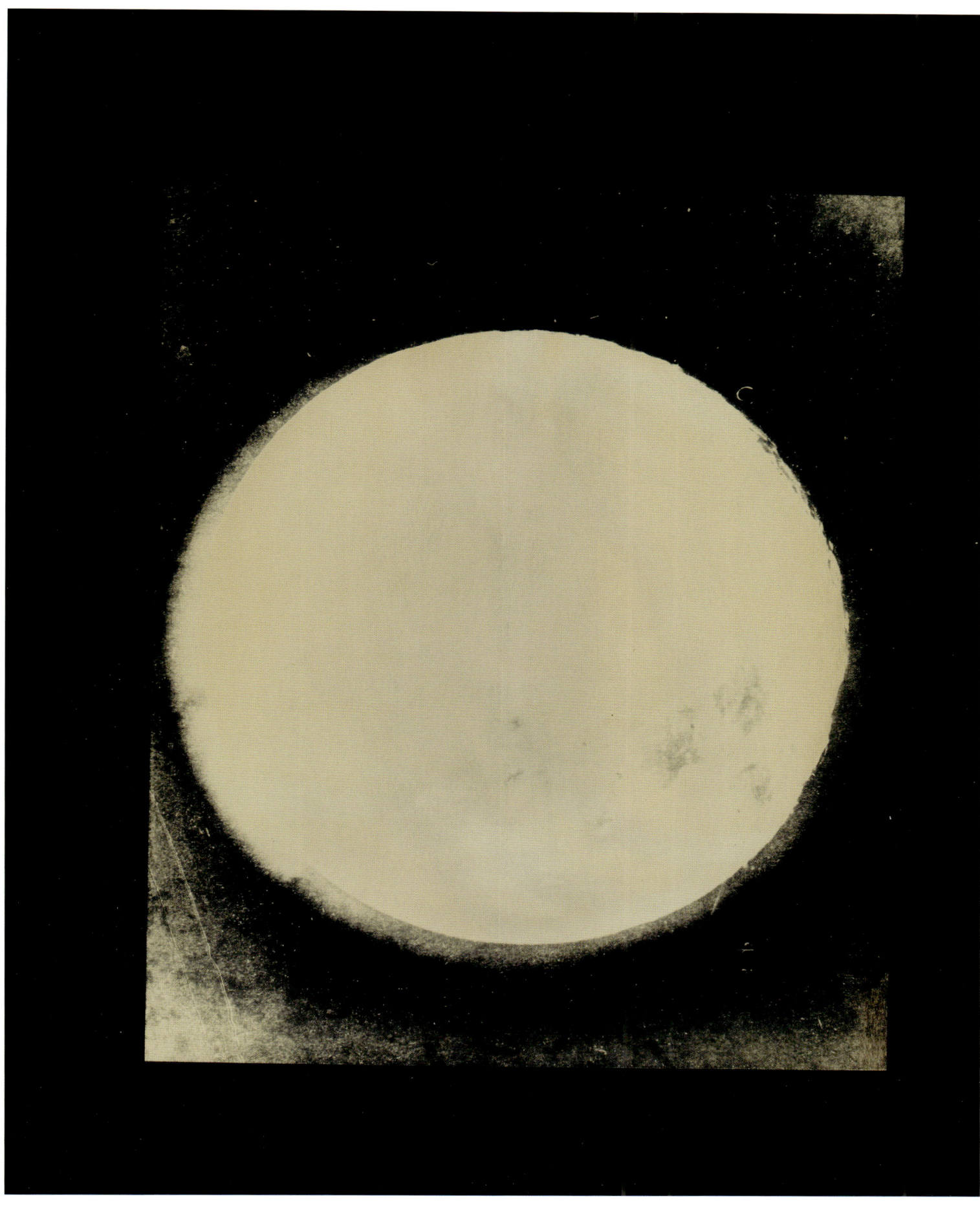

Lunagram #9 (Version 2),
2010

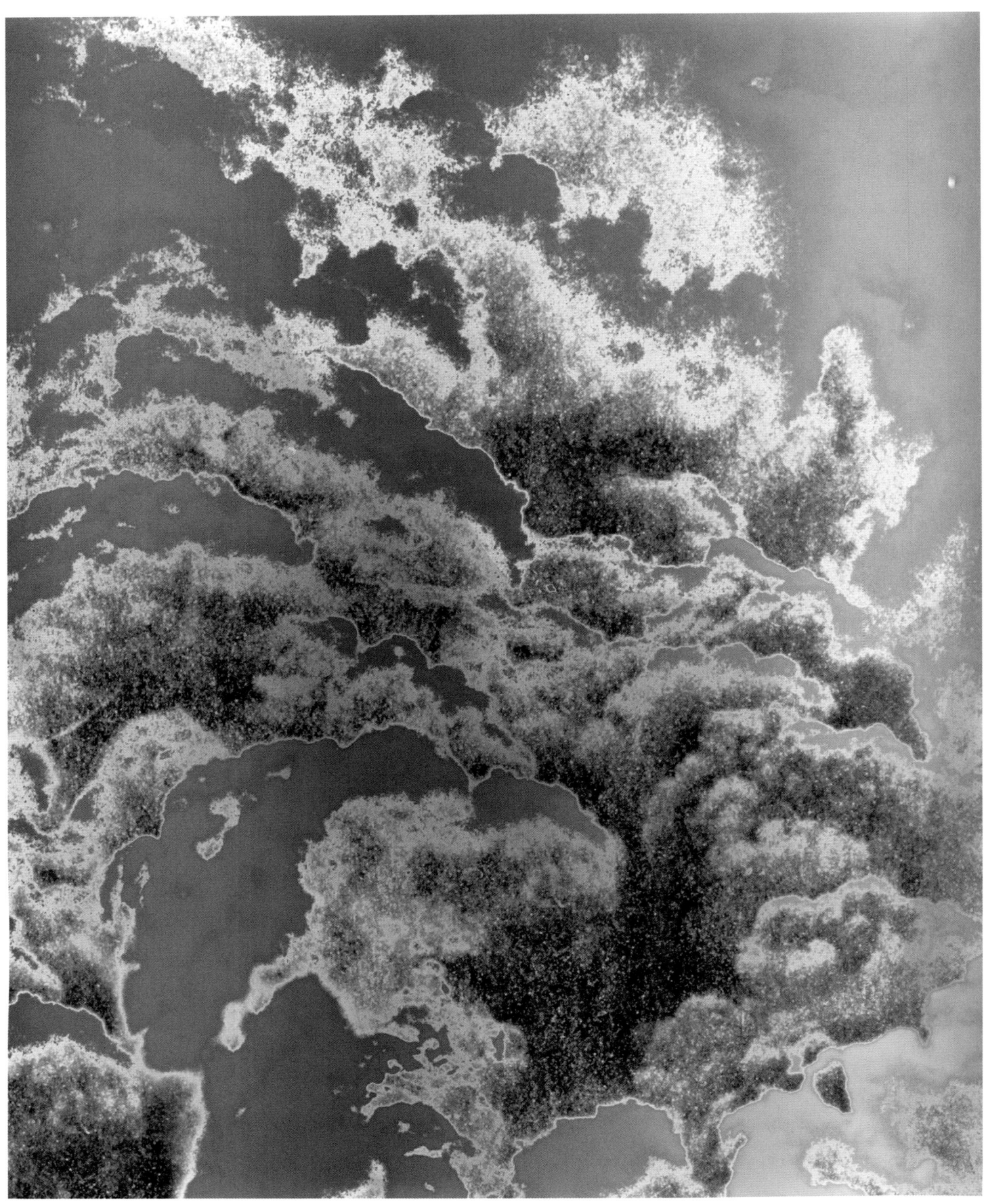

*A monstrous column of roaring flame. Star Oil Co. Loucke
No. 3 on fire since Aug. 7, 1913. Most disastrous fire in Caddo
oil field and largest single well fire in history of U.S. of A.
Daily loss of oil estimated at 30,000 barrels. 1913/2012
(Version V), 2012, from the series Smoke, 2011-12*

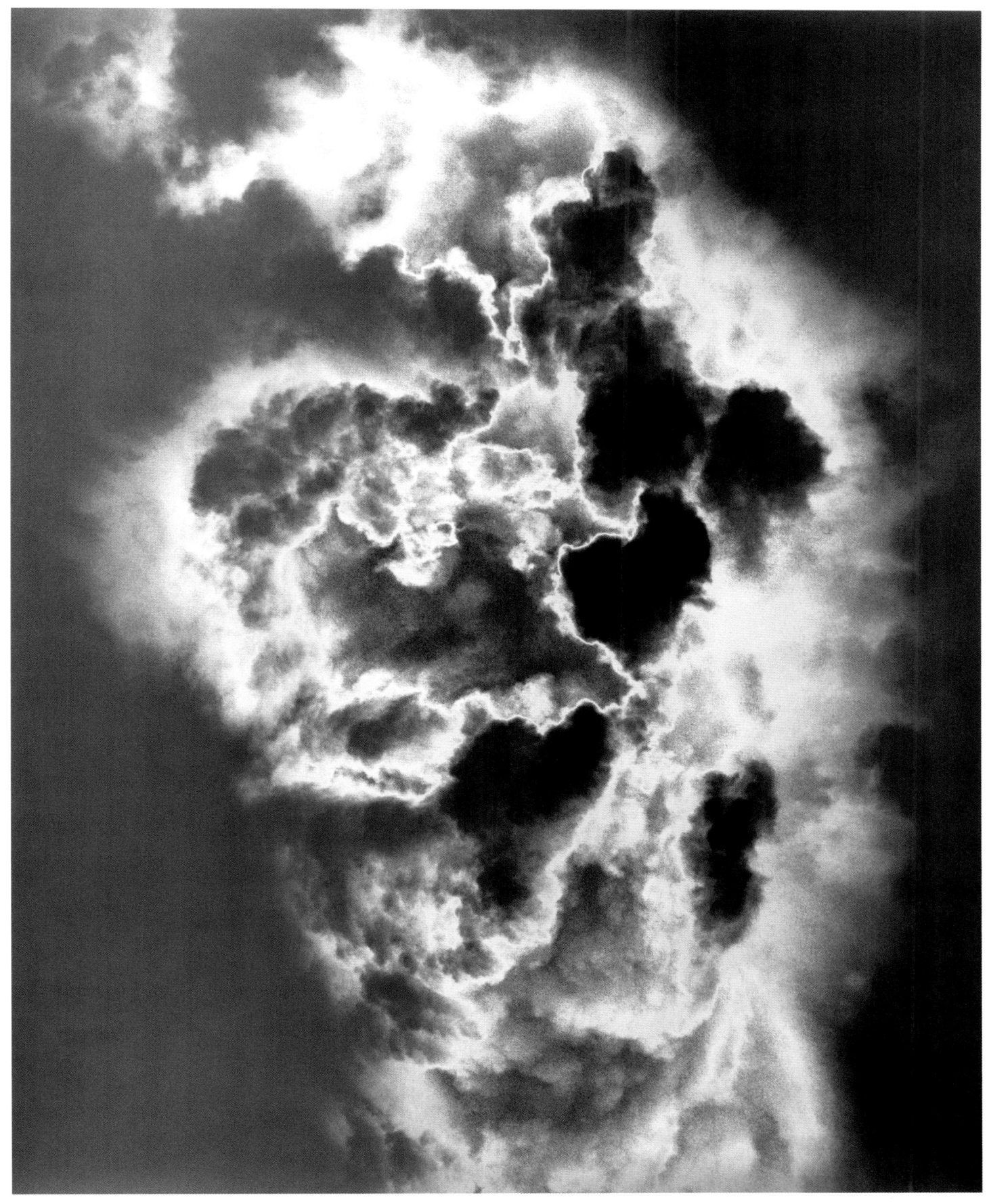

Billowing. As we were driving up to Norfolk yesterday I saw the Enfield fire; where a Sony distribution centre set ablaze by rioters was just pouring out smoke over the motorway. The sheer amount of smoke was quite surprising, and today smoke was still covering the motorway. I feel such despair at people who have taken to looting; so angry at the destruction people can cause. 2011/2012. (Version V), 2012, from the series Smoke, 2011–12

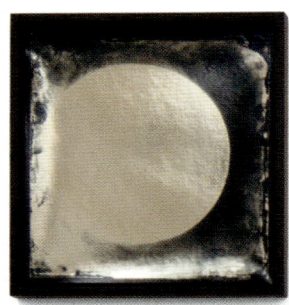

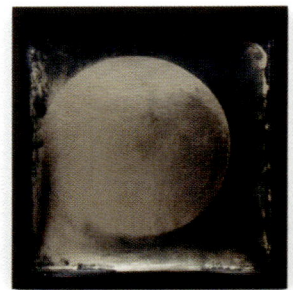

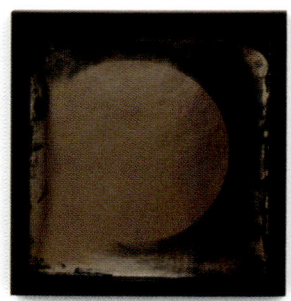

Top row: *Heliograms,*
July 8th, 1876/
December 8th, 2011, 2011
Middle row: *Heliograms,*
July 8th, 1876/
December 14th, 2011, 2011
Bottom row: *Heliograms,*
July 8th, 1876/
December 21st, 2011, 2011

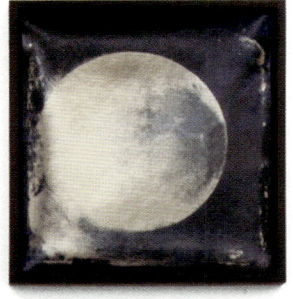

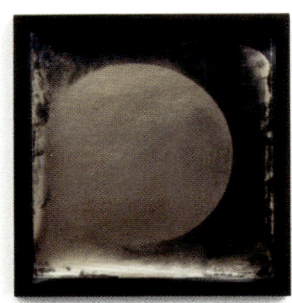

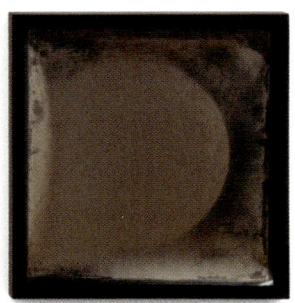

*Passage of the moon
over two hours, Arcachon,
France, ca. 1870s/2012,*
April 11, 2012

Object Lessons
Lunar Hasselblad
1968

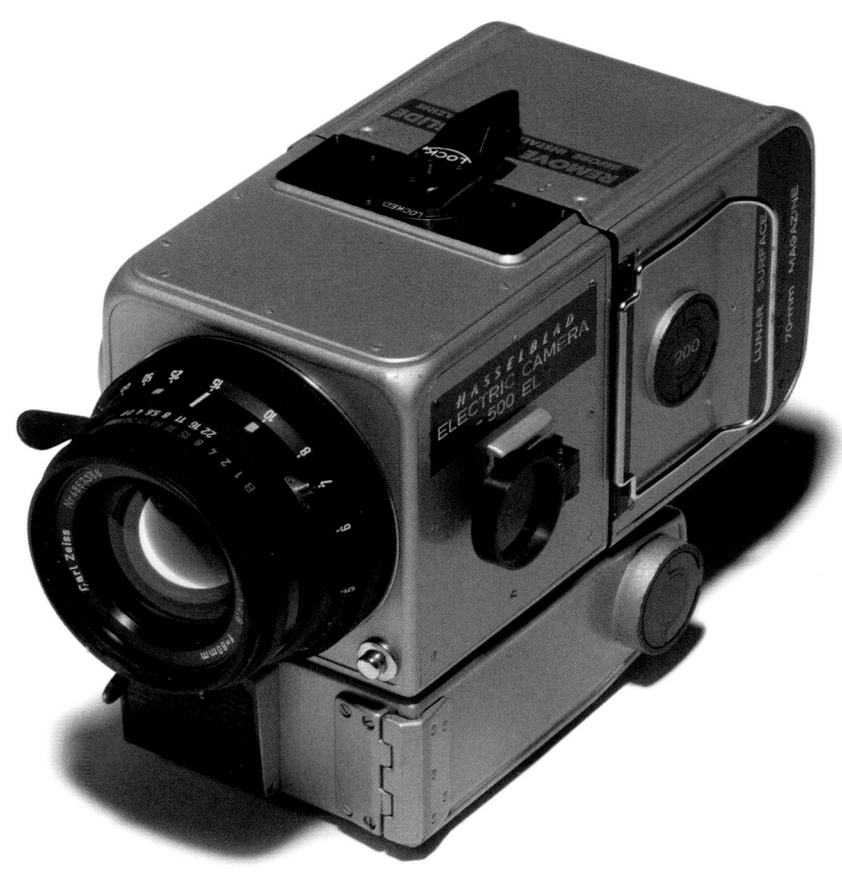

Hasselblad Electric Data Camera Photograph by Barbara Puorro/Galasso. Courtesy George Eastman House, International Museum of Photography and Film, Rochester, New York

Hasselblad Electric Data Cameras accompanied all U.S. voyages to the moon and produced many early pictures from outer space, including the iconic 1968 photograph known as *Earthrise*, shot from inside the *Apollo 8* spacecraft. Three Data Cameras were aboard the 1969 Apollo 11 mission; Neil Armstrong and Edwin "Buzz" Aldrin wore suits customized with anterior attachments to hold the cameras, which feature prominently in pictures of the space travelers: a sleek third eye fastened to their bulky spacesuits. Despite being state-of-the-art, the Hasselblad EDCs proved disposable and never returned from space; they were left behind in an effort to shed weight, their mass replaced with lunar rocks and gravel collected for study. According to the manufacturer, twelve of these cameras rest on the surface of the moon today; they might someday serve as evidence of the effects of solar cosmic deterioration on their special Zeiss Biogon lenses. The one belonging to astronaut Eugene Cernan, the last man to walk on the moon, in 1972, remains pointed at the zenith, staring into deep space, observing but recording nothing, waiting to be retrieved by the next visitor.

—The Editors